The Kingfisher

Young World
Encyclopedia

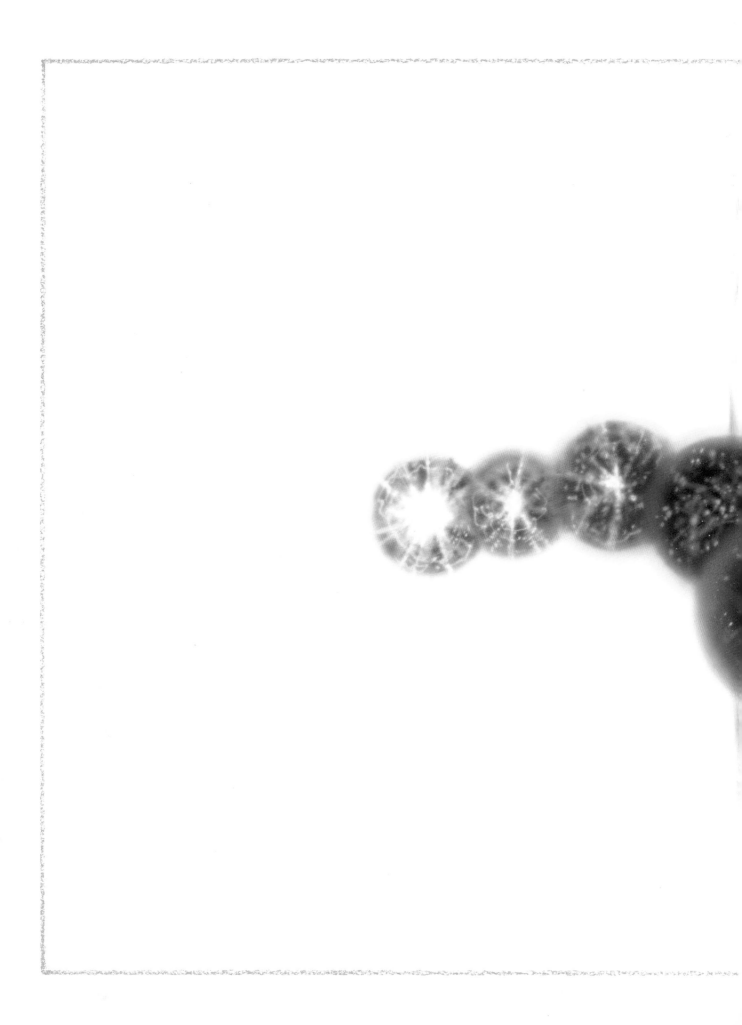

The Kingfisher

Young World
Encyclopedia

Kingfisher

NEW YORK

Project Editor Sue Grabham
Senior Contributing Editor Charlotte Evans
Assistant Editor Tara Benson
Section Editors Angela Holroyd,
Jill Thomas, John Paton
U.S. Project Editor Emily Kent

Senior Designer Janice English
Staff Designers Sandra Begnor, Siân Williams
Section Designer Ch'en Ling
Additional Design Smiljka Surla, Rachael Stone

Publishing Director Jim Miles

Art Director Paul Wilkinson

Additional Art Preparation
Matthew Gore, Andy Archer, Shaun Deal,
Julian Ewart, Narinder Sahotay, Andy Stanford,
Janet Woronkowicz

Picture Research Elaine Willis
Artwork Archivist Wendy Allison
Artwork Researcher Robert Perry

Activity Artist Caroline Jayne Church

Indexer Hilary Bird

Production Manager Linda Edmonds
Production Assistant Stephen Lang
U.S. Production Manager Oonagh Phelan

Contributing Authors
Michael Benton, Michael Chinery, Fabienne
Fustec, Keith Lye, Christopher Maynard,
Nina Morgan, Steve Parker, Barbara Reseigh,
Dominique Rift, Jean-Pierre Verdet,
Florence and Pierre-Olivier Wessels,
Brian Williams

Specialist Consultants
Martyn Bramwell M.A. (Natural Sciences writer);
David Burnie B.Sc. (Natural Sciences writer);
David Glover B.Sc., Ph.D. (Science writer);
Ian Graham B.Sc., Dip.J., F.B.I.S., M.C.I.J.
(Technology writer);
Professor B.W. Hodder B.Lit., M.A., Ph.D
(School of Oriental and African Studies, University
of London);
Keith Lye B.A., F.R.G.S. (Geography writer);
James Muirden B.Ed. (Publications Consultant at
School of Education, University of Exeter, and
astronomy writer);
Dr. Elizabeth McCall Smith M.B., Ch.B., M.R.C.G.P.,
D.R.C.O.G. (General Practitioner, Edinburgh);
Julia Stanton B.A. Dip.Ed. (Australasia consultant);
Dr. David Unwin B.Sc. Ph.D. (Royal Society Research
Fellow, Bristol University)

KINGFISHER
Larousse Kingfisher Chambers Inc.
95 Madison Avenue, New York, New York 10016

First American edition 1995
2 4 6 8 10 9 7 5 3 1

Copyright © Larousse plc 1994
All rights reserved under International and Pan-American Copyright
Conventions

Library of Congress Cataloging-in-Publication Data

Young world encyclopedia.
1st American ed.
p. cm.
Includes Index
1. Children's encyclopedias and dictionaries.
[1. Encyclopedias and dictionaries.]
Kingfisher Books.
AG5. C56 1995   94-29226
031–dc20   CIP AC

ISBN 1-85697-519-3
Printed in Italy

Foreword

We had clear goals when putting this encyclopedia together—to make it informative, interesting, and intriguing, but above all fun for the young children who would use it. We certainly had a great time making it. It was fun to create a team of inventive cartoon characters and to have them demonstrate the wide range of activities in science, crafts, and the arts. And introducing children's stories and legends from all over the globe to expose the young reader to the world of literature—that too was enjoyable.

Other features, such as the Word Boxes for explaining troublesome words and the Find the Answer panels for encouraging children to test their comprehension, are all aimed at making this book a pleasure to use.

The illustrations, and there are many on every page, will, we hope, captivate and enlighten whether the words are read or not. But the true test of this encyclopedia is whether children will sit down with it again and again simply because they enjoy doing so. We feel certain they will.

More than three hundred people have been involved in the creation of this book and all should really sign this foreword. Unfortunately, I alone have that privilege.

Jim Miles

Jim Miles

Contents

Machines

Science

People and Places

About *Young World*

Your *Young World Encyclopedia* is packed with interesting information, colorful pictures, exciting stories, and activities to give you hours and hours of fun. Watch for the six cartoon characters shown below. They appear on many of the pages to help you with each activity. On the next two pages, they also show you how to use your encyclopedia. Can you see their pet cat and dog too?

Your encyclopedia

Each page is filled with information and pictures to tell you about all your favorite topics. Also, many pages have **Find the answers** quizzes, **Activities**, stories, and **Word boxes**. Here, the cartoon characters are showing you how each of these work to help you use your encyclopedia more easily.

The yellow triangles warn you when something could be dangerous.

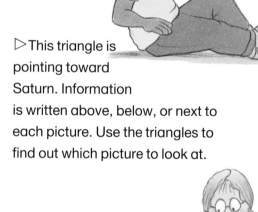

▷ This triangle is pointing toward Saturn. Information is written above, below, or next to each picture. Use the triangles to find out which picture to look at.

Word box
Word boxes are on the first page of each chapter. Two or three words are listed in **dark** print. They are explained to help you read the information on the pages in that chapter.

Find the answers

Watch for the **Find the answers** quizzes.

You will find the answers by reading the information on the page.

△ The symbols, or pictures, at the top of each page will help you find out which part of the book you are in. Each section, or chapter, has a different title and symbol.

Stories from around the world

There are fun stories to read, exciting movies to remember, and many characters to meet in your encyclopedia. Pictures or photographs are next to each one of them. Have you heard about these farmyard animals in the story called The Rain Puddle, *by Adelaide Holl?*

Look at the other end of this line to find the rings around Saturn. Many of the pictures are labeled like this.

Activities

There are lots of things to make, games to play, puzzles to solve, and experiments to try. The cartoon characters will show you what to do.

Activities

Before you start each activity, collect everything you need and make sure there is a clear space. Wash your hands before cooking and wear gloves when touching dirt. Wear an apron for gluing, cooking, and using paints. If an adult is needed, ask for their help before you start.

Afterward, make sure you clean up any mess and put everything away.

▷ Here are some of the materials that you might need for the **Activities**. **Always** ask an adult before using anything that is not yours.

Recipe

4 cups flour
3/4 cup of salt
1 cup of water
food coloring

Make dough

Make dough for some of the modeling activities. Mix flour and salt in a bowl. If making colored dough, add food coloring to water. Add as much water as needed to flour and salt, a little at a time. Stir. Turn out onto floured surface. Knead into a smooth dough. Make models. When finished, ask an adult to put them in the oven, on a low heat, for five hours. Paint the models when cool.

The Universe

What is the universe?

The universe is everything that exists. The Earth is part of the universe. So are the Sun, the Moon, and all the planets. Stars and clouds of gas and dust are also part of the universe.

Scientists use telescopes and probes to learn about the universe. We know a great deal, but there is still much that we do not know.

Word box
Planets are the nine huge ball-shaped objects moving around the Sun. Some planets are made of rock and some of gas.
Stars are enormous balls of burning gases. They are much larger than planets. Our Sun is a star, and like all stars it gives out heat and light.

△ Scientists think the universe began with a massive explosion called the Big Bang. They believe that the universe is growing larger. This means that the huge groups of stars called galaxies are moving farther and farther apart.

△ We can see stars, planets, galaxies, comets, and clouds of dust and gas in the night sky by looking through a telescope.

Make your own universe

Use a dark felt-tip pen to draw lots of small galaxies onto a balloon. Use the shape shown as a guide. The balloon is your universe.

Watch the balloon in a mirror as you blow it up. You can see the galaxies moving farther and farther apart, just as scientists believe the galaxies in the universe are moving apart.

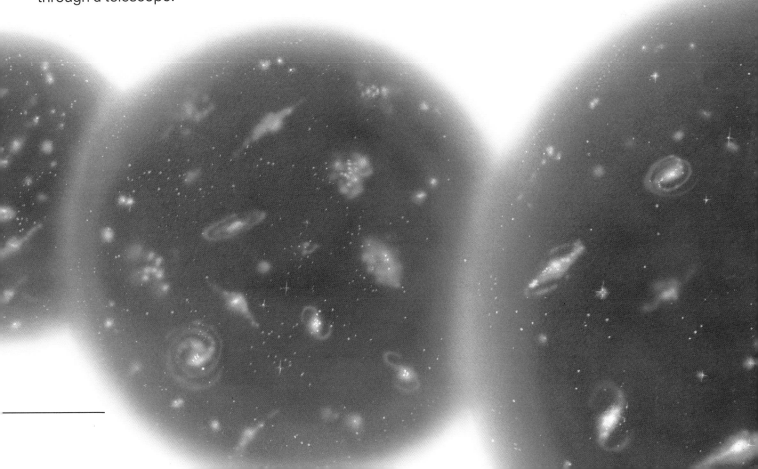

Looking at the sky

Scientists who study the universe are called astronomers. They study the sky using large telescopes in special buildings called observatories.

You do not need a telescope to study the sky. Before telescopes were invented, astronomers watched the sky with the naked eye. They could not see as much as we can now, but they made many important discoveries. We can learn a lot by regularly watching the night sky.

△ Observatories are often built on mountains where the air is clear. Here there are no other lights, so the stars can be seen clearly.

△ If we look up at the night sky, we can see hundreds of stars and the Moon.

△ With binoculars, we can see that the Moon's surface is covered with craters.

△ A small telescope helps us to see smaller craters on the Moon and many more stars.

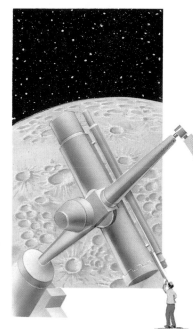

△ We see millions of stars and the Moon's surface in closeup with a big telescope.

Be an astronomer
Make sure it is a clear night, and you are warmly dressed. Use a flashlight covered with red tissue paper to look at a star map. The map will help you to name the brightest stars. Use binoculars to see the fainter stars. Write down what you see in a notebook.

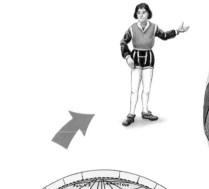

△ Later, a Polish astronomer, Copernicus, suggested that the Earth orbits, or circles, the Sun. But few people believed him.

△ Early astronomers thought that everything in the universe circled around the Earth. They were wrong.

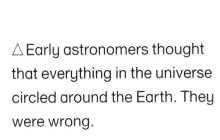

△ Then, a scientist, Isaac Newton, discovered what keeps the Earth traveling around the Sun. It is a force called gravity.

The Sun, our star

The Sun is a star. It is the closest star to us in the universe. Like all stars, the Sun is a ball of hot, glowing gases.

Jets of gas, called prominences, often erupt from the Sun's surface. Dark patches, called sunspots, are very common. Sunspots are much cooler than the rest of the Sun's hot surface.

Never look directly at the Sun. Its light will damage your eyes.

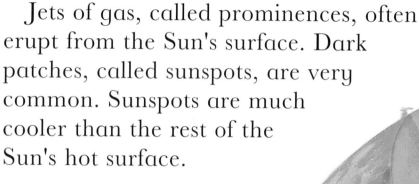

core

prominence

▷The hottest part of the Sun is its core. The surface is called the photosphere.

▽The largest prominences look like huge arches and may last for hours or days.

sunspot

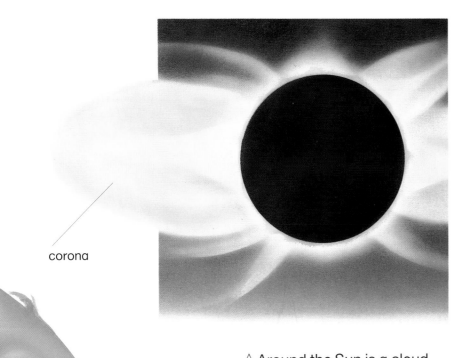

corona

△ Around the Sun is a cloud of gases called the corona. Astronomers can see this cloud during an eclipse, when the Moon hides the Sun.

Make a smiling Sun
Make dough using the recipe at the beginning of this book. Shape into a flat circle. Ask an adult to put this in a very low oven for five hours. Leave to cool, then paint a smiling face onto the circle in bright, sunshine colors.

photosphere

Apollo, the Sun god
The people of ancient Greece believed in a Sun god called Apollo. They thought he drove the Sun across the sky each day in his chariot.

Word box
Core is the center of a star or planet.
Orbit is the path followed by planets traveling around the Sun. It is also the path followed by a moon traveling around a planet.

Spinning in space

Although we cannot feel it, the Earth is always moving. It orbits, or circles, the Sun. It takes one year to travel all the way around the Sun. At the same time, the Moon is circling the Earth. It takes the Moon about a month to travel around the Earth.

All the time, the Earth, Moon, and Sun each spin on an imaginary line called an axis.

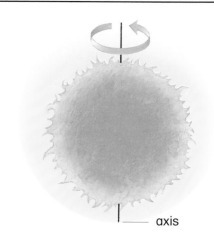

△ The Sun takes 27 days to spin around once on its axis.

▽ The blue arrow shows the Earth's orbit, or path, around the Sun.

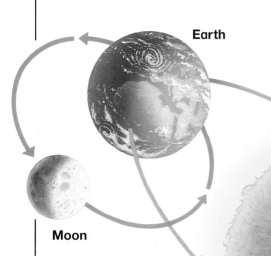

Earth

Moon

Sun

△ The green arrow shows the Moon's orbit around the Earth. The Moon travels once around the Earth every 29 days and 13 hours.

△ The Earth takes 24 hours to spin around once on its axis.

△ The Moon spins around once on its axis every 29 days and 13 hours.

Marking time

As the Earth spins, first one side of its surface is turned toward the Sun, then the other. This gives us day and night.

We have different seasons because Earth's axis is tilted at an angle. As Earth travels around the Sun, the seasons change.

△ It is day when our side of the Earth is turned to the Sun's light.

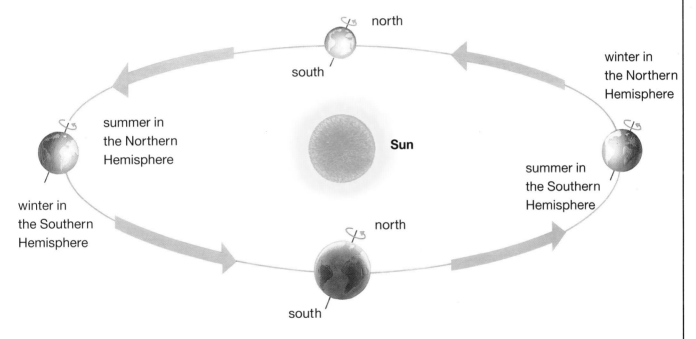

north

south

winter in the Northern Hemisphere

summer in the Northern Hemisphere

Sun

summer in the Southern Hemisphere

winter in the Southern Hemisphere

north

south

△ The northern half of the Earth is called the Northern Hemisphere. When the Northern Hemisphere tilts toward the Sun, it is summer there. But in the Southern Hemisphere, it is winter. Six months later, the Southern Hemisphere tilts toward the Sun. Then it is summer in the south, but winter in the north.

Make a shadow clock
Outside, on a sunny day, push a pencil into a ball of modeling clay and stand it on a sheet of cardboard. Mark the pencil's shadow and write the time beside it. Do this every hour until the Sun goes down.

Time zones

To measure time around the world, the Earth is divided into 24 time zones—one zone for each of the 24 hours in a day. The clocks in each zone all show the same time. But the clocks in the next zone are different by one hour.

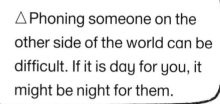

△ Phoning someone on the other side of the world can be difficult. If it is day for you, it might be night for them.

△ Imagine each time zone as a slice of the Earth.

▽ This shows the slices laid out flat and in a row. The time in London is five hours ahead of the time in New York because they are five time zones apart.

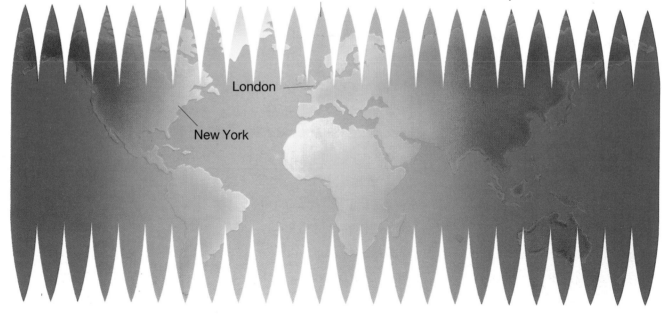

12 P.M.   5 P.M.

London

New York

Heat and light

Without the Sun there would be no life on Earth. It would be too dark and far too cold for any living thing to survive.

Plants use the Sun's light to make food so they can grow. The Sun heats us and gives us light. We can also use the Sun to heat our homes.

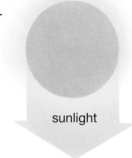

sunlight

oxygen

△ Plants make food from sunlight and give off oxygen. We need this to breathe.

△ Solar panels trap and store heat from the Sun, which is then used to heat this house.

The huntress and the mouse
(An Inuit folk tale)

An Inuit girl left her coat in the Sun too long and it shrank. She was so angry, she trapped the Sun using three strong hairs. Daylight ceased. Mouse, the largest animal in those days, gnawed at the hairs. By the time the Sun was free, Mouse had shrunk and his fur was gray.

The Moon

The Moon is Earth's nearest neighbor in space.

We can see the Moon in the sky because it reflects light from the Sun. The Moon seems to change shape. This is because as it orbits Earth, different parts of the side facing us are lit up by the Sun's light.

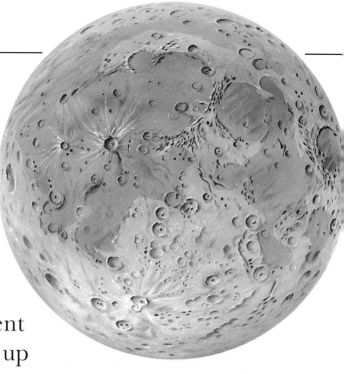

△ The Moon has no air or water. Nothing can live there.

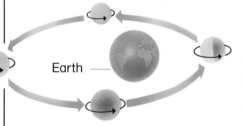

Earth

◁ Only one side of the Moon ever faces Earth, because the Moon spins on its axis in the same time it orbits Earth.

The king who wanted to walk on the Moon
(A Persian folk tale)

All the trees in the kingdom were used to make a box tower for the king to climb to the Moon. But still he needed one more. Foolishly, he asked his people to pass up the bottom box. When he fell to the ground, he wisely gave up the idea.

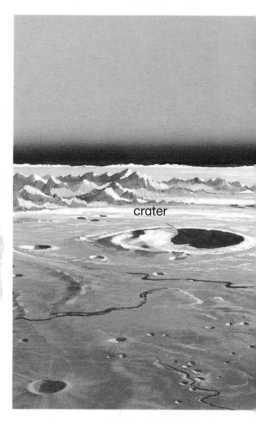

crater

△ The craters on the Moon were made when lumps of rock and iron, called meteoroids, crashed into the Moon's surface.

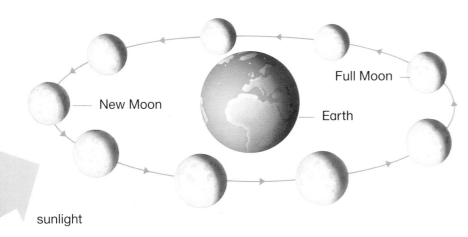

New Moon

Full Moon

Earth

sunlight

◁ When the Moon is between Earth and the Sun, the side facing us is so dark we cannot see it. This is a New Moon. At Full Moon, all of the facing side is sunlit so the Moon appears round.

▽ These changes are called the phases of the Moon.

Keep a Moon diary

To see the Moon's changing phases, record how the Moon looks each night for one month. Draw up a chart with the days of the week at the top and four rows underneath. Each night write down, or draw, what you see, even if it is cloudy and you cannot see the Moon.

Moon and tides

Each day the sea rises and falls in a movement we call the tides. Tides are caused by the pull of the Moon. There are two high tides and two low tides every day.

On the side of Earth nearest to it, the Moon pulls the sea up into a bulge. The shorelines on this part of the Earth are having a high tide. On the opposite side of Earth, the sea also bulges into a high tide.

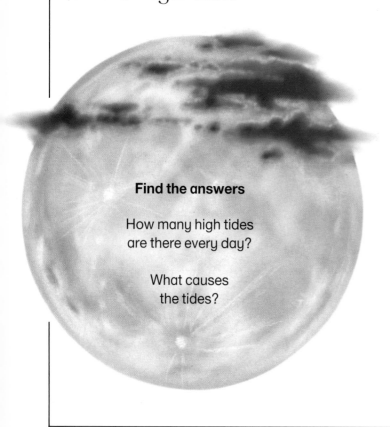

Find the answers

How many high tides are there every day?

What causes the tides?

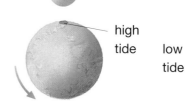

high tide   low tide

△ One high tide occurs when the shore is facing the Moon.

△ There is a low tide about six hours after the high tide.

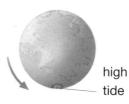

Moon

high tide

low tide

△ The second high tide is when the shore is opposite the Moon.

△ About six hours later, there is a second low tide.

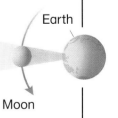

An eclipse

Sometimes, as Earth orbits the Sun, it comes between the Sun and the Moon. It throws a shadow across the Moon. This is called a lunar eclipse.

If the Moon comes between Earth and the Sun, it stops sunlight from reaching a part of Earth for a few minutes. This is called a solar eclipse.

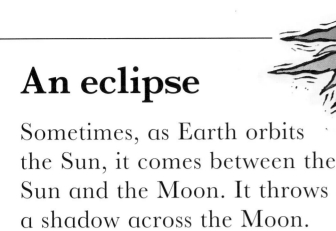

A Sun-eating dragon

The ancient Chinese had a story to explain solar eclipses. They thought a dragon had swallowed the Sun. They banged drums and shouted to scare the dragon away. This seemed to work, because the Sun always came back!

lunar eclipse

solar eclipse

Earth

Sun

Moon

Sun

Earth

Moon

△ A lunar eclipse can last more than an hour. The Moon seems very faint during an eclipse.

△ During a solar eclipse the bright Sun disappears for a few minutes.

27

Pictures in the sky

It is not easy to keep track of the thousands of stars in the sky. To make it easier, people since ancient times have grouped stars together. These groups are called constellations. Some are named after animals, others are named after ancient heroes or gods.

There are 88 constellations across the whole sky. As Earth orbits the Sun, we can see the different constellations.

Find the answers

How many constellations are there in the whole sky?

Are there more bright stars in the northern sky or in the southern sky?

△ If you look out on a cloudless night you can see thousands of stars shining brightly in the sky.

Make a constellation viewer

Put a circle of black paper on a sheet of modeling clay. Copy a constellation from the opposite page by pushing a sharp pencil through the paper several times. Attach the paper to a cardboard tube with a rubber band. Attach a circle of black paper, without a constellation, to the other end. Point the viewer to the light to see the constellation.

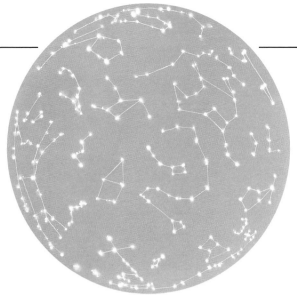

Northern Hemisphere

△ People in the Northern Hemisphere, the northern part of the world, see different stars from people living in the south.

Southern Hemisphere

△ There are more bright stars to be seen in the Southern Hemisphere, the southern part of the world, than in the north.

△ Ursa Minor is a constellation in the Northern Hemisphere. It is also called the Little Dipper. Ursa Minor can be seen in North America and Northern Europe all year round.

△ The Crux is a constellation in the Southern Hemisphere. It is also called the Southern Cross. The Crux is seen by most Australians throughout the year.

Coyote's star trip
(A Native American folk tale)

One night, Coyote was told to arrange the stars. Feeling sleepy and not looking where he was going, Coyote tripped! The stars flew off in different directions, making the bright patterns we see each night.

Word box
Constellations are the groups of stars that we can see in the night sky. **Galaxies** are the massive groups of stars that make up the universe.

The life of a star

When you look up at the night sky, the stars you see are all different ages. Some are brighter than others.

New stars are being formed all the time. When old stars grow cold and dim, a lot of the material, such as dust and gas, is thrown out into space. Later, this material may be recycled through nebulae into new stars.

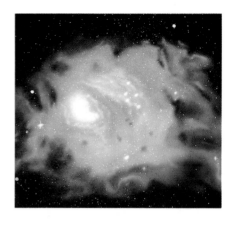

△ New stars are being born all the time from clouds of dust and gas called nebulae.

Make star-shaped glasses

Using this shape as a guide, cut out two stars large enough to cover your eyes.

Ask an adult to help you cut out the eye holes.

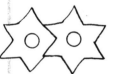

Glue the stars together so that they overlap.

Stick colored cellophane onto the back of each eye hole.

Use tape to attach a stick to your glasses.

Stars are not really this shape, but when they twinkle in the sky, they can look like it.

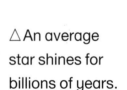

△ An average star shines for billions of years.

△ Then its gases puff outward and it swells up into a red giant. It will then become either a supergiant or a white dwarf.

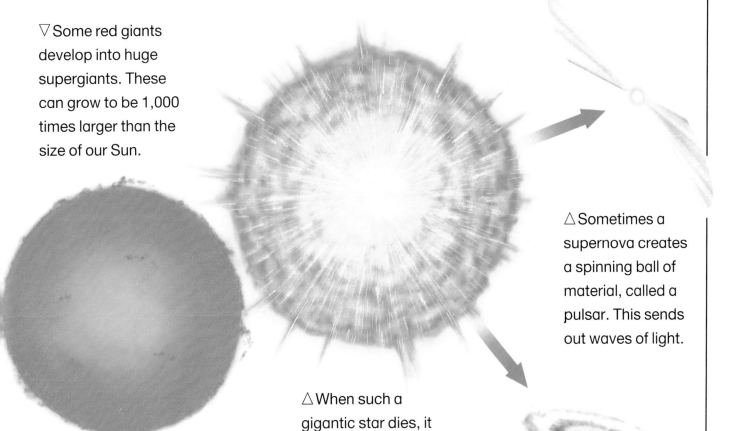

▽ Some red giants develop into huge supergiants. These can grow to be 1,000 times larger than the size of our Sun.

△ Sometimes a supernova creates a spinning ball of material, called a pulsar. This sends out waves of light.

△ When such a gigantic star dies, it collapses and causes a massive explosion. This is called a supernova.

△ A black hole may be left behind when a supernova collapses.

△ The red giant's outer gases slowly escape into space. Eventually, only the center is left.

△ The star shrinks, becomes hotter, and turns into a white dwarf. Although it is so hot, its small size makes it appear faint.

△ After millions of years, the white dwarf slowly cools and fades to become a cold, black dwarf.

Galaxies

On a clear night, you may be able to see a ribbon of white across the sky. This is the Milky Way. It is our galaxy, the huge group of stars that is our home in space.

The Milky Way is just one of billions of galaxies in the universe. Galaxies come in many shapes and sizes.

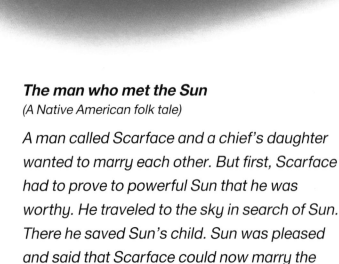

Sun

The man who met the Sun
(A Native American folk tale)

A man called Scarface and a chief's daughter wanted to marry each other. But first, Scarface had to prove to powerful Sun that he was worthy. He traveled to the sky in search of Sun. There he saved Sun's child. Sun was pleased and said that Scarface could now marry the chief's daughter. Scarface walked back down to Earth along the pathway called the Milky Way.

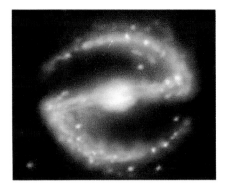

△ Spiral galaxies have arms
that slowly revolve around
a central mass of stars.

△ Certain galaxies are simply
a great mass of stars. These
are called elliptical galaxies.

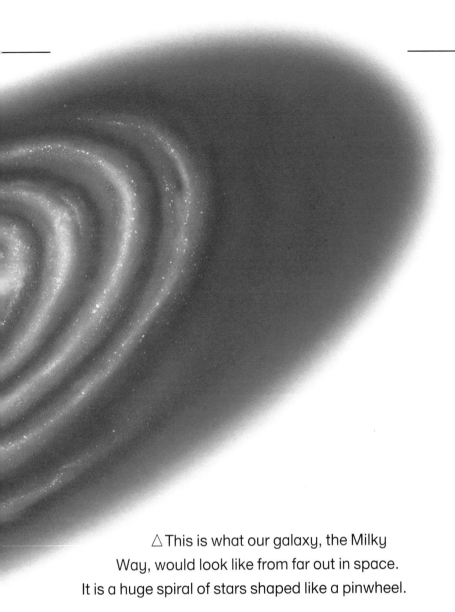

△ This is what our galaxy, the Milky
Way, would look like from far out in space.
It is a huge spiral of stars shaped like a pinwheel.

Make a galaxy picture
On a large sheet of stiff, black
paper, draw a spiral galaxy in
glue. Sprinkle glitter all over
the glue. To reveal your galaxy
picture, bend up the sides
of the paper and pour
the spare glitter
into a container.

△ Some galaxies do not seem
to have any shape at all. They
are called irregular galaxies.

The Solar System

The Sun's family is called the Solar System. It includes all the planets, moons, comets, and lumps of rock, dust, and ice that orbit the Sun.

Planets are made up of rock, metal, or gas. All the planets belong to the Solar System, but there are great differences between them.

Uranus

Saturn

▷There are nine planets in the Solar System. Jupiter is the largest. It is so large, all the other planets would fit inside it. Very little is known about Pluto, the smallest planet.

Sun

Mercury

Venus

Earth

Mars

Jupiter

◁These are the planets in the Solar System.

▷ Most of the planets were named by astronomers after Greek and Roman gods. They chose a god to fit each planet's appearance.

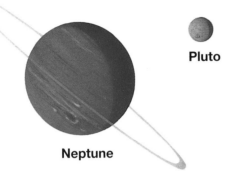

Neptune

Pluto

Mercury, the winged god

Venus, the goddess of love

Mars, the god of war

Jupiter, king of the gods

Saturn, father of Jupiter

Uranus, father of Saturn

Neptune, god of the sea

Pluto, god of the underworld

Sun

Mercury

Earth

Jupiter

Venus

Uranus

Mars

Saturn

Pluto

Neptune

Make a planetarium

Make the planets and the Sun from modeling clay balls of different colors and sizes. Use the main picture as a guide. Cut and paint cardboard tubes to make stands.

Cover a table with paper. Place the Sun on a stand and put it in a corner of the table. Put the planets in their correct order from the Sun, as shown in the picture above.

Word box

Solar System is the Sun and everything that orbits the Sun.

Comets are huge lumps of ice, gas, and dust that orbit the Sun.

Moons are natural, rocky balls that orbit planets.

35

Mercury

Mercury is the closest planet to the Sun. It is bare and rocky, and has no water or air.

Mercury's days are hotter than the hottest desert on Earth and nights are freezing cold. Mercury takes only 88 days to orbit the Sun.

◁ The probe *Mariner 10* flew past Mercury and sent back photographs of its rocky surface.

Mercury, the winged god

Mercury was a Roman god who had wings on his feet. He traveled very quickly. The planet was named after him because it travels quickly around the Sun.

crater

Mercury
▽

△ Mercury is covered with craters made by rocks from space.

Venus

The second planet from the Sun is Venus. It is covered with thick clouds of hot, poisonous gases. These clouds hide its volcanic surface and trap heat. It is so hot on Venus that you could bake a cake in a few seconds, without using an oven.

◁ Several probes have landed on Venus. They sent back information, but were then destroyed by the heat.

Seeing Venus

Venus is the brightest planet in the sky. The ancient Maya people built temples from which they could watch the Sun, stars, and Venus.

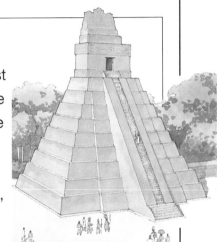

top of volcano

lava

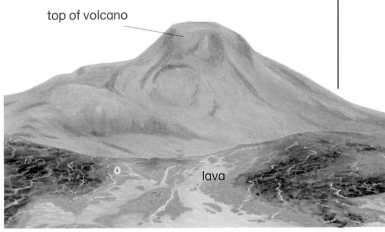

Venus
▽

△ Venus's surface is covered with old volcanoes and lava.

Mars

Mars looks red because its rocks are full of rusted iron. Huge dust storms also make the sky look pink.

On Mars there are channels that look like dried-up river beds, but there is no water there. There are deep valleys and old volcanoes.

▷This is one of Mars's two small, odd-shaped moons.

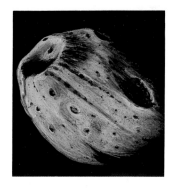

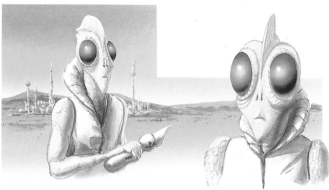

Martians

Before we knew that there was no life on Mars, people used to believe there were strange creatures living there. People called these creatures Martians.
Many stories have been written about Martians, such as The War of the Worlds, *by H.G. Wells.*

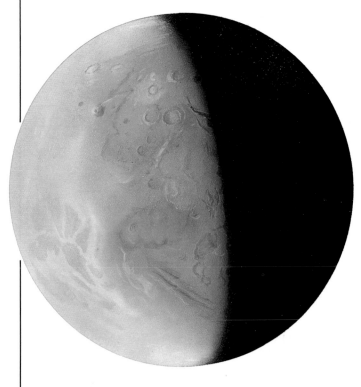

Mars
▽

Olympus Mons

△ Olympus Mons is the tallest mountain in the Solar System.

Jupiter

Jupiter is the biggest planet in the Solar System. It is a huge ball of liquid and gas. In 1979, a probe discovered a ring of dust around it.

Jupiter has 16 moons. The three largest moons are all bigger than our own Moon.

Make marbled Jupiter paper
Mix turpentine with drops of pink and orange oil paint. Put drops into a bowl of water and swirl gently with a paintbrush. Place a piece of paper lightly on the surface. Lift the paper off and leave to dry.

△ The huge red spot on Jupiter is a giant storm three times bigger than Earth.

Io   Europa   Ganymede   Callisto

Jupiter
▽

△ Jupiter's four largest moons were first seen by Galileo in 1610.

Saturn

Saturn is a giant ball of liquid and gas. From Earth, it looks as if Saturn is surrounded by two wide rings. In fact, these rings are made up of thousands of narrow rings.

Saturn has at least 18 moons, more than any other planet in the Solar System.

Make a Saturn window pane
Fold a sheet of black paper in half. Cut out a Saturn shape, as shown.

Open out and tape tissue paper on one side. Fold and glue together. Prop up by a window.

△ Each of Saturn's rings are made up of dust and tiny bits of ice and rock.

Saturn
▽

Titan

△ Titan is Saturn's biggest moon. It is surrounded by gas.

Uranus

Uranus is the only planet in the Solar System to orbit the Sun tipped over on its side. Uranus has at least 11 narrow rings and 15 moons. Ten of Uranus's moons are so small they were not discovered until the probe *Voyager 2* flew past in 1986.

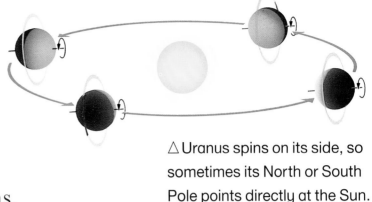

△ Uranus spins on its side, so sometimes its North or South Pole points directly at the Sun.

Miranda and Ariel
(From a play by William Shakespeare)

Miranda and Ariel are the names of two of the moons that orbit Uranus. They are also the names of two characters in The Tempest, *a play by William Shakespeare.*

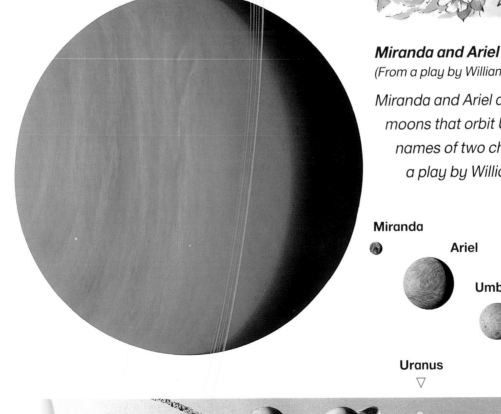

Miranda

Ariel

Umbriel

Titania

Oberon

Uranus
▽

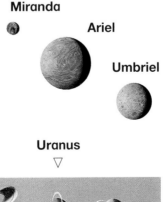

△ These are Uranus's five biggest moons. Titania is the largest.

Neptune

Neptune is an enormous ball of liquid and gas. Some of the fastest winds in the Solar System blow across this planet's surface. The winds can reach speeds of up to 1,200 miles an hour.

Neptune has eight moons in all, but only two can be seen from Earth.

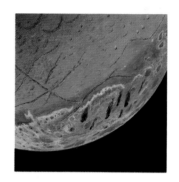

▷ Neptune's biggest moon, Triton, has a surface of ice that is split by giant cracks.

▷ *Voyager 2* flew past Neptune in 1989. Its pictures showed that Neptune is surrounded by rings.

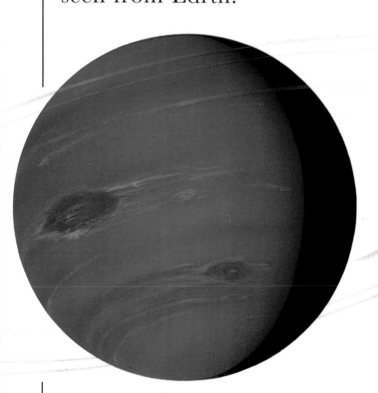

Neptune, god of the sea

Neptune is too faint to be seen without a telescope. When astronomers discovered it in 1846, they named the new planet after the Roman god of the sea.

Neptune
▽

Pluto

Pluto is usually the most distant planet from the Sun, but until 1999 it will be closer than Neptune. We know little about Pluto because no probe has visited it.

Astronomers wonder if there might be a tenth planet farther away than Pluto. But so far, none has been found.

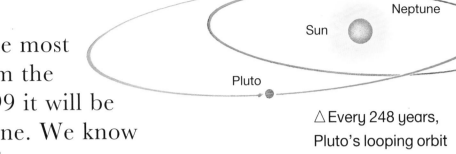

△ Every 248 years, Pluto's looping orbit brings it closer to the Sun than Neptune.

Charon the boatman

Pluto's moon is named after Charon, the boatman in the Greek story Orpheus in the Underworld. *Charon took Orpheus across the river Styx.*

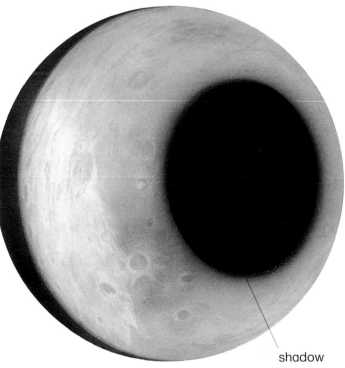

shadow

Charon

◁ Pluto's one moon, Charon, is about half as big as Pluto. Charon is so close to Pluto that it often throws a shadow onto the planet's surface.

Pluto
▽

◁ Do you think there is another planet in our Solar System?

43

Comets and meteors

Meteors are brief, bright trails in the sky. They happen when grains of dust from space burn up in the Earth's air.

Asteroids are much bigger lumps of rock. Millions of asteroids orbit the Sun between Mars and Jupiter.

Comets are made up of rocks, ice, and dust. When comets come close to the Sun, they may have a glowing tail.

△ Meteors are also called shooting stars. They may be pieces of asteroids or comets.

▽ As a meteor enters the Earth's atmosphere, it burns up. This leaves a glowing trail for a second or two.

△ Ceres is the largest known asteroid. It measures about 600 miles across.

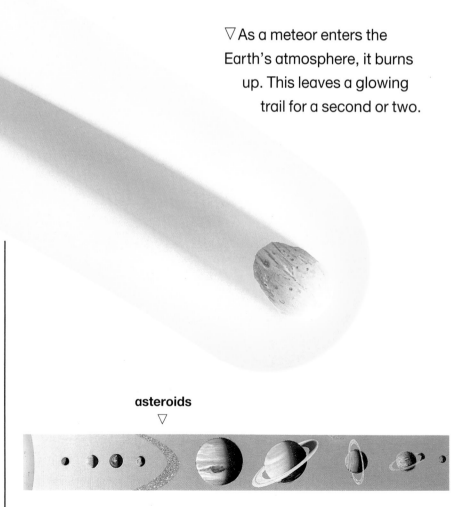

asteroids
▽

tail of comet

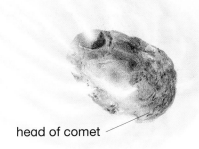

head of comet

△ The head of a comet is only a few miles wide, but its tail can be millions of miles long.

▽ Comets usually have long, looping orbits. The tail always points away from the Sun.

△ Comets are like dirty snowballs. As they near the Sun the ice melts, and dust and gas form a tail.

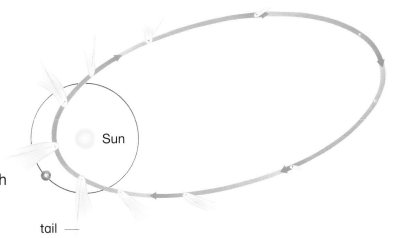

Sun

tail —

▽ When an asteroid collides with Earth, it is called a meteorite. Long ago, a meteorite caused this huge crater in Arizona.

Make a crater
Fill a tray with flour. From a height, drop a small ball of clay into it. Carefully remove the ball to see the crater it has made.

Astronauts

Living in space is very different from living on Earth. In space, nothing has weight and there is no air. An astronaut must wear a spacesuit with its own air supply to go outside the spacecraft.

Spacecraft are designed to make astronauts as comfortable as possible. This way, people can stay in space for days, weeks, or even months at a time.

camera — visor

backpack

footstrap

▷Everything in space is weightless, so astronauts have to get used to floating around like a balloon.

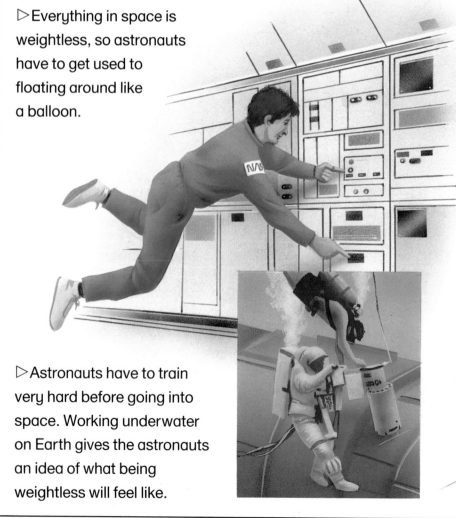

△Without a spacesuit, an astronaut would either burn up in the heat of the Sun or freeze in the cold shadows where sunlight does not reach. A backpack holds air and a visor protects the astronaut from the Sun's glare.

▷Astronauts have to train very hard before going into space. Working underwater on Earth gives the astronauts an idea of what being weightless will feel like.

Find the answers

When do astronauts have to wear spacesuits?

Why do astronauts strap themselves into their sleeping bags?

▽ Astronauts still have to exercise to keep fit and healthy. You cannot pedal a bike like this on Earth!

▽ Astronauts have to strap themselves into their sleeping bags so that they do not float away in their sleep.

▽ Keeping clean in space is not easy. Some spacecraft have special showers where the water is sucked away.

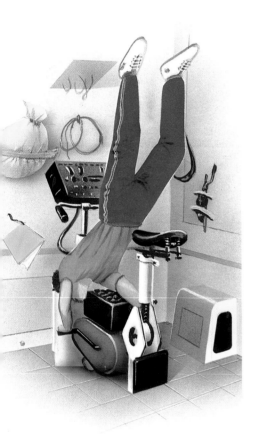

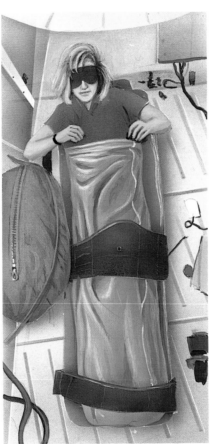

The Adventures of Tintin
(A story by Hergé)

In one of his adventures, Tintin became an astronaut and traveled to the Moon. On the way, he had to rescue his friend, Captain Haddock, before they could continue their journey.

Word box

Astronauts are travelers in space. They collect information for scientists to study. They are also called cosmonauts.

Satellites are spacecraft sent to orbit a planet. They collect information and radio back to Earth.

Rockets

Rockets are used to carry things into space. They are the only machines powerful enough to take spacecraft away from Earth. Rockets have carried hundreds of satellites and probes into space. Rockets also launch astronauts into space. The largest rocket ever made was *Saturn V*. It carried the first astronauts that landed on the Moon.

command module

△ Every trip into space is run from a mission control center. Here, controllers keep track of the rocket on their computers.

▷ This is *Saturn V* blasting off into space. The rocket was 355 feet tall. Most of it held fuel. Only the small command module returned to Earth, with three astronauts inside.

Find the answers

What is *Ariane 5* designed to do?

When did astronauts first land on the Moon?

◁ On July 20, 1969, the American astronauts Neil Armstrong and Edwin Aldrin were the first people to land on the Moon. They collected rocks and set up instruments to study the Moon.

upper part

fuel tank and engine

ariane 5

esa   esa

Make a balloon rocket

Thread a long piece of strong thread onto a needle and drop the needle through a straw. Tie the ends of the thread to chairs as far apart as possible. Blow up a long balloon and seal it with a spring clip. Tape the balloon to the straw, as shown. Release the clip to see your rocket fly.

▷ *Ariane 5* is designed to lift several heavy satellites and probes into space at once. *Ariane 5* has two parts. The first is a huge fuel tank and powerful engine. The cargo is carried in the second upper part.

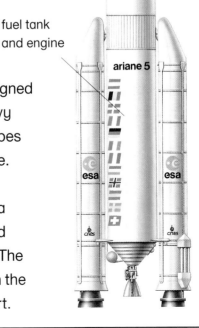

49

The space shuttle

flight deck

The space shuttle can lift off into space like a rocket and then come back to Earth like a glider.

The shuttle is more powerful than 100 jumbo jets. It takes eight minutes to travel into space. Unlike rockets, the shuttle is a spacecraft that can be used again.

space lab in payload bay

▷The shuttle can carry a crew of up to seven astronauts. It can also carry loads as big as a bus in its payload bay.

Make a shuttle glider

Enlarge the two shape guides and trace onto cardboard. Cut the shapes out. Cut a slit in each shape, as shown. Fit the pieces together and tape in place. Staple the nose to give it weight, then glide your shuttle.

50

△ The space shuttle is launched using a huge fuel tank and two booster rockets.

▷ This faulty satellite has been brought into the space shuttle's repair bay to be mended. The astronauts have to be attached so they do not float away.

◁ When the space shuttle returns to Earth, it lands just like a glider.

Satellites and probes

Hundreds of satellites have been put into orbit around Earth. Some bring us television pictures from the other side of the world. Others are used to help ships or planes find their way.

Probes do not carry any astronauts. They are sent on long journeys into space and never return to Earth. Most are used to study the other planets in our Solar System.

△ Meteosat is a satellite that follows the Earth's weather.

▷ The Hubble Space Telescope sends us pictures of distant stars and galaxies.

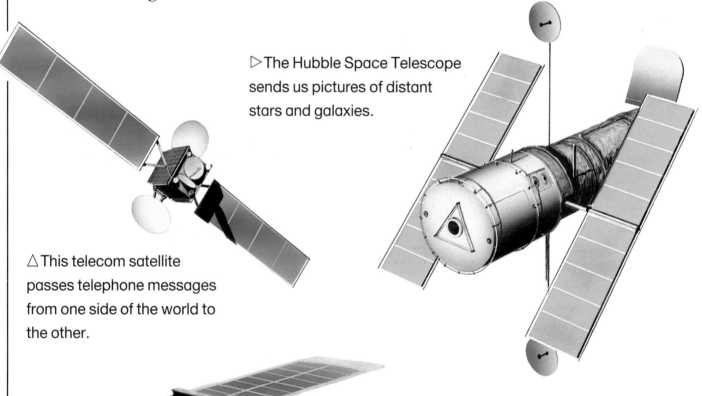

△ This telecom satellite passes telephone messages from one side of the world to the other.

◁ SPOT takes photographs of the Earth's surface as it passes over.

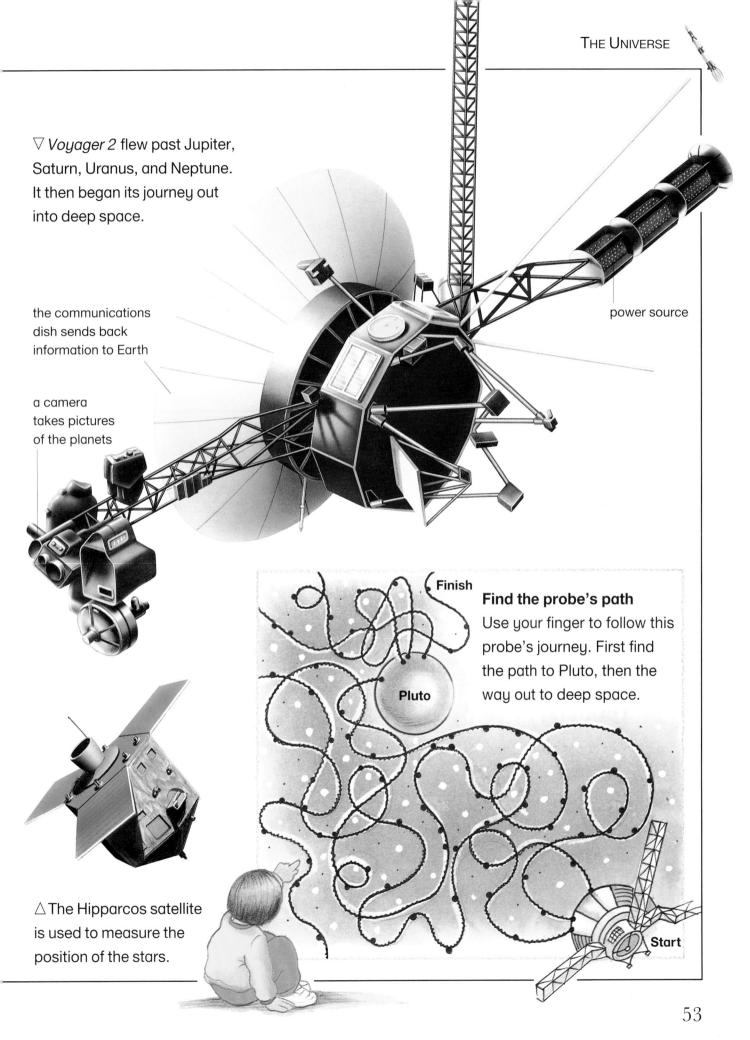

▽ *Voyager 2* flew past Jupiter, Saturn, Uranus, and Neptune. It then began its journey out into deep space.

the communications dish sends back information to Earth

a camera takes pictures of the planets

power source

Find the probe's path
Use your finger to follow this probe's journey. First find the path to Pluto, then the way out to deep space.

Finish

Pluto

Start

△ The Hipparcos satellite is used to measure the position of the stars.

53

Giant telescopes

Astronomers use powerful telescopes on Earth and in space to see far across the universe. Telescopes use lenses and mirrors to see light from stars and galaxies. Many galaxies give off radio signals. Scientists can pick up these signals using radio telescopes. Radio telescopes may one day receive messages from other living beings far away in space.

◁ Hubble can see millions of distant galaxies. It sends photographs back to Earth.

△ The Hubble Space Telescope can see a lot more than ground telescopes, because it is above the blanket of air that surrounds the Earth.

▷ This giant telescope is on Mount Palomar in California, nearly 6,130 feet up. Here the air is very clear and the weather is almost always good.

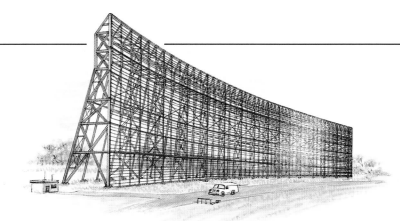

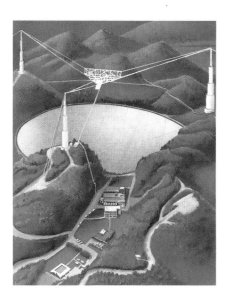

△ This radio telescope in France is fixed in one position. It can only pick up signals from stars that pass directly in front of it as the Earth turns.

▷ The biggest radio telescope in the world is at Arecibo in Puerto Rico and fills the crater of an old volcano.

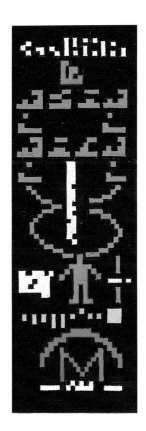

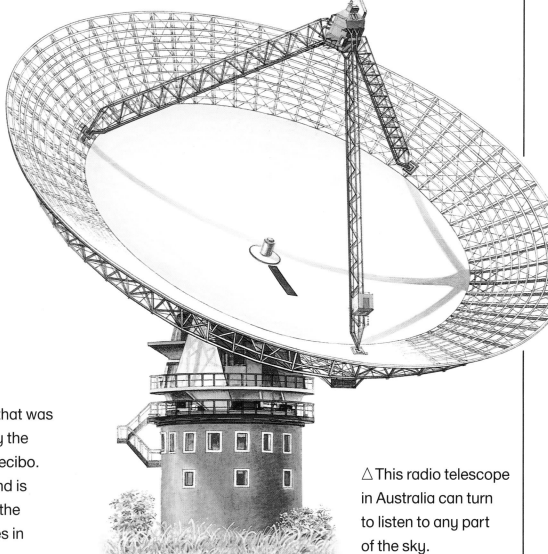

△ This is a message that was sent far into space by the radio telescope at Arecibo. It was sent in 1974 and is expected to arrive in the constellation Hercules in the year 27,000.

△ This radio telescope in Australia can turn to listen to any part of the sky.

55

Space stations

Living in space may seem impossible, but already Russian cosmonauts have lived in space for months, aboard the space station *Mir*. Scientists are now planning to build a base on the Moon.

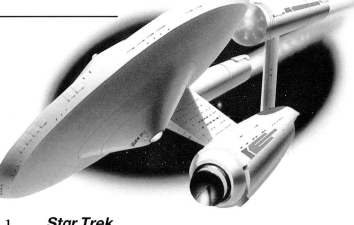

Star Trek
In the film Star Trek, Captain Kirk and his crew live aboard the Starship Enterprise.

However, scientists are a long way from inventing spacecraft like this one.

▽ When cosmonauts live on *Mir*, spacecraft without a crew bring them supplies from Earth.

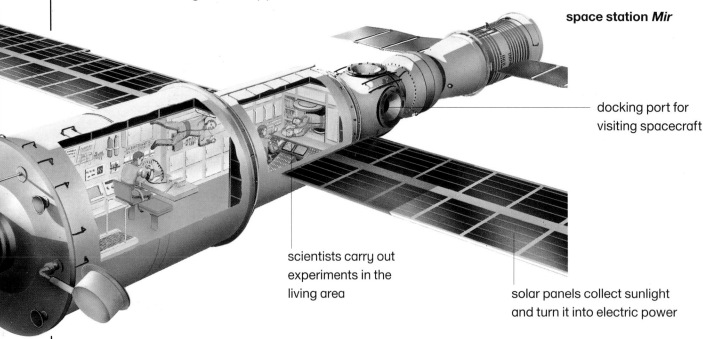

space station *Mir*

docking port for visiting spacecraft

scientists carry out experiments in the living area

solar panels collect sunlight and turn it into electric power

▷ People could be living and working on the Moon one day. The first base will probably be a mining camp and may look like this.

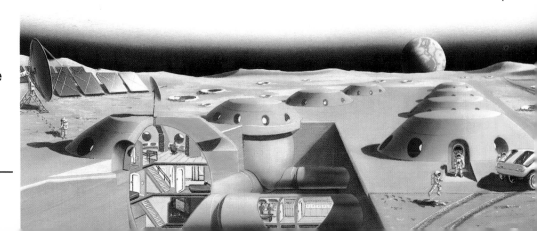

Our Planet Earth

What is Earth?

Our planet Earth is a huge rocky ball. It is one of the nine planets that travel around the Sun. From space, Earth looks blue because seas and lakes cover nearly three-fourths of its surface.

Our planet has hot deserts, steamy rain forests, and freezing cold North and South Poles. In some parts, the land rises to make high mountains.

Can you find?

1 city
2 river
3 smoking volcano
4 elephant and her baby
5 rain cloud
6 forest

Earth, Sky, and the gods
(A Polynesian folk tale)

At the beginning of time, Earth and Sky were joined together. The gods were trapped in the darkness between them and wanted to escape. They asked Forest to put his head on Earth, his feet on Sky, and push them apart. Sky fought back and started a storm, but Forest won. Earth and Sky were separated forever.

△ If you could see the Earth from space, it would look like this. The swirling patterns are clouds. They are part of a thin layer of air around the Earth called the atmosphere.

Word box
Planets are the nine huge ball-shaped objects moving around the Sun. Some planets are made of rock and some of gas.
Atmosphere is the layer of air surrounding the Earth, protecting it from too much heat and cold.

59

Under your feet

The outside of the Earth is a thin shell of hard rock with soil and water on top. The shell is called the crust. Soil is made of tiny pieces of eroded, or worn down, rock mixed with dead plants. Plants get water and food from the soil, through their roots. Many animals live underground and make their homes in the soil.

The Tale of Peter Rabbit
(A story by Beatrix Potter)

Naughty Peter Rabbit squeezed under the gate to eat the garden's delicious vegetables. The gardener chased him and Peter lost his blue coat.

Separate the soil
Wearing gloves, dig up some soil from a pet-free area. Put the soil in a glass jar, and fill it with water. Screw the lid on, and shake well. Leave for 24 hours.

The soil settles in layers, showing what is in the soil.

Word box
Crust is the outer layer of the Earth. It is a thin shell of rock covered by land and sea.
Erosion is the wearing away of rock by wind and water. Tiny pieces of eroded rock and dead plants make up soil.

▷Many animals live under the soil because it is safe and warm. Rabbits live in underground homes called warrens. Moles dig tunnels using their huge front paws.

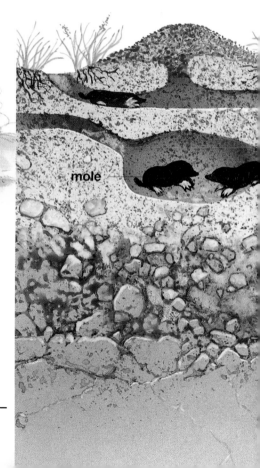

mole

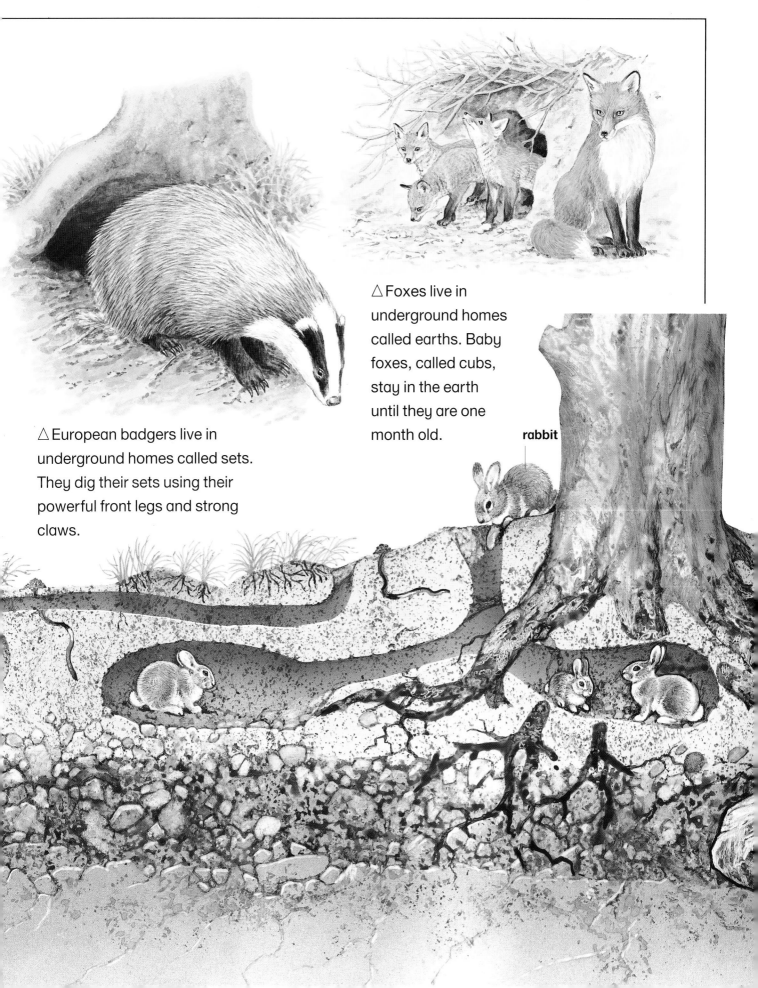

△ Foxes live in underground homes called earths. Baby foxes, called cubs, stay in the earth until they are one month old.

△ European badgers live in underground homes called sets. They dig their sets using their powerful front legs and strong claws.

rabbit

Rocks and fossils

Rocks are made in several different ways. Some form when layers of sand and seashells pile up and get squashed together. Others are made when hot, melted rock from inside the Earth erupts out of a volcano. It cools down and goes hard. Rocks can be changed by being heated or squashed again.

Fossils are often found in layered rocks, such as limestone and shale.

Find the answers

How can rock be changed?

Do you find older rock above or below younger rock?

▽ As rocks are made, they build into layers, like a pile of sandwiches. The oldest rocks are at the bottom and the newest are at the top.

1.7 billion years old

550 million years old

250 million years old

Make a twig fossil

Smear a twig with a little petroleum jelly. Press it firmly into a layer of modeling clay in a plastic pot. Remove the twig carefully. Pour some plaster of Paris over the clay. When it is set, turn out and pull away the clay to see the twig fossil.

△ Millions of years ago, ammonites lived in the sea.

△ After they had died, mud covered the ammonites' shells.

△ Over millions of years, layers of mud built up to make rock.

△ The shapes of their shells are found in the rock as fossils.

▷ Granite is a volcanic rock that hardened underground.

granite

sandstone

shelly limestone

◁ Slate is a rock with layers that split apart easily.

slate

chalk

▷ You can see the shells that helped to make this limestone.

marble

63

Volcanoes and earthquakes

The Earth's crust, or surface, is divided into enormous pieces called plates. These plates are always moving very slowly. When plates move apart, the hot, runny rock below them rushes up to the surface and a volcano erupts. The hot, runny rock that comes out of a volcano is called lava. When plates bump or scrape against each other, earthquakes occur.

Erupt a volcano
Make a cone with thick cardboard. Leave a hole at the top, as shown. Put a shallow plastic tub in the hole. Place a little red poster paint and baking soda in the tub.

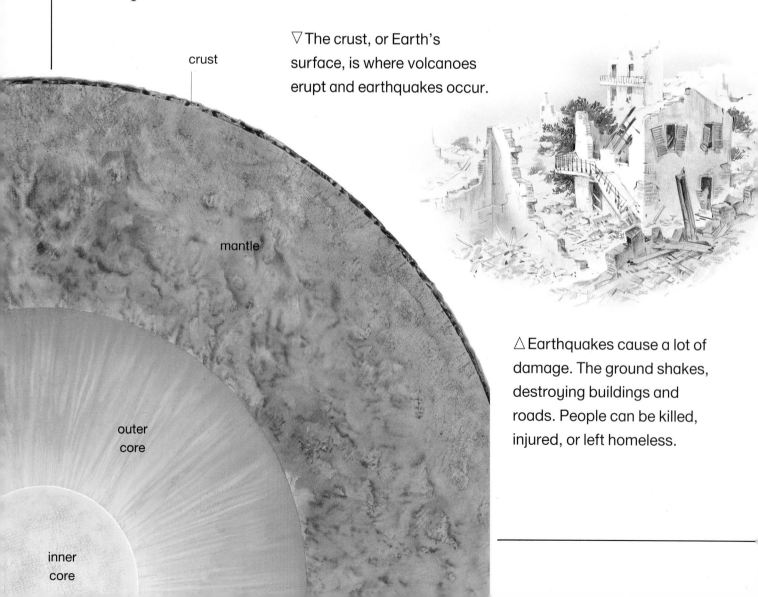

crust

mantle

outer core

inner core

▽ The crust, or Earth's surface, is where volcanoes erupt and earthquakes occur.

△ Earthquakes cause a lot of damage. The ground shakes, destroying buildings and roads. People can be killed, injured, or left homeless.

Carefully add vinegar to make the volcano erupt.

▷When volcanoes erupt, melted rock, called lava, is thrown into the air.

lava

Mountains

It takes thousands of years for mountain ranges to form. Many mountains are made when two of the crust's plates press against each other. When this happens, the rocks at the edges of the plates are squeezed together and pushed up into huge folds. A mountain becomes colder toward its peak, or top. Some mountain peaks are so cold they are snow capped all year long.

▷A slice through a mountain range would show layers of different rocks that have been folded and bent by the plates' movement.

purple
mountain
saxifrage

edelweiss

spring
gentian

◁Mountain plants must survive very cold conditions. In spring and summer, many mountains are bright with colorful flowers.

△ Older mountains have rounded peaks because they have been eroded by the weather.

Rocky Mountain goat

chamois

△ In winter, chamois usually move down the mountain to the warmer forest areas. Rocky Mountain goats have very thick coats so that they can survive nearer the top.

Heidi
(A story by Johanna Spyri)

Heidi moved to the mountains in Switzerland. She loved life in the mountains and the friends she met there.

Find the answers

Do older mountains have sharp or rounded peaks?

Are mountains colder at the top or the bottom?

Shaping the land

Wind and water are constantly wearing down, or eroding, the land. Winds blow sand up off the ground and this rubs away the rock. The rock's shape changes, very slowly, over many thousands of years. Water also erodes the land. Waves wear away cliffs by the sea. Rainwater makes tunnels and caves in limestone rock.

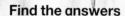

Find the answers

Can wind erode rock?

Do stalagmites point up or down?

Does hard rock erode before soft rock?

◁ Windblown sand has eroded this rock. Softer rock has worn away first, leaving the harder rock behind.

Grow a stalactite

Dissolve washing soda crystals into two jars of warm water. Stand jars on newspaper, placing a saucer between them, as shown. Twist together several strands of yarn, and place an end in each jar. Make sure there is a dip in the middle of the yarn, over the saucer. After a few days, a stalactite and stalagmite will form.

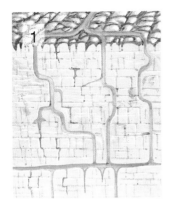

△ Rainwater trickling through the limestone makes passages.

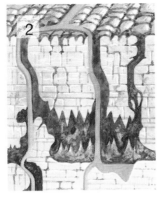

△ If a passage roof collapses, a big cave forms.

Ali Baba and the forty thieves
(An Arabian folk tale)

Ali Baba was a poor man. One day, he saw forty men walking in the wood where he was working. He followed them to a rock, and heard them say, "Open sesame!" A door in the rock sprang open, and from his hiding place Ali Baba saw a cave filled with gold. They said, "Close sesame!" to shut the door as they left.

Ali Baba realized this was stolen gold. He waited until the thieves had gone then, using the password, he entered the cave. He carried home as many sacks of gold as he could manage and shared it out among the other poor people in the town.

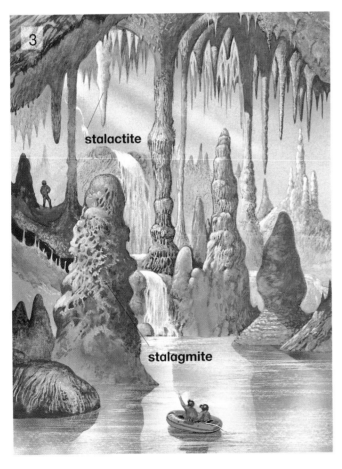

stalactite

stalagmite

△ Minerals are dissolved in the water dripping from the cave roof. This makes stalactites, which hang down from the roof, and stalagmites, which grow up from the floor.

69

The water cycle

The water cycle goes on all the time. It begins when heat from the sun turns water into an invisible gas in the air. This gas is called water vapor.

The water vapor rises, cools, and turns into drops of water. These drops join together to make clouds. Wind blows the clouds over the land.

Water in the clouds falls as rain, snow, or hail. It runs into rivers, which carry the water down to the sea, completing the cycle.

Word box
Water vapor is made of tiny drops of water held in the air.
Valleys are made when rivers wear away the land as they flow to the sea.
Glaciers are huge, slow-moving rivers of ice.

winds blow clouds over the land

water vapor rises in the air to form clouds

seawater is heated by the sun and turned into water vapor

water falls as rain, snow, or hail

Make rain in the bath
When you take a bath, water vapor rises as steam. When the vapor touches something cold, such as a mirror or window, it turns back into water again.

water runs into rivers and is carried back to the sea

The life of a river

Rivers carry water downhill to the sea. A river starts its journey in the mountains, where it falls steeply and flows quickly. It wears away deep valleys. As a river gets nearer the sea, it usually grows wider and flows more slowly. The place where the river meets the sea is called the river's mouth.

△ A river can start from a spring. A spring occurs where underground water gushes out onto the surface.

underground water

some rivers start from the end of a glacier, where the ice melts

valley

a river flows in large bends

river mouth

Make a river

Build a mound of damp sand and stones on a tray. Using a watering can or hose, slowly pour a stream of water over the top. The water will find the quickest way down the slope, carrying some of the sand with it.

△ Most waterfalls are found in mountains. They often form where rivers flow over cliffs made of hard rock, which is not worn away easily.

The discontented fish
(A folk tale from Senegal)

A big fish, who thought he was very important, lived in a river with smaller fish. The small fish hated his boasting, and told him to swim to the sea to live with other big, important fish. The vain fish did this, but was so frightened by the huge sea fish, he swam straight back, promising he would never again be rude to the smaller fish.

▽ Lakes form in large hollows. Rivers flow in and out of most lakes. The rivers bring mud and sand, so some lakes clog up and disappear.

What is air?

Air is a mixture of invisible gases. We cannot see it, taste it, or smell it, but air is all around us. We can feel air when it moves. Moving air is called wind. Wind brings the weather, hot or cold, wet or dry.

All living things need oxygen, a gas in the air we breathe. Without oxygen, there would be no plants, animals, or people on Earth.

▷Seabirds are masters at using the wind to glide and soar above the waves. Upward air currents next to cliffs help these seabirds reach their nests on high, rocky ledges.

Word box
Air is the mixture of gases surrounding the Earth. We all need it to live.
Hurricanes are violent storms with very high winds. Tornadoes are more violent, but smaller and shorter-lasting.

▷Animals, planes, and gliders would not be able to fly without air. Plants such as dandelions use the wind to carry their seeds away. Balloons are filled with air.

Find the answers

What do we call the scale for measuring wind speeds?

What do dandelions use wind for?

parachute

glider

bird

balloon

butterfly

seeds

dandelion

▷There is a scale to measure wind speeds. It is called the Beaufort scale.

Make a parachute

Fix four equal lengths of string to some modeling clay. Cut out a square, about 16 inches by 16 inches, from a plastic bag. Use tape to attach the string to each corner of the square. Hold the parachute high up, and let it drop down.

△Number 1 on the Beaufort scale is almost calm air.

△Number 4 is a breeze that shakes small branches.

△Number 7 is a gale strong enough to break branches.

△Number 10 is a strong gale. Buildings are often damaged.

The Wind and the Sun
(Based on a story by Aesop)

Wind and Sun had a competition to make a man remove his coat. Wind blew a fierce gale, but the man pulled his coat tightly around him.

Sun proved he was more powerful. He gently shone on the man, which made him take off his coat to cool down.

75

Storms and clouds

Storms bring clouds, rain, lightning, and thunder. Lightning is a giant, hot spark of electricity that jumps between a storm cloud and the ground. Thunder is the noise caused by this spark. We hear thunder after lightning because sound travels more slowly than light.

cumulus clouds

▷Clouds are made from millions of tiny water droplets or ice crystals. There are many different kinds of clouds. The largest are thunder clouds, called cumulonimbus.

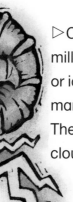

Thunder and Lightning
(A Nigerian folk tale)

Once Lightning, an angry ram, lived on Earth. Thunder was his mother. Lightning spat fire, burning down villagers' huts. Thunder followed him, shouting loudly at her son. The villagers pleaded with their king to send them away. He banished them to the sky. But you can still see Lightning's fiery rages and hear his mother, Thunder.

▽Hurricanes and tornadoes cause damage. They rip up trees and buildings.

cirrus
clouds

△ Electricity builds up inside clouds and on the ground.

cumulonimbus
cloud

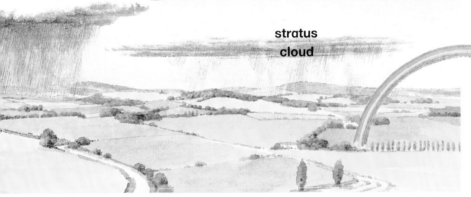

stratus
cloud

△ The electricity causes a brilliant flash of lightning.

Find the answers

Why do we hear thunder after we have seen lightning?

What are clouds made from?

△ Seconds later, there is a crash of thunder.

Rain and snow

Raindrops are made when the tiny droplets of water in clouds join together. When the drops become too heavy to stay in the cloud, they fall down to the ground as rain. Rain is very important to farmers because plants need water to grow.

Snow falls when it is very cold. The drops of water freeze into ice crystals, which fall as light, fluffy snow.

The Snow Queen
(A story by Hans Christian Andersen)

The Snow Queen was beautiful and very evil. She took a young boy to her palace and turned his heart into ice.

▷ Rice is a plant that needs a lot of water. The low walls of rice paddies, where it is grown, hold in rainwater. If there is no rain, crops will die and there will not be enough food.

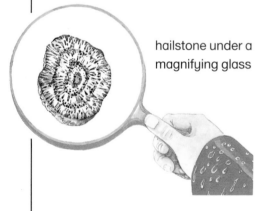

hailstone under a magnifying glass

△ Frozen water droplets are tossed about inside storm clouds and build up layers of ice. They fall as hailstones.

▽In cold places, snow can cover the land and trees for most of the year. People use snowmobiles to travel over snowy ground.

Shake a snowstorm

Find a jar with a snugly fitting lid. Glue cake decorations to the lid. Pour water into the jar until it is almost full. Add one teaspoon of glitter. Screw lid on. Shake jar and turn upside down to see the snowstorm.

▷If you look at snowflakes under a magnifying glass, you can see the patterns of the ice crystals.

Find the answers

What is the name of a field for growing rice?

What can people use to travel across snowy ground?

Why is rain important to farmers?

The seven continents

Spread out flat, the Earth looks like this map. The land is divided into seven continents. They are Africa, Antarctica, Asia, Australia, Europe, North America, and South America.

Continents have different climates. Climate is the usual weather of a place. Can you find a hot, dry desert on this map?

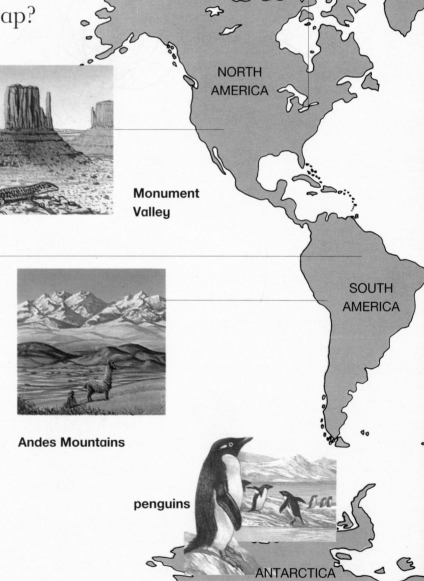

Niagara Falls

NORTH AMERICA

Monument Valley

SOUTH AMERICA

ANTARCTICA

Amazon River and rain forest

Andes Mountains

penguins

Word box
Continent is one of the seven largest areas of land on Earth.
Climate is the usual kind of weather found in a particular place.

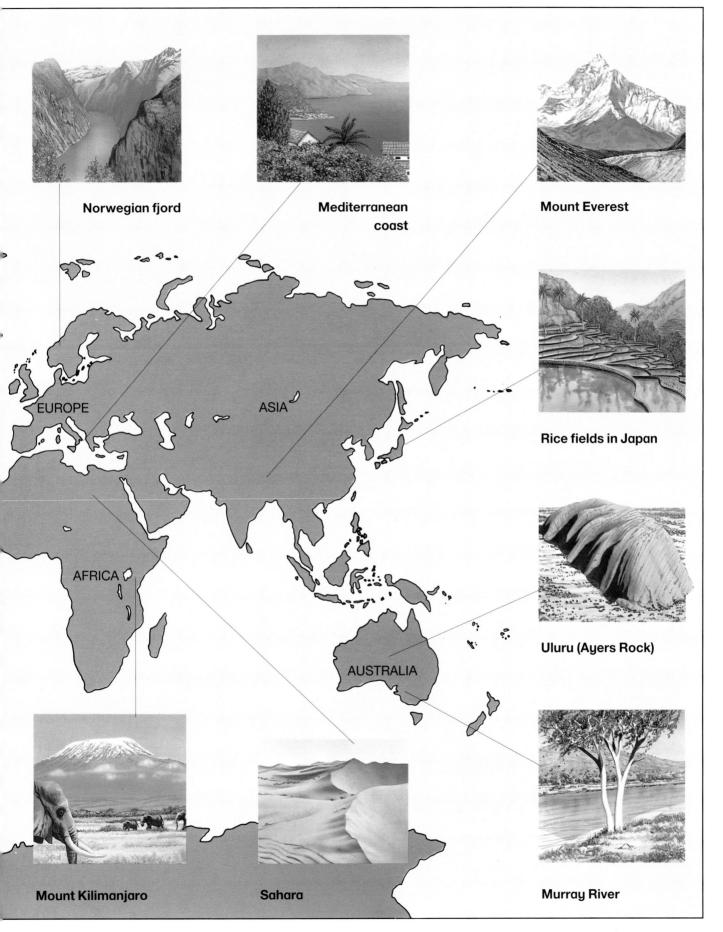

Norwegian fjord

Mediterranean coast

Mount Everest

Rice fields in Japan

Uluru (Ayers Rock)

EUROPE

ASIA

AFRICA

AUSTRALIA

Mount Kilimanjaro

Sahara

Murray River

Cold lands

The climate is very cold around the North and South Poles. Most of the Antarctic continent, around the South Pole, is covered in thick ice all year.

The Arctic Ocean, around the North Pole, is also very cold. But in summer, snow melts on the surrounding land. Plants grow, caribou come to graze, and birds come to nest.

North Pole

South Pole

△ The North and South Poles are at opposite ends of the Earth. There is no day and night. In winter, it is dark all the time and in summer, it is light all the time.

Antarctic

Can you find?
1 baby Adelie penguin
2 emperor penguin
3 Adelie penguin
4 Weddell seals
5 icebreaker
6 glacier

Arctic

Can you find?

1 herd of caribou
2 long-tailed skua
3 Arctic butterfly
4 Arctic poppy
5 bearberry flowers
6 male snow bunting
7 female Lapland bunting

Make ice pops

Pour some fruit juice into clean yogurt tubs. Put them in the freezer. As they start to freeze, push in a popsicle stick or a plastic spoon and freeze again.

Why Polar Bear Lives on the North Pole
(Based on a story by Ted Hughes)

At one time all the animals held beauty contests to decide who was the most beautiful of them all. Polar Bear always won, which made jealous Falcon want to get rid of her. When Polar Bear became vain and hated dust on her fur, Falcon told her about the spotlessly clean North Pole. Polar Bear and her admirers, the seals, moved to the North Pole. You can still see her there today.

Forests and woods

Forests and woods grow in areas where the climate is cold in winter and warmer in summer. Evergreen trees do not lose their leaves in winter. They grow in forests in northern parts of the world, where winters are long and cold. In many countries with milder climates, there are deciduous woods. Deciduous trees lose their leaves in winter.

△ The raccoon lives in the forests of North America. Raccoons are good climbers. Sometimes, they raid birds' nests for the eggs. Raccoons now come into towns for food.

evergreen forest

Can you find?

1 pine cone
2 grizzly bear
3 chipmunk
4 female moose
5 evergreen tree
6 lake

deciduous forest

Can you find?

1 green woodpecker

2 fox

3 acorns

4 deer

5 jay

6 deciduous tree

▽ Kookaburras live in Australia. They eat lizards, snakes, and insects as well as other small animals.

Find the answers

What happens to deciduous trees in winter?

What does evergreen mean?

Fir Tree and Bramble
(Based on a story by Aesop)

Fir Tree often boasted of his height and beauty. This upset humble Bramble, who knew he was ugly. But Fir Tree soon wished he was short and ugly too, when he saw men coming to chop him down for firewood.

Grasslands

In places with long dry seasons, it is mainly grass that grows.

In Africa, many animals live on the savanna, which is grassland with some trees. It is hot all year. In the dry season the grass is brown and dry. During the short wet season it becomes lush and green.

△ Termites are small insects that live in hot grasslands all over the world. They are able to build nests that are much larger than they are.

Can you find?
1 lioness and cub
2 zebras
3 gazelles
4 elephant
5 giraffes

86

A giraffe jigsaw puzzle

Trace the giraffe shown and draw it on a piece of cardboard. Color it in. Carefully cut the giraffe out and then cut it into several pieces. Mix all the pieces up. Can you figure out where the pieces go to make the giraffe whole again?

3

Australia's grassland is called the bush. Kangaroos and emus feed on the grasses there.

kangaroo

emu

Hot deserts

Deserts cover large parts of the world. They get very little rain, so they have few plants and animals, just a lot of sand and rock. Wind blows the sand into huge hills called dunes.

In some deserts, plant seeds lie in the ground for years. The seeds only grow when a rainstorm gives them enough water.

△ The scorpion's tail has a very nasty sting at the end. Some scorpions' stings can kill people, but they do not usually attack unless they are annoyed.

▷ The fennec fox lives in North Africa and Arabia. Its huge ears help it listen for insects to eat and also help it to keep cool.

Find the answers

Where do cactus plants store water?

What is a camel's hump full of?

What do we call the huge hills of sand in deserts?

Can you find?

1 jerboa
2 camel train
3 desert city
4 sand dunes

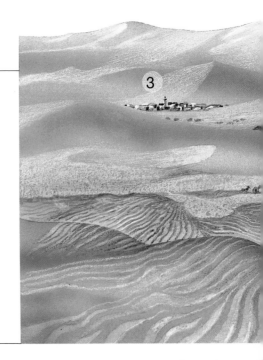

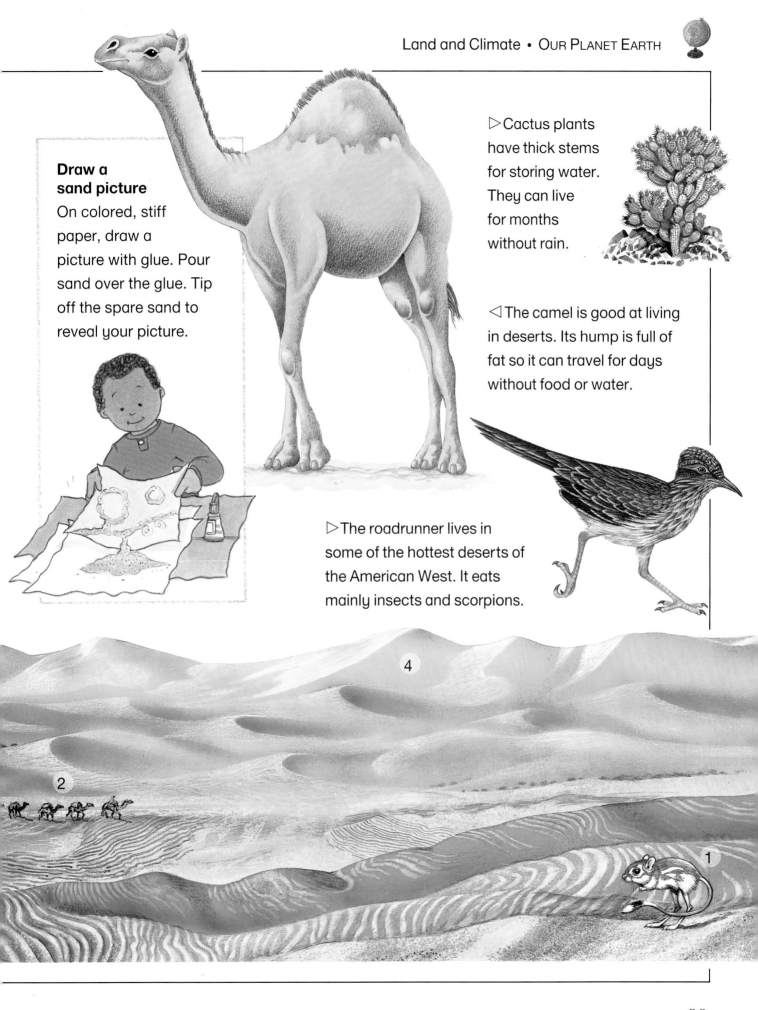

Draw a sand picture
On colored, stiff paper, draw a picture with glue. Pour sand over the glue. Tip off the spare sand to reveal your picture.

▷Cactus plants have thick stems for storing water. They can live for months without rain.

◁The camel is good at living in deserts. Its hump is full of fat so it can travel for days without food or water.

▷The roadrunner lives in some of the hottest deserts of the American West. It eats mainly insects and scorpions.

Rain forests

Rain forests grow in countries that are hot and have a lot of rain. More than half the world's animals and plants live in these forests. The animals live among the thick undergrowth and tall trees. In the treetops, the branches meet and form a roof called a canopy. The world's rain forests are in danger because people are cutting them down and turning them into farmland.

△ Tree frogs have suction pads on their toes to grip twigs and leaves. Tree frogs are tiny and very colorful.

◁ Leaf-cutting ants march along the forest floor. They bite off pieces of leaf and carry them back to their nests.

Make a mask
Fold a piece of cardboard in half. The cardboard should be 12 inches by 8 inches. Draw half of an animal's head and color it. Cut it out. Make a hole at each side. Thread elastic through to finish the mask.

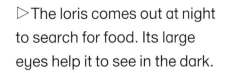

▷ The loris comes out at night to search for food. Its large eyes help it to see in the dark.

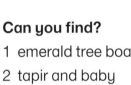

◁ The gibbon's long arms help it to swing from tree to tree, high up in the rain forest's canopy.

Can you find?

1 emerald tree boa
2 tapir and baby
3 howler monkey
4 crowned eagle
5 hummingbird
6 butterfly
7 ocelot
8 toucan
9 macaw

Day and night

The Earth is spinning on an imaginary line called its axis. It is this spinning that gives us day and night.

The part of the Earth facing the Sun gets sunlight. This is daytime. As Earth spins around, that part turns away from the Sun and it becomes dark. This is nighttime. The Earth takes 24 hours to make a whole turn.

Never look straight at the Sun. It will damage your eyes.

Word box
Axis is the imaginary line that goes through the center of the Earth.
Poles are the two ends of the Earth's axis. The North Pole is at the north end. The South Pole is at the south end.
Equator is an imaginary line around the middle of the Earth. Places on or near the equator are very hot.

▷The axis is an imaginary line from the North Pole through the center of the Earth to the South Pole. The Earth makes one whole turn every 24 hours.

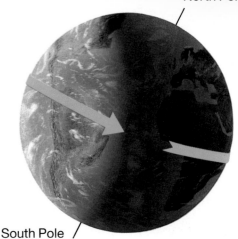

North Pole

South Pole

Earth

◁ As well as spinning on its axis, the Earth moves around the Sun. It takes Earth one year to travel all the way around the Sun.

Sun

Moon

△ The Moon travels around the Earth once every 29 days. It is only a quarter of the size of Earth.

Find the answers

What is an axis?

How long does the Earth take to travel once around the Sun?

Are places near the equator hot or cold?

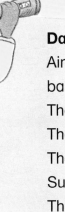

Day and night
Aim a flashlight at a ball in a dark room. The light is the Sun. The ball is the Earth. The side facing the Sun is light, or day. The other side is dark, or night.

△ During the day, the Sun gives us light. At nighttime, streetlights light the streets.

93

Seasons

The four seasons in most parts of the world are summer, fall, winter, and spring. Other places have only two seasons.

We have seasons because the Earth tilts. First one half leans toward the Sun, then the other. It is summer in the part of the world tilted toward the Sun.

Find the answers

How many seasons does the Arctic have?

When is the first day of summer in the southern half of the world?

▷ June 21 is the day of the year when the land above the equator first leans toward the Sun. It is the first day of winter in the southern half of the world.

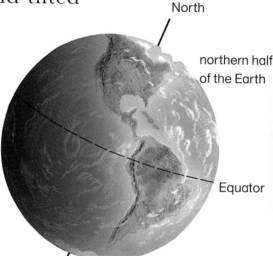

North

northern half of the Earth

Equator

South

△ In spring, days are warm, and nights cool.

△ In summer, days are hot, and nights warm.

△ In the fall, days and nights are cooler.

△ In winter, days and nights are cold.

△ The Arctic and Antarctic regions have just two seasons. During the summer, the Sun never sets. In winter it does not rise.

△ In some places near the equator, there are only two seasons. After the long, hot, dry season, there is a wet season.

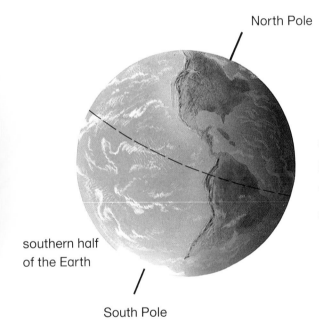

North Pole

southern half of the Earth

South Pole

◁ December 21 is the first day of the year that land below the equator leans toward the Sun. It is the first day of winter in the northern half of the world.

Paint a summer tree
Use pencils and felt-tip pens to draw a winter tree with no leaves. Change it into a summer tree by adding leaves. Mix up different shades of green paint, and fingerprint summer leaves onto the branches.

Changing our Earth

People change the Earth. They often turn land that was once forest into farmland. As the number of people grows, more land is used for farming.

People need houses. Today, many people live in towns and cities. As more houses are built, towns and cities grow. Cars, buses, trains, and planes take people from one place to another.

△ Much of the land was once covered in forests. Hundreds of different plants and animals lived there.

△ People cut the forest down and sold the wood.

△ The land was used to graze animals and grow crops for food.

△ To begin with, there may have been only one small farm.

△ The farming families then set up a small village.

△ Other people came to shop or visit. Villages often grew into towns and people built new houses on the farmland.

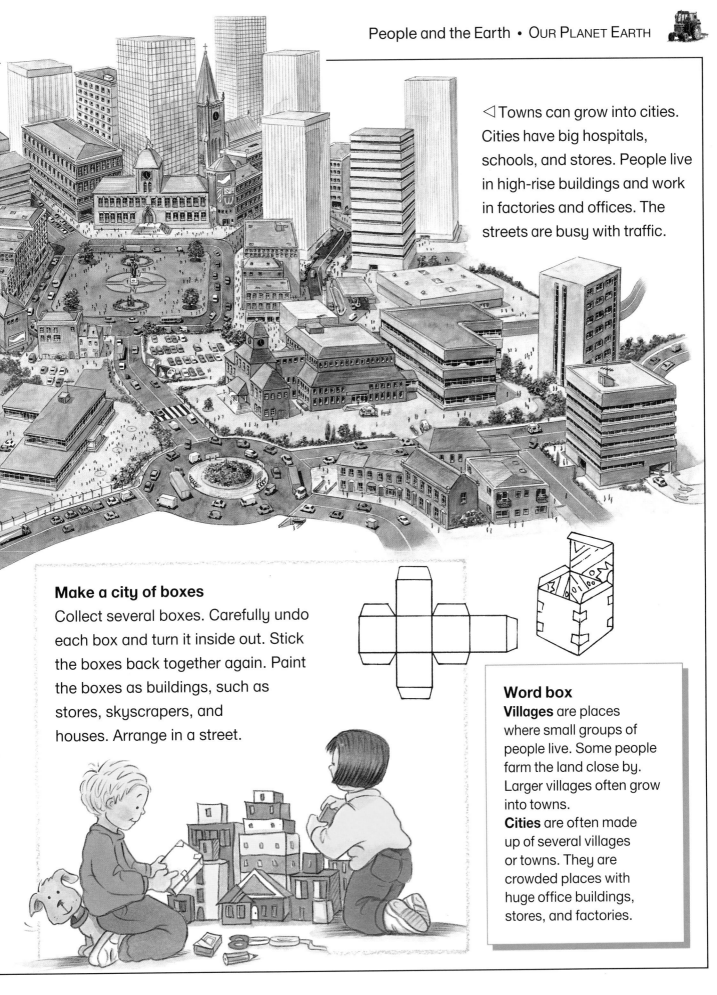

▷ Towns can grow into cities. Cities have big hospitals, schools, and stores. People live in high-rise buildings and work in factories and offices. The streets are busy with traffic.

Make a city of boxes

Collect several boxes. Carefully undo each box and turn it inside out. Stick the boxes back together again. Paint the boxes as buildings, such as stores, skyscrapers, and houses. Arrange in a street.

Word box

Villages are places where small groups of people live. Some people farm the land close by. Larger villages often grow into towns.

Cities are often made up of several villages or towns. They are crowded places with huge office buildings, stores, and factories.

97

Food and farming

The Earth provides us with many resources. Resources are the things we need. Land is a resource. All over the world, farmers use the land to grow crops to feed people and animals.

The most important crops grown are grains including corn, rice, and wheat. As well as growing food crops, farmers keep animals on the land.

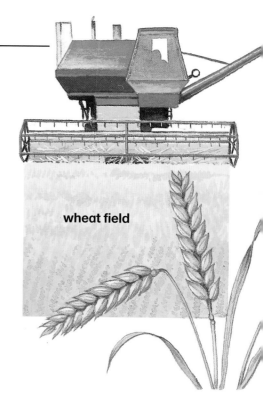

wheat field

▷Wool can be obtained from several different animals. A sheep's wool is called its fleece. It is cut off with shears. This is like a haircut and does not hurt. The sheep soon grows a new woolly fleece.

▽The wool is cleaned and spun into long threads called yarn. Then the wool is dyed with color and wound into balls, ready to sell.

◁People buy balls of wool for knitting clothes, such as this sweater.

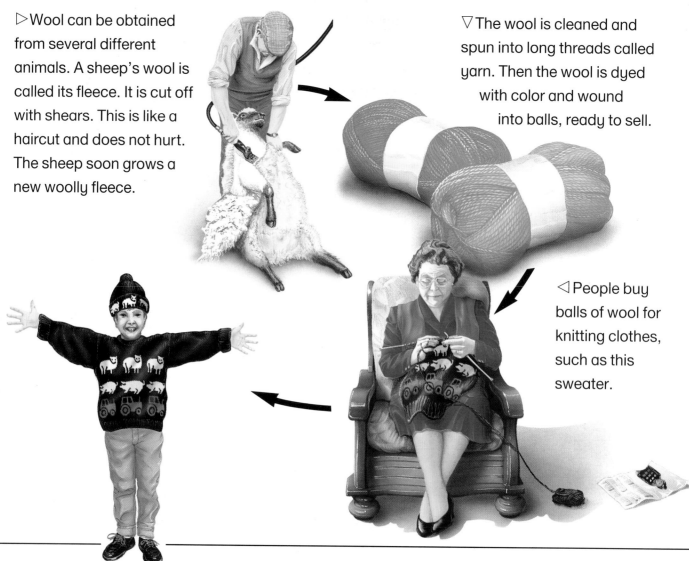

◁ Wheat is grown in large, open fields. It is harvested with huge machines called combine harvesters. Wheat flour is used to make bread and pasta.

bread

wheat plant

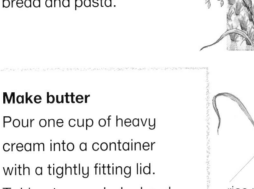

rice field

cooked rice

rice plant

Make butter

Pour one cup of heavy cream into a container with a tightly fitting lid. Taking turns, shake hard until butter forms. This may take 30 minutes. Drain off any liquid. Stir in some salt and spread on bread or crackers.

△ Rice is grown in many countries. Rice plants are grown in flooded fields. The rice is often harvested by hand.

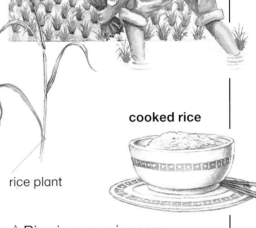

△ Cows provide us with milk. Some of their milk is used to make butter and cheese.

△ Hens lay eggs. Hens are kept on large and small farms all over the world.

The Earth's riches

The Earth is rich in resources. Crops are grown on the land and fish are caught from the sea. Forests give us timber. Metals are mined from rocks.

Coal, gas, and oil are important natural resources. They provide us with energy to light our homes and power factories. But they will not last forever. People are looking for new ways of making energy, using such things as the wind and the Sun.

sap

Rubber trees provide sap for making rubber. Car tires are made from rubber.

▽ Huge forests of trees are grown for their valuable timber. When the trees are cut down, new trees must be planted. This makes sure there will be a supply of wood in the future.

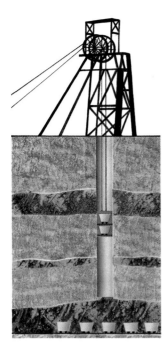

△ Coal is used as fuel. Miners dig it out of the ground. Most coal is dug from near the surface, but some coal mines are very deep.

△ Oil and gas are found on land and under the sea. Miners on a rig drill holes into the rock and pump up the oil or gas.

◁ Timber is used for building houses and making furniture. Even the paper in this book is made from wood.

Find the answers

Which resources might we use for making energy in the future?

What do we use coal, oil, and gas for?

What is timber used for?

Spoiling our planet

By learning to use the Earth's riches we have made our lives easier. But we are also spoiling our planet. Factories, cars, and power stations pump smoke and gases into the air. This pollutes, or damages, the air. Pollution harms our own health and kills wildlife.

▽ Towns and factories pump sewage and poisonous chemicals into rivers and the sea. This pollution harms water plants and animals.

Find the answers

What do factories, cars, and power stations pump into the air?

What do towns and factories pump into rivers and the sea?

▽ Exhaust fumes from traffic and fumes from burning waste can kill plants and make people sick.

▽ Farmers use chemicals to produce more food, but some of them can damage soil and rivers. Accidents at sea mean tankers spill oil into the water.

▽ Many people litter our planet with their trash. What can we do about it?

Saving our planet

Everyone can help make the Earth a cleaner, healthier place to live on. We can help to keep the Earth beautiful by planting trees. We can help keep the Earth clean by being careful with our trash. A lot of this can be recycled, by making new things from old materials.

△ It is useful to plant trees. They provide food and homes for animals and help to keep the air clean.

◁ Always make sure you put your litter in a trash can.

△ Old glass, metal, paper, rubber, and clothes can be recycled. Bottle banks are used to collect glass.

Recycle paper
Tear newspaper into small pieces. Place in a bucket of warm water. Leave until soggy. Collect paper in a strainer to drain off water.

Squeeze water out of the mixture with a rolling pin, using plenty of newspaper to soak it up. Leave to dry. Paint a picture on it.

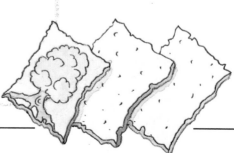

The Sea

Our blue planet

If you looked down at the Earth from space, you would see that most of our planet is covered by water. This huge amount of water is separated into five areas, called oceans, by the land. The oceans are the Arctic, Antarctic, Atlantic, Indian, and Pacific. Smaller areas of the oceans are called seas. Two of the largest seas are the Caribbean and Mediterranean.

△ There is more water than land on the Earth's surface. Nearly three-fourths of the Earth is covered in water.

▷ The oceans and seas are all joined up, so you can travel from one to the other without crossing any land. Because the Earth is round, if you set off from the Pacific Ocean and kept on sailing right, you would eventually return to the Pacific again.

Word box
Oceans are the five vast areas of salty water that surround all the land on Earth.
Plankton are tiny creatures and plants that drift in seawater and fresh water.

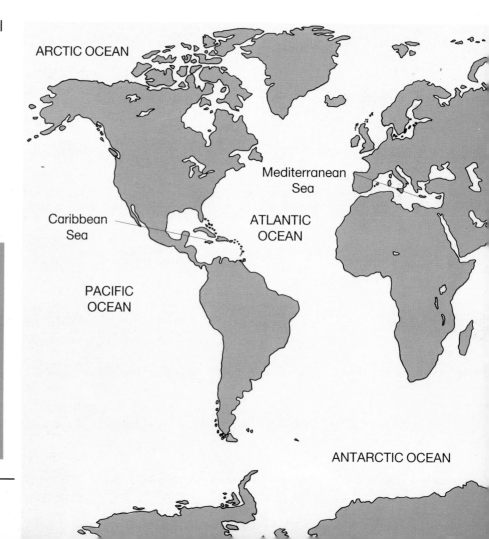

ARCTIC OCEAN

Mediterranean Sea

Caribbean Sea

ATLANTIC OCEAN

PACIFIC OCEAN

ANTARCTIC OCEAN

▽ Life on Earth began in the sea millions of years ago. Now it is home to many plants and animals, from tiny plankton to the huge blue whales that feed on them.

plankton

blue whale

PACIFIC
OCEAN

INDIAN
OCEAN

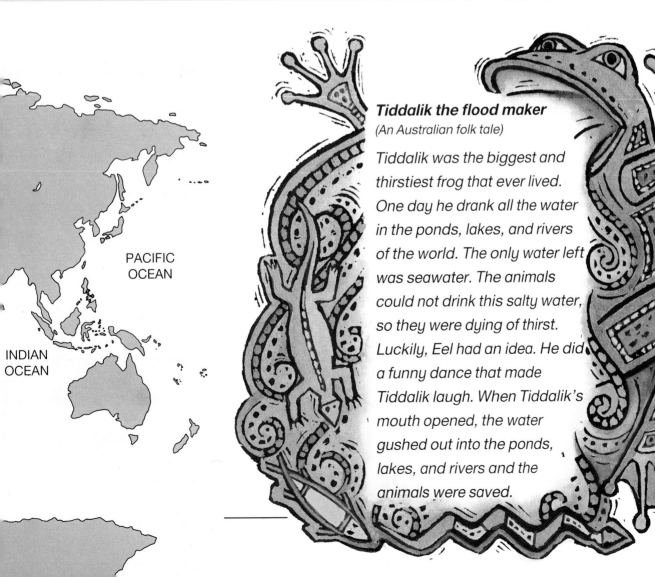

Tiddalik the flood maker
(An Australian folk tale)

Tiddalik was the biggest and thirstiest frog that ever lived. One day he drank all the water in the ponds, lakes, and rivers of the world. The only water left was seawater. The animals could not drink this salty water, so they were dying of thirst. Luckily, Eel had an idea. He did a funny dance that made Tiddalik laugh. When Tiddalik's mouth opened, the water gushed out into the ponds, lakes, and rivers and the animals were saved.

What is seawater?

If you have ever swum in the sea and tasted seawater, you will know that it is salty. Most of the salt comes from rocks on the land. When rocks are worn down by wind and rain, the salt they contain is washed into the sea by the rivers. It builds up and makes the water salty.

All seawater is not at the same temperature. Sunlight warms the water near the surface of the sea. Where the sun shines longest the water is warmest.

△ Around the North and South poles the water is so cold that it freezes. The huge, flat pieces of floating ice are called ice floes.

▷ Around the equator, the Sun heats the water for many hours each day. But at the poles there is much less sunlight and the water is cold.

△ Because of the Sun, the tropical seas around the equator stay warm all year long.

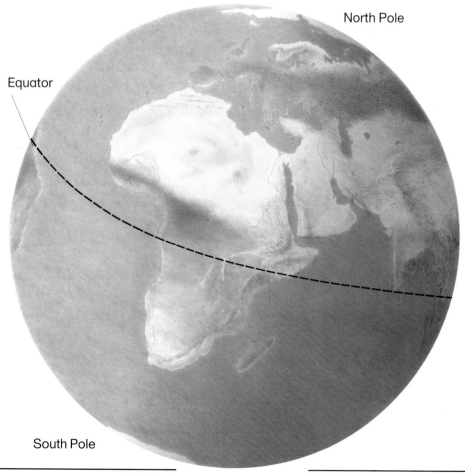

North Pole

Equator

South Pole

Find the answers

Why is seawater salty?

Is water near the equator warm or cold?

Where is the sea least salty?

△ River water does not taste salty because the amount of salt it contains is very tiny. We call it fresh water.

△ Seawater does taste salty. This is because so much salt has been washed into it and collected there over the years.

▽ The least salty part of the sea is in the Atlantic Ocean, off South America. There, the Amazon River pours millions of gallons of fresh water into the sea every day.

Weather and the sea

The sea helps to control our weather. It does this by soaking up heat from the Sun and slowly releasing it. Unlike the land, the seawater warms up and cools down slowly. This means places near the sea have milder winters and cooler summers than those inland.

The sea is never still. Currents, like huge rivers, carry water from one part of the world to another. Some flow near the surface. Others flow deep down, along the ocean floor.

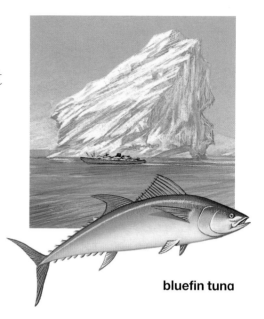

bluefin tuna

△ Icebergs and sea animals are moved around by currents. Bluefin tuna use the currents to travel across the Atlantic Ocean.

▷ The sea is part of the water cycle. In the cycle, the Sun's heat turns some seawater into an invisible gas called water vapor. This rises into the air and forms clouds. The water in the clouds falls back to the sea as rain or snow. Even water that falls on land eventually flows back to the sea in streams and rivers.

ATLANTIC
OCEAN

△ Currents are like huge rivers in the sea. Some of them are shown on this map. As the wind blows them along, the currents bend around the land and change direction. Some animals, such as tuna, use the currents to travel to different parts of the world.

Word box
Water vapor is made of tiny drops of water in the air, which we cannot see.
Currents are made by water or air that is always on the move.

111

Waves and tides

The sea is never still. Waves and tides keep the water moving. Most waves are made by the wind. The stronger the wind, the bigger the waves. They are fun for surfing on, but dangerous for ships out at sea.

Twice a day the tides come in and go out. At high tide the water moves farther onto the land. At low tide, it moves away from the land.

King Canute and the tides
Long ago lived a king called Canute. People believed he could do anything, even stop the tides. But he showed them that no one can stop the tides.

wind

▽ In a storm, strong winds blowing across the top of the sea make huge waves with foamy edges. These waves are called whitecaps.

Find the answers

What happens at high tide?

What starts a tsunami?

What is a whitecap?

Make waves in the bathtub

Waves look as if they go forward, but really they only move up and down. To see this, put a toy into the bathtub and make some waves with your hands. The toy will bob up and down on the waves.

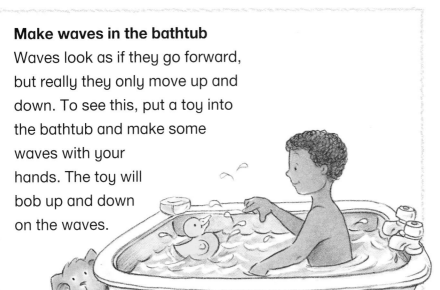

▽ When the water near to the shore rises and gets deeper it is high tide. When the water falls, it is low tide. Boats in a harbor may be left sitting on the mud at low tide.

▽ Waves called tsunamis (soo-nah-mees) can cause a lot of damage to the land. They are started by underwater earthquakes and volcanoes.

Along the coast

A coastline is where the land meets the sea. When the wind and the waves beat against the coastline they wear it away and change its shape. This is called erosion. Big rocks break away from the land and fall into the sea. They are knocked against each other by the waves and break up into small rocks. Eventually, tiny bits of broken-up rock and shell become grains of sand.

▷A bay forms when the waves wear away soft rock in the cliff. Harder rock may be left sticking out as a headland. Sometimes the waves carve out caves, arches, and stacks.

Make a paperweight
Wash and dry a smooth pebble.
Paint a sea creature or monster on it.
Varnish the picture with some clear nail polish.
When it is dry, use it as a paperweight.

Word box
Erosion is the wearing away of rocks and land by the weather and the sea.
Sediment is tiny pieces of sand and rock carried along by rivers and the sea.

cliff

bay

cave

headland

△ Erosion goes on all
the time, so the shape
of a coastline changes.
Some buildings have been
built on the coastline and have fallen
into the sea when erosion has eaten away the cliff.

△ Waves rub boulders of rock against each other.

△ Rocks are broken up and worn down.

△ Sand is made of tiny pieces of broken rock and shell.

stack

arch

The water's edge

The coastline is home to many different animals and plants. Some of them live in rock pools on the beach. Others live on the cliffs high above the beach. The sea provides plenty of fish and tiny creatures and plants called plankton for the animals to catch and eat.

Why the crab has no head
(An African folk tale)

Goddess Nzambi was making all the animals. She started Crab just before bedtime and did not have time to finish him. "Come back tomorrow and I'll give you a head," she said.

"Nzambi's taking two days to make me because I am so important," Crab boasted to all the other animals.

Nzambi heard about Crab's pride and decided not to give him a head.

Crab went to hide under a rock in shame. To this day, he has to poke his eyes out from under his body shell, as he still has no head.

puffin

gannet

guillemot

◁ Different birds live along the coastlines of the world. Puffins build their nests in burrows on the clifftop. Gannets make nests from seaweed. Guillemots lay their eggs on rocky ledges.

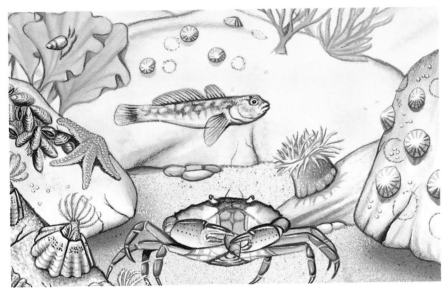

△ Wild thrift grows along many of the coastlines around the world.

△ When the tide is in, animals in the rock pools look for food. Barnacles open their shells and stick out their feathery arms to catch plankton.

▷ When the tide goes out, barnacles and mussels close their shells up tight. Snails and limpets cling to the rocks. Crabs and starfish hide.

Make a treasure chest

Collect shells from the seashore. Glue them carefully onto a cardboard box, covering the whole box with your design.

Paint the words "Treasure Chest" on the lid and use it to keep all the things you find washed up on the seashore.

Seaweed

Seaweeds live along rocky shores. These plants do not have roots because there is no soil for them to dig into. Instead, they grip tightly to the rocks with sticky pads called holdfasts.

Seaweeds live at different depths in the water. They all bend with the water so that they do not get damaged by the waves, tides, and currents.

△ Giant seaweeds called kelp grow in deep water. Seals hide from their enemies in the kelp forests.

▽ Bladderwrack and some other seaweeds have swellings full of gas so that they can float and move easily with the water.

grass kelp

sea lettuce

bladderwrack

holdfast

oarweed

Find the answers

What do seals use the giant kelp for?

Why do seaweeds bend with the water?

Do seaweeds have roots?

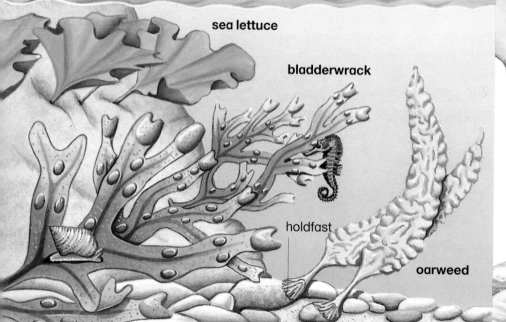

In the sand

On sandy shores, the wind often blows the sand into small hills called dunes. Down on the beach, animals burrow into the sand to protect themselves when the tide is out.

△ Grasses grow on sand dunes and hold them in place.

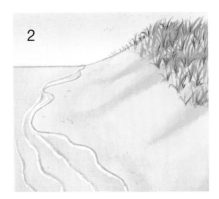

△ As more sand is piled up by the wind, the dunes become larger.

Build a sand sculpture
Try building a giant turtle or an imaginary monster in the sand. Use shells, seaweeds, and sticks to decorate it.

▷ Some shellfish use a special kind of foot to dig themselves into the sand. When the tide is in, they stick out tubes called siphons and suck in seawater. The water contains tiny bits of food.

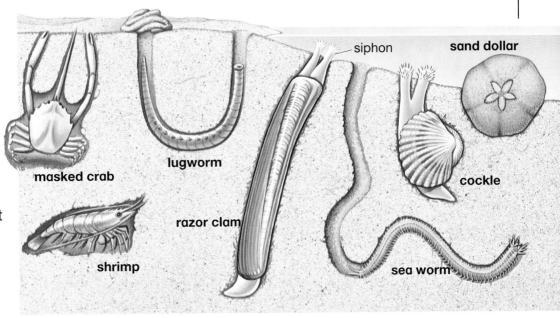

masked crab

lugworm

shrimp

razor clam

siphon

sand dollar

cockle

sea worm

Estuaries and deltas

When a river flows into the sea, we say it has reached its mouth. If the river has a wide mouth it is called an estuary. Here, there is a mixture of fresh river water and salty seawater. Some rivers dump huge amounts of stones and sand into the estuary and a muddy piece of land, called a delta, is made. Many animals live on this land.

◁ The stilt's long legs help it wade through the water on estuaries and deltas. Its long pointed beak searches for food in the mud.

▽ Fresh water flows into an estuary from a river. When the tide comes in, salty water moves into it from the sea.

▷A delta is a triangular area of mud dumped into an estuary by a river. The river makes pathways through the delta so that it can flow into the sea.

Make stilts

Take the lids off two small, empty paint cans. Trap the middle of a long piece of thick string under each lid. Turn the cylinders upside down. Wind tape around each cylinder several times to keep the string tightly in place.

Place one foot on each cylinder, hold the ends of the string, and walk forward.

▽ Many birds live on deltas. They poke into the mud with their specially shaped beaks to find worms and other creatures to eat.

curlew   oystercatcher   redshank   turnstone

Marshes and swamps

Where the land meets water, there are sometimes wet strips of land called marshes and swamps. Plant roots stop sand, gravel, and mud from being washed away. This helps build up the coast. Marshes and swamps provide food and shelter for many animals.

▷ The heron wades through marshes looking for fish to eat. It catches them with its long pointed beak.

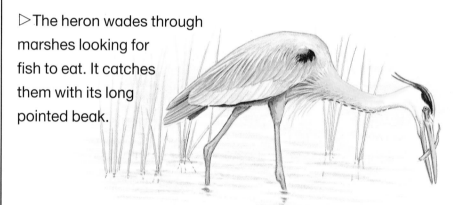

Puck, the mischievous elf

*Have you heard of Puck?
He is the naughty elf in William Shakespeare's play
A Midsummer Night's Dream.
He was based on the flickering light that is caused by burning marsh gas (methane) formed when plants decay.*

▷ Marshes have no trees. The roots of grasses trap sediment, or bits of sand and mud, in the water.

▷ Large marsh pinks grow in salt marshes on the coast of North America.

marsh

Make a dragonfly

Blow up a long balloon. Make two twists to form the head and body and tie with string. Glue on bits of newspaper to cover it. Paint when dry. Make wings from wire bent into shape and cover with tracing paper. Attach wings with wire. Stick on pipe cleaners for legs.

▷Mangrove trees grow in tropical swamps. Their long roots grow high above the mud, holding the tree in place, and keeping the rest of the tree above water. The archer-fish shoots down insects by spitting drops of water. The mudskipper fish breathes air.

swamp

◁The water moccasin lives in some of the swamps in North America. It eats many of the other swamp animals.

Zones

Sea animals live in different zones, or areas, of the sea. Some zones are deeper than others. Most animals and plants live in the top zone, where it is warm. Here, there is enough sunlight for plants to grow. Not many animals are able to live at the bottom of the sea, where it is cold and dark.

Find the answers

What are prey?

Where do sea plants grow?

▷Animals that hunt other animals are called predators. They usually live in the same zone as their prey, the animals that they eat. Creatures living in the bottom zone also eat bits of food that fall down from above.

Word box
Predators are animals that hunt and kill other animals for food.
Prey are the animals hunted by predators.

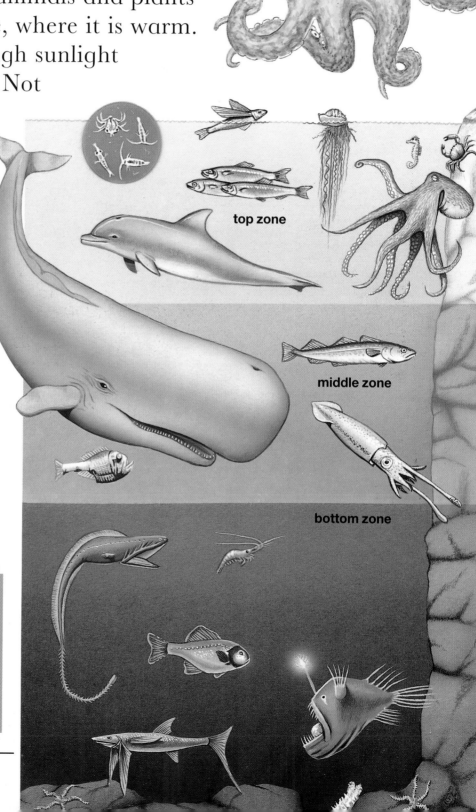

top zone

middle zone

bottom zone

Plankton

Plankton are the smallest living things in the sea. They live near the surface of the water and are food for many sea animals. Some plankton are plants and others are animals. Animal plankton eat plant plankton.

△ Most plankton are so small that you can see them only with a microscope.

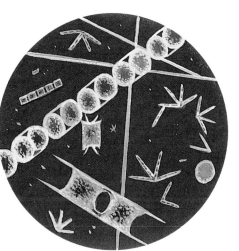

plant plankton
under a microscope

animal plankton
under a microscope

▷ Blue whales, the largest animals in the sea, feed on animal plankton. One whale can eat four tons a day!

mackerel

jellyfish

sea anemone

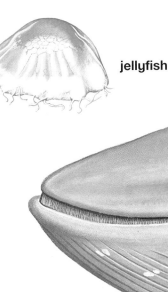

△ Sea anemones, jellyfish, and fish such as mackerel eat plankton.

Staying alive

All the animals in the sea need food. Many of the smaller creatures eat tiny sea plants. Bigger animals hunt and eat the smaller creatures, and even larger animals eat them. This is called a food chain.

To stay alive in the sea the animals must find food and also try not to be eaten. They hide and protect themselves in different ways.

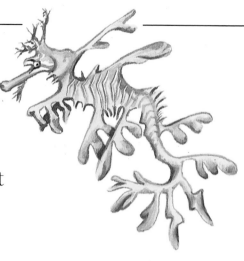

△ The sea dragon is hard to see because it looks like a piece of seaweed.

▷ There are thousands of different food chains in the sea. Here is one of them. Killer whales eat harbor seals, which eat cod, which eat herring, and so on.

∇ Mackerel travel together in large groups called schools to protect themselves. Some may be caught by predators, such as barracuda, but the rest are able to escape.

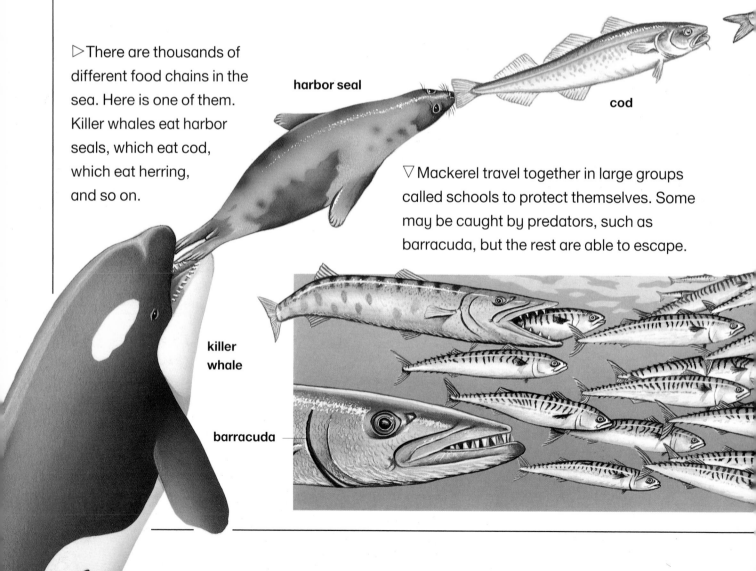

harbor seal

cod

killer whale

barracuda

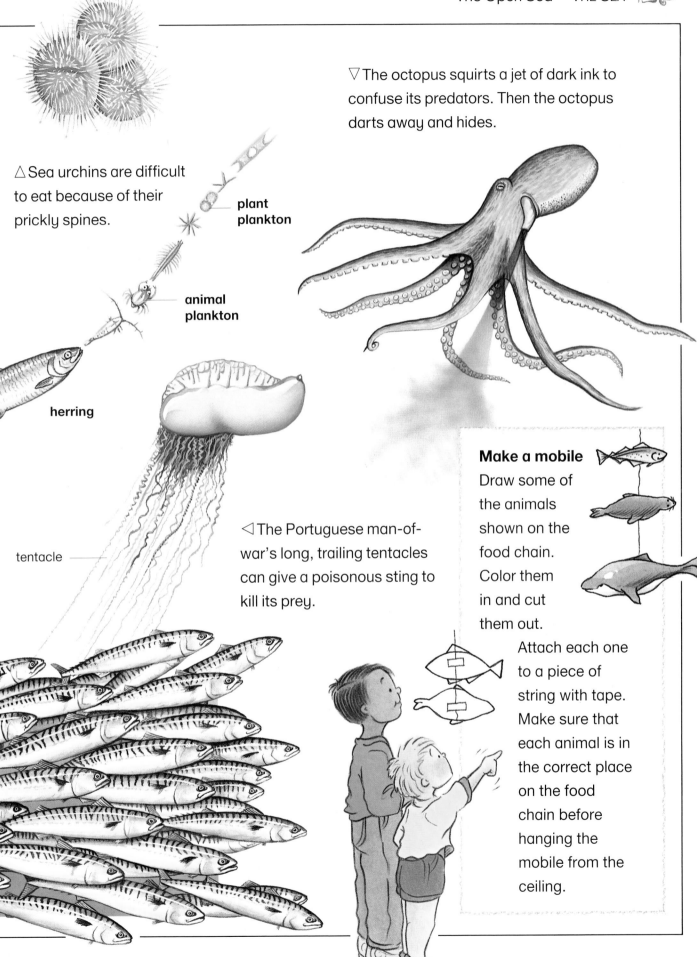

▽ The octopus squirts a jet of dark ink to confuse its predators. Then the octopus darts away and hides.

△ Sea urchins are difficult to eat because of their prickly spines.

plant plankton

animal plankton

herring

tentacle

◁ The Portuguese man-of-war's long, trailing tentacles can give a poisonous sting to kill its prey.

Make a mobile
Draw some of the animals shown on the food chain. Color them in and cut them out.

Attach each one to a piece of string with tape. Make sure that each animal is in the correct place on the food chain before hanging the mobile from the ceiling.

Fish

There are about 13,000 types of fish living in the sea. They live in different areas. Seas, like countries, can be cold or warm. Some fish live in the colder open sea, far away from the shore. Others live in the warmer and shallower waters of the tropical seas. Many of the tropical fish have beautiful colors and patterns.

The magic fish
(A Scandinavian folk tale)

One day a poor fisherman caught a magic fish. "Let me go and I'll grant you a wish," said the fish. The fisherman wished for a big house and his wish came true.

He caught the magic fish again and again, asking for more and more wishes. Each wish came true. But when the fisherman asked for the Moon

cold open sea

Can you find?

1 marlin

2 ray

3 tuna

4 cod

5 sawfish

6 mackerel

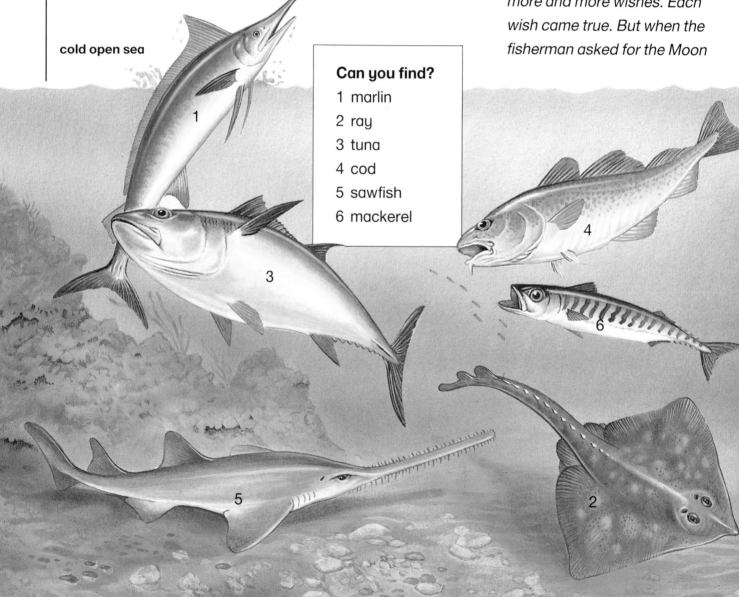

and the stars, the fish decided that the fisherman had become too greedy and took all the gifts away. The fisherman was poor again.

Make a fish scene

Paint the inside of a shoebox bluish-green and turn it on its side. Draw, color, and cut out tropical fish.

Attach the fish to the top of the box with tape and string. Add colorful sponges and stones.

warm tropical sea

Can you find?

1 angelfish
2 cowfish
3 parrot fish
4 butterfly fish
5 lionfish
6 trumpetfish

Deep-sea fish

It is cold and dark in the deepest parts of the sea. Not many animals can live here, as there is not much food. Most deep-sea fish are small and do not have to eat very often. Some have sharp teeth, enormous mouths, and glowing lights to help them catch other fish to eat.

▽ Many deep-sea fish hunt other fish. The gulper eel waits for tiny fish to swim into its big, open mouth. The deep-sea anglerfish dangles its glowing light so that other fish think it is a tasty worm.

Flip the fish game
Cut out fish shapes from tissue paper. Line the fish up. Each player moves one fish along by waving a newspaper up and down. Whoever reaches the other end of the room first wins.

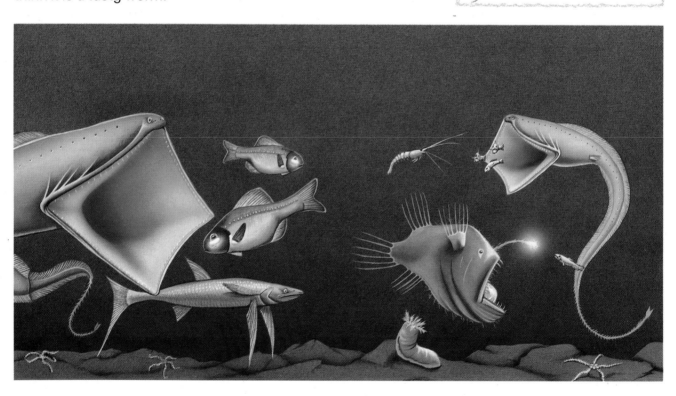

Sea journeys

Many sea creatures make long journeys. Some eels swim all the way across the Atlantic Ocean. They are born in the warm waters of the Sargasso Sea, but some swim to the rivers of Europe to grow up. They swim all the way back to the Sargasso Sea to lay their eggs.

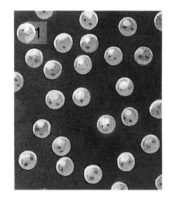

△ Eel eggs are laid and hatch in the Sargasso Sea.

△ The baby eels travel across the Atlantic Ocean.

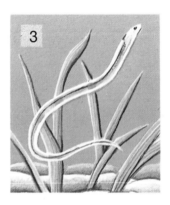

△ They grow up in the rivers of Europe.

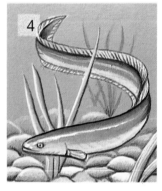

△ Grown eels swim to the Sargasso Sea.

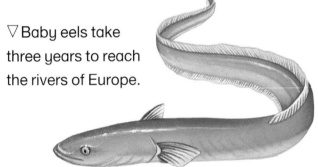

▽ Baby eels take three years to reach the rivers of Europe.

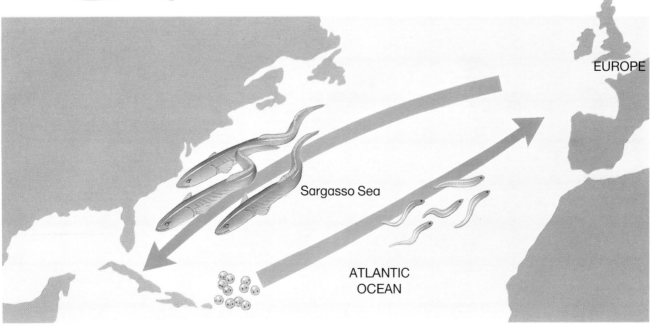

EUROPE

Sargasso Sea

ATLANTIC OCEAN

Dolphins and whales

Dolphins and whales are not fish. They are mammals like dogs and horses. Fish take in the oxygen they need from the water, but whales and dolphins have to come up to the surface for air. They breathe through a blowhole on the top of their heads. Most fish lay eggs, but mammals give birth to their babies and feed them with their own milk.

△ Dolphins feed their babies with milk from their bodies.

◁ Dolphins are lively animals. They often leap out of the water when they are playing.

▽ Humpback whales have strips of whalebone called baleen instead of teeth. The whale takes a gulp of water and the baleen traps all the plankton like a giant sieve.

△ Meat-eating whales, such as killer whales, have teeth.

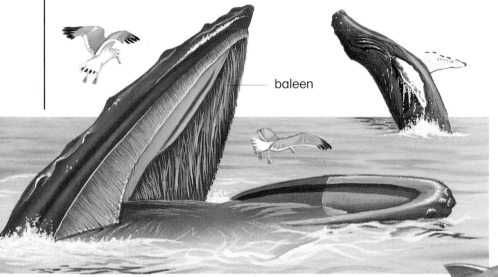

baleen

◁ Dolphins and whales make clicking sounds to find other sea animals to eat. The clicks bounce off the animals like an echo.

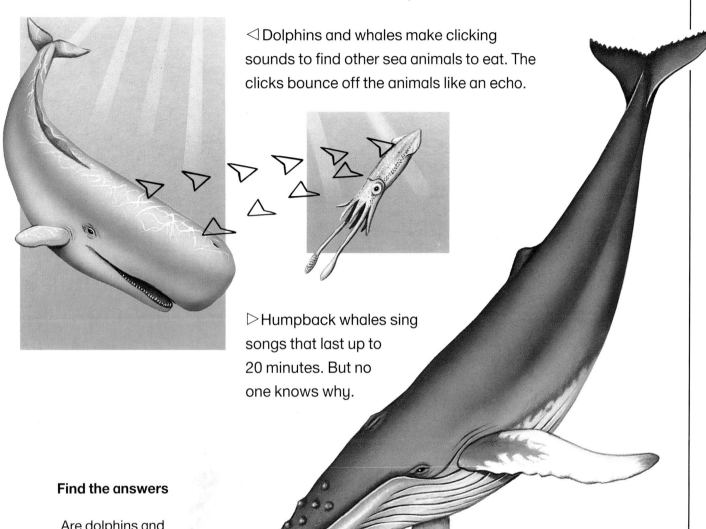

▷ Humpback whales sing songs that last up to 20 minutes. But no one knows why.

Find the answers

Are dolphins and whales fish?

What does a humpback whale have instead of teeth?

Jonah and the whale
In a Bible story, a man called Jonah was swallowed by a whale. He was spat out onto the land after three days.

A changing world

The surface of the Earth is made of 13 huge pieces, called plates. They fit closely together, but are moved around by hot, runny rock that lies underneath them. When a plate moves, the land and the sea on top of it move too.

The land and the sea are slowly changing shape all the time. Today, there are seven large pieces of land on the Earth. These are called the continents. Two hundred million years ago, there was only one continent.

△ The surface of the Earth is made up of huge pieces, called plates. The land and the sea are on top of these plates.

▽ The plates are floating on hot, runny rock from inside the Earth. When this rock moves, it pulls the plates apart or pushes them together.

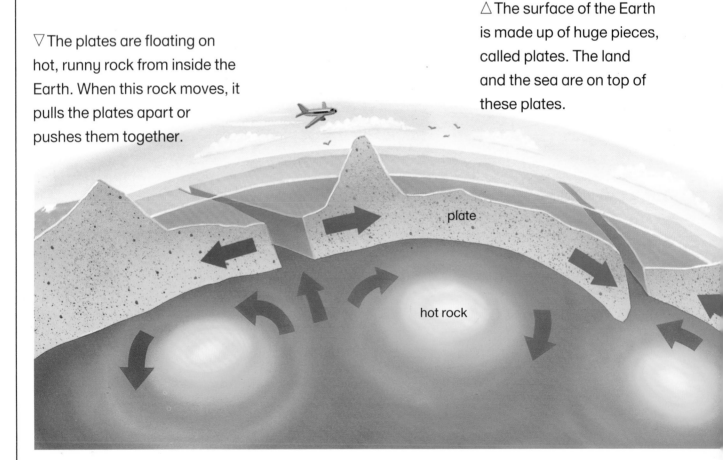

ATLANTIC OCEAN

plate

hot rock

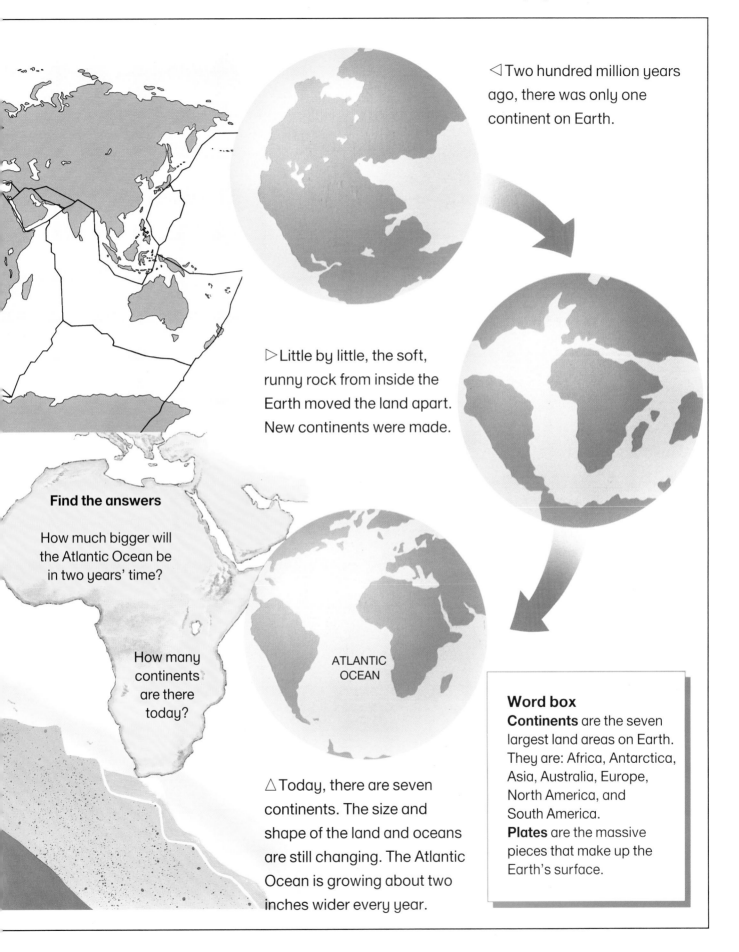

◁ Two hundred million years ago, there was only one continent on Earth.

▷ Little by little, the soft, runny rock from inside the Earth moved the land apart. New continents were made.

Find the answers

How much bigger will the Atlantic Ocean be in two years' time?

How many continents are there today?

ATLANTIC OCEAN

△ Today, there are seven continents. The size and shape of the land and oceans are still changing. The Atlantic Ocean is growing about two inches wider every year.

Word box
Continents are the seven largest land areas on Earth. They are: Africa, Antarctica, Asia, Australia, Europe, North America, and South America.
Plates are the massive pieces that make up the Earth's surface.

135

The seabed

The bed, or bottom, of the sea is not all flat. It has mountains and valleys, just like the land. The deepest valleys and the tallest mountains on Earth are found underneath the sea. An underwater mountain is made when a volcano erupts under the sea. When a volcano grows tall enough to be above the water, it forms an island.

△ On April 14, 1988, three men were fishing in the sea near Sabah in Malaysia. Suddenly, they saw a volcano erupt and an island appeared before their very eyes!

▽ At some places on the seabed, hot water bubbles up through rocks that look like chimneys. Giant worms and blind crabs live near to these hot spots.

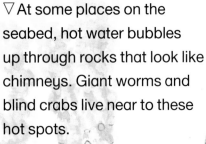

▷ There are mountains and valleys at the bottom of the sea. The very tallest mountains make islands.

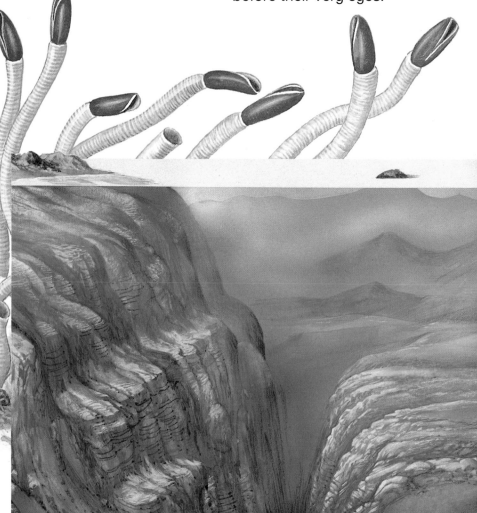

Make an underwater scene

Make some mountains from modeling clay. Put them into an old bowl. Pour water into the bowl to see how many islands there are.

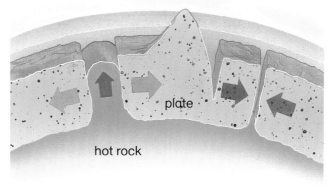

hot rock

plate

△ Underneath the sea are plates. They float on hot, runny rock inside the Earth. Some plates move apart, while others move closer together.

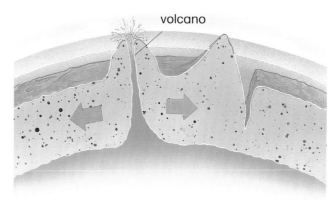

volcano

△ When the plates move apart, hot, runny rock, called lava, bursts up onto the surface of the sea, like a volcano erupting. When the lava cools down, it turns into hard rock.

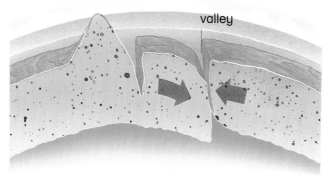

valley

△ When the plates move together, one plate is pushed below the other one and a deep valley is made. This takes millions of years.

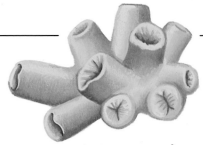

orange cup coral

Coral islands and reefs

When an island is made in warm parts of the world, tiny animals called corals may come to live in the warm, shallow water around it. The corals attach themselves to the rocks. When they die, new corals grow on top of their old shells. As old corals die and new corals grow on top of them, a reef builds up around the island. The reef is home to masses of colorful plants and animals.

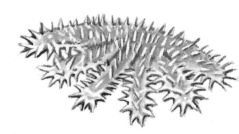

△ The crown-of-thorns starfish destroys coral reefs by eating the coral.

▷ Many types of animals and plants live in and around coral reefs, because they can find a safe place to live and plenty of food to eat.

sea fan   brain coral

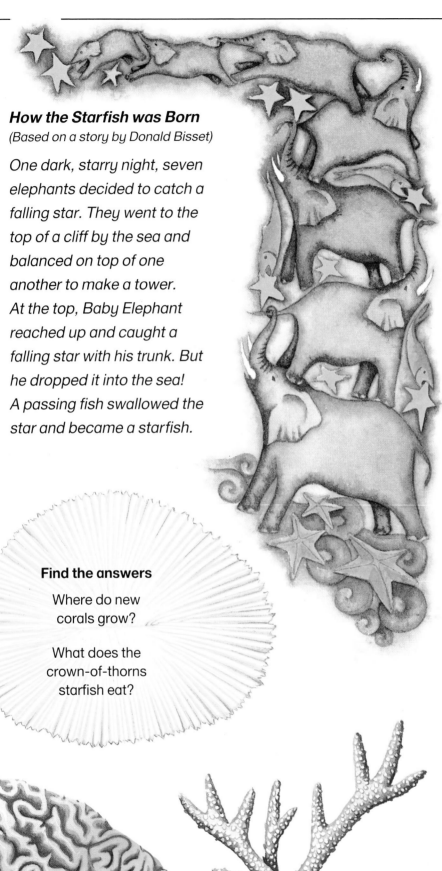

How the Starfish was Born
(Based on a story by Donald Bisset)

One dark, starry night, seven elephants decided to catch a falling star. They went to the top of a cliff by the sea and balanced on top of one another to make a tower. At the top, Baby Elephant reached up and caught a falling star with his trunk. But he dropped it into the sea! A passing fish swallowed the star and became a starfish.

Find the answers

Where do new corals grow?

What does the crown-of-thorns starfish eat?

staghorn coral

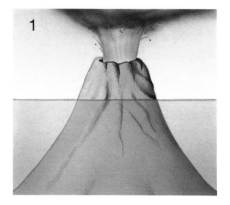

△ A new island is made by an underwater volcano.

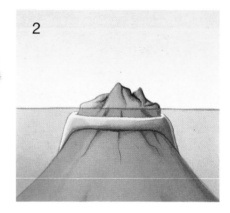

△ In warm seas, corals attach themselves to the new island. As they die, other corals grow on top of their shells.

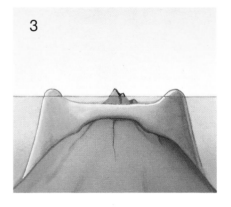

△ As the volcano sinks, the coral builds up, leaving a ring.

Fishing

Many sea fish are caught and eaten each year. People go out to sea in fishing boats and use sonar to find out where the fish are swimming. Different nets are used to catch fish in different areas of the sea. The nets are hauled into the boats and fish are packed in ice to keep them fresh.

▷ Sonar uses echoes to find out where fish are swimming. Beeps of sound are sent down into the sea. If a large school of fish gets in the way, an echo bounces back to the fishing boat. This can be seen on a screen.

Word box
Trawlers are boats that drag nets along the bottom of the sea to catch fish.
Sonar is a device used to find fish, shipwrecks, and icebergs. It is also used to explore underwater.

Play the fishing game
Cut out fish shapes from cardboard. Use tape to attach a paperclip to each fish.
Make a fishing rod by attaching a small magnet to a stick with string. Players take turns trying to catch as many fish as they can at one time.

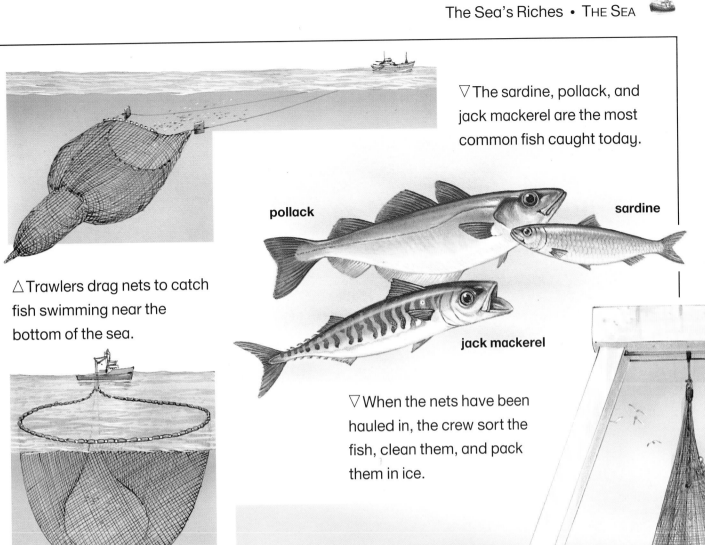

▽ The sardine, pollack, and jack mackerel are the most common fish caught today.

pollack

sardine

jack mackerel

△ Trawlers drag nets to catch fish swimming near the bottom of the sea.

△ Purse seine nets surround fish in a giant net bag.

△ Long drift nets float on the surface of the water and hang like a curtain.

▽ When the nets have been hauled in, the crew sort the fish, clean them, and pack them in ice.

Farming the sea

In many parts of the world, the sea is farmed. Fish, mussels, and seaweed are grown. Most of the fish are sold to be eaten, but some are put back into the sea to lay more eggs. These fish will provide food for the future. The mussels are eaten. Some seaweed is grown for food, but giant seaweed called kelp is also grown to be burned as fuel.

▷ Mussels are grown on tall poles. When they are fully grown, people collect them at low tide.

△ At fish farms, fish hatch from eggs in tanks of water. When they are adults, some are put back into the sea to lay more eggs.

△ Edible seaweed is farmed in some parts of the world.

▷ Giant kelp grows very quickly. It is harvested by divers.

Mining the sea

Salt, oil, and gas are mined from the sea. Salt is found in seawater. Oil and gas are buried deep beneath the seabed. Oil rigs drill narrow holes down to the oil and gas and pump it up to the surface. Tankers and underwater pipes carry it to factories on the shore.

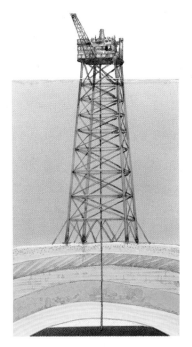

△ Oil and gas are pumped up from beneath the seabed and taken to the shore.

△ In hot, sunny places, people build shallow ponds to trap seawater. The heat of the Sun dries up the water, and leaves the salt behind. People collect the salt to use and sell.

Why the sea is salty
(A Norwegian folk tale)

Once a sailor stole a magic mill that would grind anything he asked for. He took it out to sea in his boat and asked it to grind salt. When there was enough, he wanted the mill to stop, but did not know the magic words. Soon there was so much salt that the boat and the mill sank to the bottom of the sea. The mill continued to grind salt. It is still grinding today, and that is why the sea is salty.

Power

The sea is very powerful. People have used the moving tides for hundreds of years to turn water wheels. The seawater was used to turn large wheels that ground grain into flour. Today, the tides are also used in power stations to make electricity.

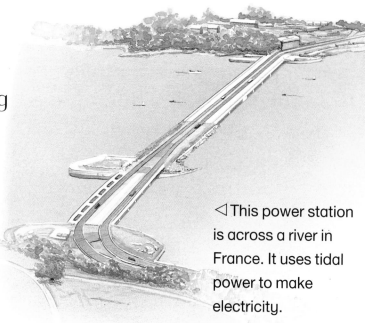

◁ This power station is across a river in France. It uses tidal power to make electricity.

Make a water wheel

Use this pattern to cut out four pieces of cardboard. Fold each piece in half. Glue each piece onto a thread spool. Push a pencil through the spool. Hold it under a gently running faucet. The force of water turns the water wheel around.

fold

sea

water wheel

pond

△ When seawater comes in at high tide, it turns the water wheel in a tidal mill. As the tide goes out, it turns the wheel the other way.

Treasure

The sea is full of treasure. Precious minerals, pearls, and beautiful shells can be found on the seabed. When ships sink, their treasures are left at the bottom of the sea. Divers may find them years later.

Blackbeard the pirate
Pirates used to attack and rob treasure ships. Blackbeard was one of the most well-known and feared pirates of them all.

▽ Beautiful shells are often washed up onto the shore. People enjoy collecting them.

△ Lumps of valuable minerals lie deep down on the seabed.

△ Shipwrecks can show scientists how people lived long ago.

◁ Pearls form inside oyster shells.

Find the answers

What can you find on the seabed?

Who might find the treasures of a sunken ship?

Studying the sea

People who study the sea are called oceanographers. They can explore the sea with sonar. Sonar uses echoes to measure the depth of the sea and find things underwater. Satellites in space are also used to study the sea. They send out radio waves to measure the height of waves and locate icebergs.

In shallow seas, divers study the seabed. They also carry out important repair jobs to underwater pipes, cables, and oil rigs.

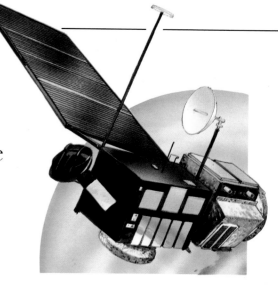

△ Satellites in space are valuable because they can take pictures of the Earth. The photographs give scientists information about the shape of the seabed and the temperature of the water.

▷ Satellites also measure the amount of light reflected from the sea. If a blue-green color shows up on the screen it means there are plankton. People use this to find fish, because fish eat plankton.

Word box
Oceanography is the study of the sea.
Scuba equipment allows divers to breathe underwater.

screen

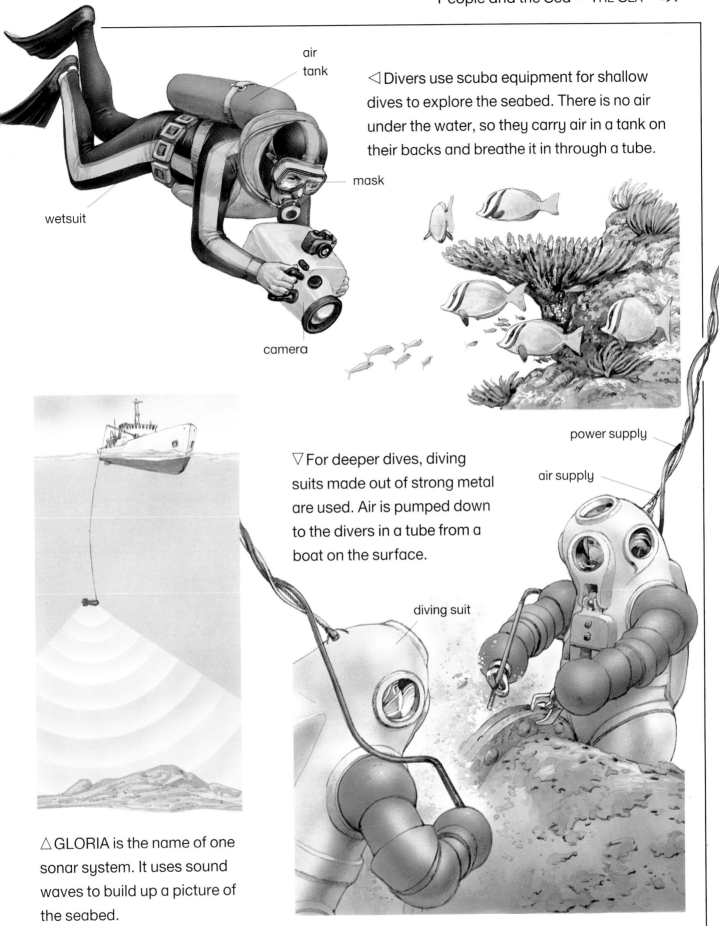

◁ Divers use scuba equipment for shallow dives to explore the seabed. There is no air under the water, so they carry air in a tank on their backs and breathe it in through a tube.

air tank

mask

wetsuit

camera

▽ For deeper dives, diving suits made out of strong metal are used. Air is pumped down to the divers in a tube from a boat on the surface.

power supply

air supply

diving suit

△ GLORIA is the name of one sonar system. It uses sound waves to build up a picture of the seabed.

Submarines and ships

Underwater craft, called submarines take people to the deepest parts of the sea. For very deep and dangerous dives, remote operated vehicles (ROVs) are used. They need no crew, and are controlled from a ship on the surface.

The sea is a very busy place. Ships travel in shipping lanes that are like expressways across the water.

ferry

ferry

▽ A minisub is launched from a ship at sea. During the trip the crew keeps in touch with the ship by telephone.

△ The crew of a minisub can work underwater for up to eight hours. Then they return to the surface.

Make a bottle submarine
Make a large hole in the bottom of an empty dishwashing liquid bottle. Attach a piece of plastic tube over the nozzle.

oil tanker

container ship

bulk carrier

△ Different ships carry different things. Huge tankers carry oil. Bulk carriers carry grain and other dry goods. Some goods are put in containers. Ferries carry people, cars, and trucks.

▽ Some ROVs have robot arms that can hold tools to carry out repairs. This ROV is scraping seaweed and shells off the legs of an oil rig.

remote operated vehicle (ROV)

Push the bottle down into the water so that it sinks. Blow hard down the plastic tube. As the air goes into the bottle, it pushes some of the water out, so the bottle rises.

Spoiling the sea

When people dump waste into the sea they are polluting, or dirtying, the water. Pollution like this harms the plants and animals that live there. Sometimes the sea is used as a dump. When oil is spilled from tankers it is washed ashore. It takes a lot of hard work to clean up the coastline.

▽ Waste flows into the sea through pipelines. Much of it is from towns and cities.

▽ Some factories let poisonous waste flow into rivers and down to the sea.

△ Fertilizers from farms also run into the sea. Many of them can harm sea life.

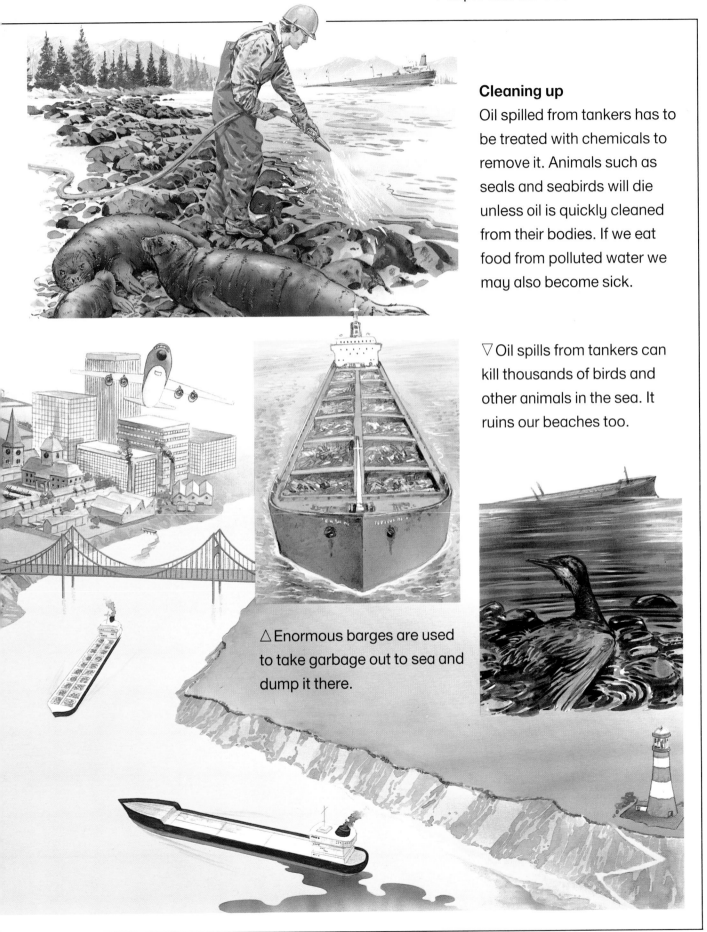

Cleaning up

Oil spilled from tankers has to be treated with chemicals to remove it. Animals such as seals and seabirds will die unless oil is quickly cleaned from their bodies. If we eat food from polluted water we may also become sick.

▽ Oil spills from tankers can kill thousands of birds and other animals in the sea. It ruins our beaches too.

△ Enormous barges are used to take garbage out to sea and dump it there.

Saving the sea

The sea is beautiful and valuable. Everyone should do all they can to help protect it. Many people are trying to stop the harm we are doing to the sea. The world is beginning to realize how important the sea is, but there is still a lot to do. What can you do?

▷ You and your friends could start by clearing up your own litter when you visit the seashore.

△ If you look at a globe you will see just how much of our planet is covered by the sea. Do you know which is the largest ocean?

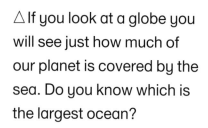

▽ The sea is a wonderful place to have fun. The best beaches are clean beaches.

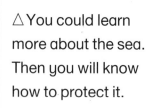

△ You could learn more about the sea. Then you will know how to protect it.

All Kinds of
Animals

What is an animal?

Animals are living things. So are plants. They both need energy to live, but they get their energy in different ways. Plants use the Sun's energy. Animals cannot do that. Animals get their energy from the food they eat. Some animals eat plants, some eat other animals, and some eat plants and animals. There are many different kinds of animal. Scientists arrange them in groups.

the frog is an amphibian

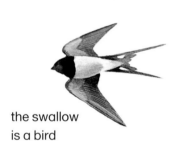

the swallow is a bird

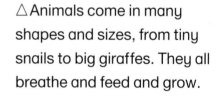

△ Animals come in many shapes and sizes, from tiny snails to big giraffes. They all breathe and feed and grow.

the mouse is a mammal

the cricket is an insect

Word box
Vertebrates are animals with backbones as part of their skeletons.
Invertebrates are animals without backbones. Some have a hard outside, a bit like armor. This is called an external skeleton.

the turtle is a reptile

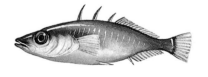

the stickleback is a fish

▽ These animals are all mammals. They are more closely related to each other than to birds or reptiles or fish. Can you find mammals on the chart below?

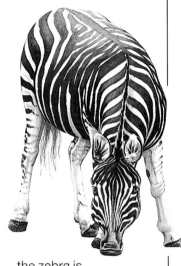

the panda is a mammal

the fox is a mammal

human beings are mammals

the zebra is a mammal

Tiny animals

Many animals are so small that we need a powerful microscope to see them.

animal under a microscope

▽ There are more than a million different kinds of animal. Scientists divide them into two main groups. Animals with backbones are called vertebrates. Animals without backbones are called invertebrates.

| 4,000 amphibians | 4,150 mammals | 6,500 reptiles | 8,800 birds | 21,500 fish | more than 1 million |

Vertebrates

Invertebrates

Animals in danger

The area an animal lives in is called its habitat. Today many of these habitats are in danger of being destroyed. The animals that live there will die. Some kinds of animal will become extinct, which means they will disappear forever. This map shows some of the animals in most danger.

Noah's ark

The very old story of Noah's ark tells how one man and his family saved all the animals from a terrible flood. By finding out why the animals on this map are in danger you might be able to do something to help animals too.

whooping crane

NORTH AMERICA

woolly spider monkey

SOUTH AMERICA

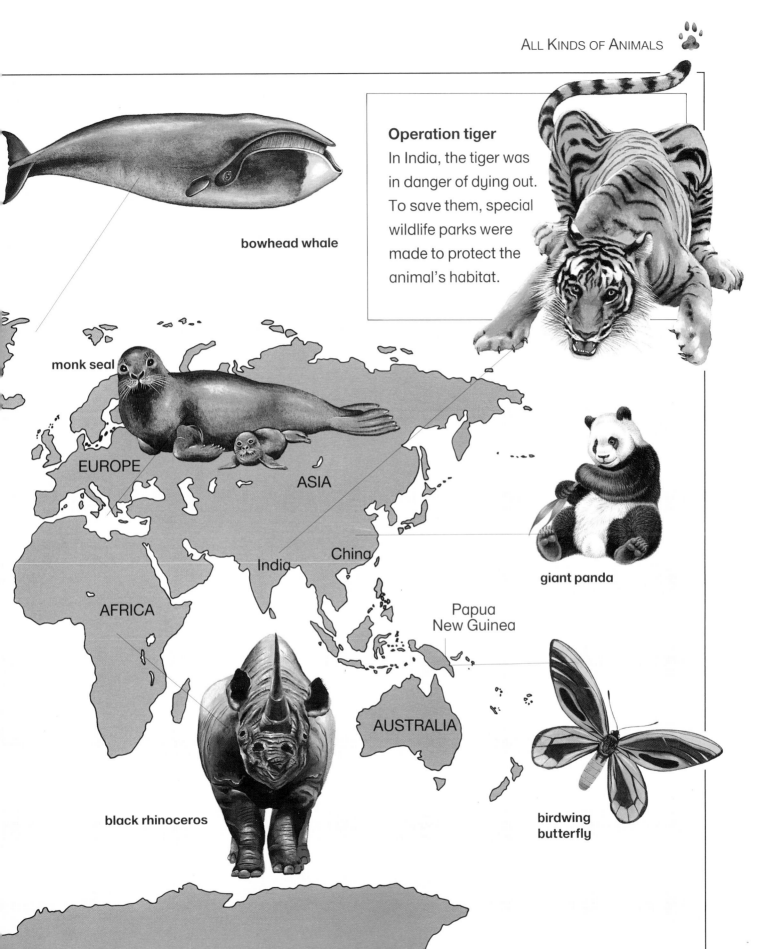

bowhead whale

Operation tiger
In India, the tiger was in danger of dying out. To save them, special wildlife parks were made to protect the animal's habitat.

monk seal

EUROPE

ASIA

India

China

giant panda

AFRICA

Papua
New Guinea

AUSTRALIA

black rhinoceros

birdwing
butterfly

ANTARCTICA

What is a mammal?

A mammal is an animal with hair or fur. This often helps to keep its body warm. Young mammals are fed with milk produced by their mother's body.

Mammals live almost everywhere, from freezing cold Antarctica to scorching hot Africa. Most mammals live on the land. Some, such as whales, live in water. Bats are the only mammals that can fly.

Find the answers

Which mammals can fly?

What do rabbits use their whiskers for?

◁ Human beings are mammals. We are often fed with our mother's milk when young.

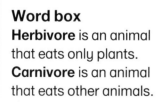

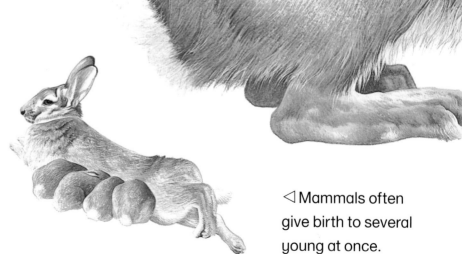

Word box
Herbivore is an animal that eats only plants.
Carnivore is an animal that eats other animals.

◁ Mammals often give birth to several young at once.

▽ Most mammals are good at seeing, hearing, and smelling things around them. Rabbits use whiskers to feel things, too.

hair or fur

whiskers

most mammals move on four legs

Design a mammal game
Each player thinks of a mammal. First player draws its head at the top of a page. The page is folded over and passed to the next player, who draws the torso of their mammal. The next player draws the lower body and feet of their mammal. Open papers out to find new mammals.

▷ Most mammals give birth to live babies, but the platypus lays eggs with leathery shells.

◁ Some mammals hibernate. They eat a great deal in the fall, then curl up and sleep through the cold winter. This dormouse will not wake up until spring.

Monkeys and apes

Most monkeys and apes spend a lot of time in trees, so they need to be good at balancing. They grasp things with their hands, and use their arms and legs to swing through the trees.

Apes are different from monkeys because they do not have tails. Gorillas are the largest of all the apes.

△ The gibbon is an ape. With its long arms, fingers, and toes, it is a good climber.

◁ This spider monkey is using its strong tail, as well as its hands and feet, to hold onto the branches.

Pick up monkeys game
Trace the monkey shape onto cardboard. Cut out ten monkeys. Players take turns picking up monkeys using the arms and tails. The player who makes the longest chain wins.

▷ Baby monkeys and apes are carried by their mothers until they are old enough to look after themselves.

△ Gorillas may look fierce, but they are shy and gentle. Like us, gorillas live in families, cuddle their babies, and play together.

▷ Apes are clever. This chimpanzee is using a stick to poke out tasty termites from their nest.

△ Orangutans are apes. They like to live alone, but a mother always looks after her young.

161

Cats

All cats are meat-eaters. They use their good sight, hearing, and sense of smell to hunt.

Cats have padded paws, so they can quietly creep up on another animal. Their long, sharp teeth and claws help to grip and kill it.

Alice's Adventures in Wonderland
(A story by Lewis Carroll)

Alice met some very strange characters in Wonderland. The Cheshire Cat slowly disappeared, starting with his tail, leaving his broad grin until last!

◁ Tigers are the biggest cats. They live in forests and grasslands.

▽ Some of the big cats are very fast. A cheetah is the fastest animal on land. Cats' long tails help them keep their balance when they run and jump.

cheetah

black panther

cat　　**wildcat**　　**lynx**　　　　**leopard**　　　　　**lions**

Living in a herd

Some mammals live in groups or herds. Herbivores, or plant-eaters, are safer in a herd. If one animal sees, hears, or smells danger, it warns the rest. Some carnivores, or meat-eaters, hunt in groups called packs.

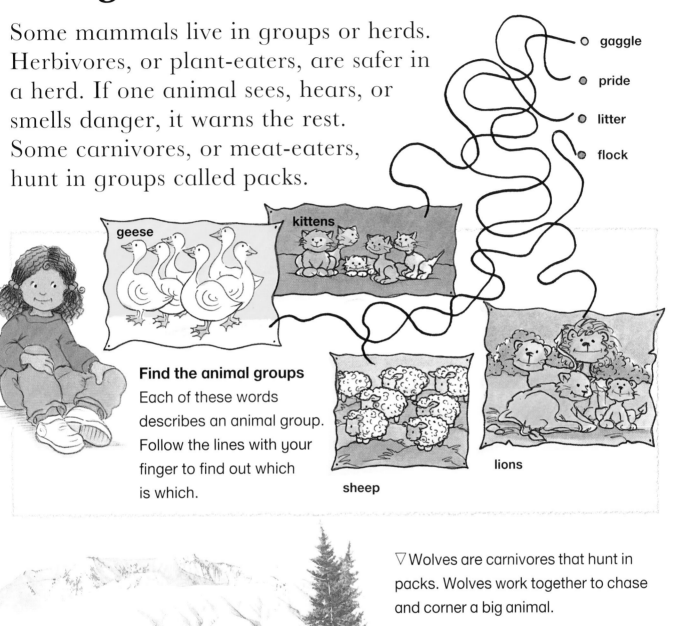

○ gaggle

○ pride

○ litter

○ flock

geese

kittens

Find the animal groups
Each of these words describes an animal group. Follow the lines with your finger to find out which is which.

sheep

lions

▽Wolves are carnivores that hunt in packs. Wolves work together to chase and corner a big animal.

Biggest of all

African elephants are the biggest land animals. They can grow as tall as eleven and a half feet and weigh as much as six tons. The biggest of all animals is a mammal that lives in the sea. The blue whale is the largest animal ever to have lived on Earth.

▽ The blue whale has no teeth, but has strips of whalebone called baleen. It eats tiny shrimps, called krill, which it filters out of the water through its baleen.

How the Whale Got Its Baleen
(Based on a story by Rudyard Kipling)

A whale swallowed a ship-wrecked man and his raft, but the man refused to be eaten. He made the whale take him home. The man wove his suspenders and raft together and pulled it into the whale's mouth to stop it from swallowing anyone else. The whale could not spit it out or swallow it, so it became his baleen.

▷Elephants live in herds. They use their trunks to take food and water to their mouths. They are strong enough to push trees over to get at the leaves.

Make elephant chains
Fold a long piece of paper into wide zigzags. Draw an elephant on the top of the paper. Make sure that the tail and trunk reach each side, as shown. Cut out the elephant shape and unfold to make an elephant chain.

△Blue whales can be as long as six or more elephants.

165

Water mammals

Some mammals spend a lot of time in water. The hippopotamus lives in Africa and stays in the water to keep cool during the burning hot days.

Most seals live in cold water. They have a thick layer of blubber, or fat, which helps them stay warm.

Polar bears live in the Arctic. They are good swimmers. Their thick, white coats keep them warm.

▽ Seals like to sunbathe on rocks. Their flippers make them excellent swimmers, but they are clumsy on land.

▽ The hippopotamus usually leaves the water at night to feed on plants. Hippopotamus means water horse.

▷ Polar bears are large and fierce hunters. To catch a seal, a polar bear waits beside a hole in the ice until a seal comes up for air.

Busy rodents

Rodents are mammals with strong, sharp front teeth that they use to gnaw, or chew. Rodents gnaw at almost anything. Rats sometimes eat the walls of buildings.

▽ Beavers gnaw down trees to dam streams and make a lake. They build homes, called lodges, in the lake.

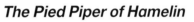

The Pied Piper of Hamelin
(Based on a poem by Robert Browning)

The townspeople of Hamelin promised a piper gold if he rid them of rats. He played his pipe, and the rats followed him to the river and drowned. But the town refused to pay him, so he played a new tune, and led away all the town's children to a new land.

▽ Marmots live in groups called colonies. They dig underground homes called burrows.

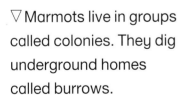

△ The squirrel holds a nut with its front paws and uses its teeth to crack it open.

Marsupials

Marsupials are mammals that have a pouch where their young grow. Baby marsupials are born very small. They crawl straight into their mother's pouch. Here they are kept safe while they feed on their mother's milk. When they are strong enough they leave the pouch.

▷Wombats live in Australia. Marsupials live only in Australia and the Americas.

▽ Koalas are often called bears, but they are not real bears at all. They eat no meat, just eucalyptus leaves.

△Kangaroos use their strong, thick tails to balance. Their babies are called joeys.

Make a kangaroo puppet

Stitch a pocket to the palm of a mitten. Glue on paper eyes, nose, ears, and mouth.

Cut out and color in a joey to fit in the pocket. Wear the puppet and bend your fingers to make a nose.

Bats

Bats are the only mammals that can fly. Their wings are folds of skin, stretched over long, thin fingers.

Many bats make high-pitched squeaks when they fly. The sounds bounce off objects all around them and they hear the echoes. This is how these bats find their way.

△ Bats sleep upside down in caves or trees. Most bats are nocturnal, which means they sleep in the day and hunt at night.

◁ Most bats eat insects such as moths. Some bats can snatch fish from the water with their feet.

Flying fox

Some bats eat fruit. A bat called the flying fox eats fruit. It is the largest bat of all.

Batman

Batman is a superhero who comes out at night, as bats do. He cannot fly, though. Batman drives around Gotham City in his Batmobile.

What is a bird?

A bird is an animal with feathers and wings. Birds live in most parts of the world, and nearly all of them can fly.

The smallest bird is the bee hummingbird, which is only two inches long. The largest is the ostrich, which can grow to more than eight feet tall.

A bird's ears are on either side of its head, hidden by feathers

pigeon

The Ugly Duckling
(A story by Hans Christian Andersen)

The cruel animals teased the Ugly Duckling for his ugliness. But by spring, he had grown into a beautiful swan.

Word box
Preening is the way a bird keeps itself clean. A bird preens its feathers with its beak.
Birds of prey are birds that hunt other animals for food.

Print a peacock
Using bright paints, make hand prints on paper. When dry, cut them out and glue in a fan shape to make a peacock's tail. Cut out a body and glue it in the middle of your picture.

beak or bill

Canada geese

△ When a bird flaps its wings, its feathers push the air back and down, so the bird moves forward and up.

birds have two feet with claws for gripping

ostrich

△ A few birds, such as the huge ostrich, cannot fly. But the ostrich can run very fast.

171

Feathers

Birds are the only animals with feathers. Feathers give birds their colors and help to keep them warm.

Birds often preen, or clean their feathers. They use their beaks to rub in oils from their body. Birds pull out old feathers where newer ones have grown.

◁ The hummingbird beats its wings more than 60 times a second while it drinks nectar, a sweet liquid, from flowers.

△ A flamingo's feathers are pink because it eats pink shrimps.

▽ The patterns on a pheasant's feathers help it to hide in grasses. Parrots' brightly colored feathers make them easy to see.

Find the answers

Which animals have feathers?

Why are a flamingo's feathers pink?

golden pheasant

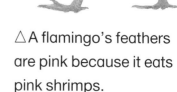

parrots

◁ A peacock spreads his tail feathers into a beautiful fan to attract a mate.

Beaks and bills

All birds have hard beaks, or bills. Birds' beaks give clues to what they eat. Sparrows have stubby little bills for crushing seeds. Eagles have sharp, curved bills for tearing meat.

◁ Curlews have long, thin bills for poking into sand and mud.

△ Toucans have long, strong bills that are good at pushing leaves apart and picking fruit and nuts.

▷ Wrens have pointed beaks for snatching insects.

◁ Pelicans have a pouch of skin under their beaks to scoop up fish.

Make a bird beak card
Fold some cardboard in half; cut a slit in the middle. Fold back corners. Push folds inside out. Glue to a piece of cardboard. Do not glue beak. Draw a bird's face around the beak. Open and close cardboard to move beak.

173

Nests and eggs

Most birds build nests to protect their eggs. The nests must be hidden out of reach from their enemies.

Usually, nests are made with leaves, twigs, and grasses. Other birds build their nests by pushing stones into a pile. When the female is ready, she lays her eggs. Then she sits on them, spreading her feathers to keep them warm, until her chicks hatch.

▽ Storks build a big, untidy nest of twigs, high up, away from their enemies.

stork

▽ The tailorbird makes a neat little nest by sewing leaves together.

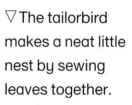

tailorbird

1

embryo

2

△A bird's egg contains an embryo that grows into a chick. The chick gets bigger and bigger. When it is ready to hatch, it cracks the shell with a special part of its beak, called the egg tooth, and crawls out.

3

4

▷The woodpecker uses its strong, hard beak to make a hole in a tree for its nest.

▽The chaffinch uses springy, soft moss and warm feathers to make a cozy nest.

woodpecker

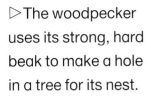

chaffinch

The Goose that Laid the Golden Eggs
(Based on a story by Aesop)

Long ago a farmer had a goose that laid golden eggs. Soon he became greedy. He thought that if he cut open his goose, she would have many more golden eggs inside. But when he cut open the goose, there were none. He never had a golden egg again.

kingfisher

chaffinch

wren

starling

golden eagle

▷Different birds lay eggs of different size and color. Usually, the bigger the bird, the bigger its egg will be. Eggs contain all the food and water needed by the tiny chick inside the shell.

Find the answers

What do chicks use to break the shells of their eggs?

What are birds' nests usually made from?

Flying hunters

Birds that hunt animals are called birds of prey. Some birds of prey soar high above the ground, using their excellent sight and hearing to spot any movement below them. When the bird finds its prey, it swoops silently for the kill.

▽ Most owls sleep in the day and hunt at night. This barn owl is taking a rat to its chicks.

△ Eagles have long, sharp talons to catch their prey. They hunt during the day.

talon

Why owls hoot
(A Scandinavian folk tale)

It was day when the king of the animals gave birds their songs. At night, when the owls awoke, all the songs were gone. Nearby a musician was playing "hoo-hoo" on his double bass. So the owls copied that sound and used it as their song.

Swimmers and divers

Some birds spend a lot of their time in water. Most waterbirds have short, powerful legs with webbed feet, which they use as paddles. Some swim on top of the water, others dive beneath it. Often, birds that seem clumsy on land are skillful swimmers.

▷ Penguins use their wings as flippers when they swim.

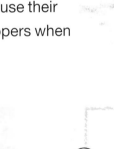

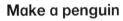

Make a penguin
Copy the penguin shape onto cardboard. Color it in and cut it out. Cut out two yellow triangles for feet. Paint a cardboard tube black. When the paint is dry, stick the body and feet onto the cardboard tube.

△ The kingfisher perches by a stream. When it sees a fish, it dives into the water with folded wings. It grabs the fish with its strong, pointed beak.

What is a reptile?

Crocodiles, snakes, lizards, and turtles are all reptiles. Reptiles are cold-blooded animals. This means that they cannot keep their bodies warm in cold weather. They need lots of sunshine to keep warm, so most reptiles live in hot countries. Reptiles that live in cold countries sleep all winter and wake up in spring. This is called hibernation.

Gila monster

△ Reptiles bask in the Sun to get warm. If a reptile gets too hot, it hurries into the shade or into some cool water.

reptiles have scaly skin

ocellated lizard

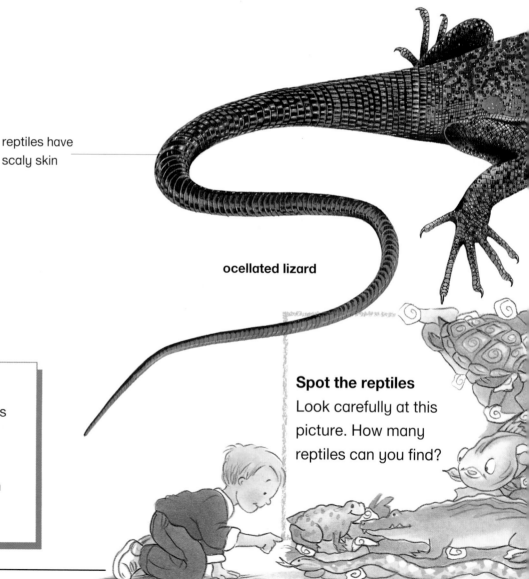

Word box
Warm-blooded animals keep themselves warm by eating.
Cold-blooded animals need heat from the Sun to keep warm.

Spot the reptiles
Look carefully at this picture. How many reptiles can you find?

marine turtle

△ Some reptiles live longer than any other animal. Large turtles can live for more than 100 years.

Find the answers

Is a crocodile a reptile?

How do reptiles get warm?

Are reptiles' eggs hard like birds' eggs?

many reptiles are brightly colored

◁ Geckos have sucker-like pads on their feet. This helps them to run up walls when hunting for insects.

▷ This king snake is hatching from its egg. Reptiles' eggs are not hard like birds' eggs, but soft and leathery.

▷ As it grows, a king snake will shed its skin. It has a brand new skin underneath. The snake rubs its head against something rough until the old skin splits open. Then the snake wriggles out.

Snakes

All snakes are carnivores. They can open their mouths very wide to swallow animals that are bigger than they are. Snakes do not chew their food, they swallow it whole. Some snakes use a poison called venom to kill their prey. When they bite, their sharp fangs inject venom into the animal.

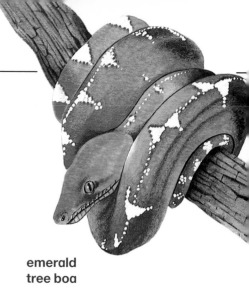

emerald tree boa

△ Some snakes live in the trees. They coil around the branches.

▷ Poisonous snakes often warn animals to keep away by hissing, spitting, or rattling their tails.

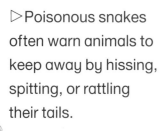

fang

rattlesnake

Find the answers

How do poisonous snakes warn off other animals?

How do anacondas kill their prey?

Do snakes chew their food?

▽ Some snakes kill by coiling around an animal and squeezing it until it cannot breathe. Boa constrictors and pythons do this. The anaconda is a boa constrictor that lives near the water.

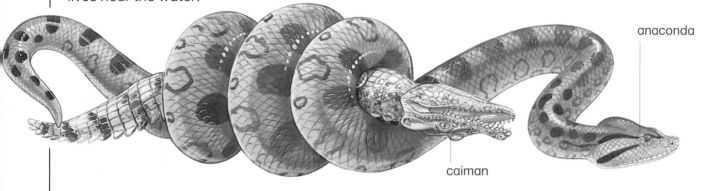

anaconda

caiman

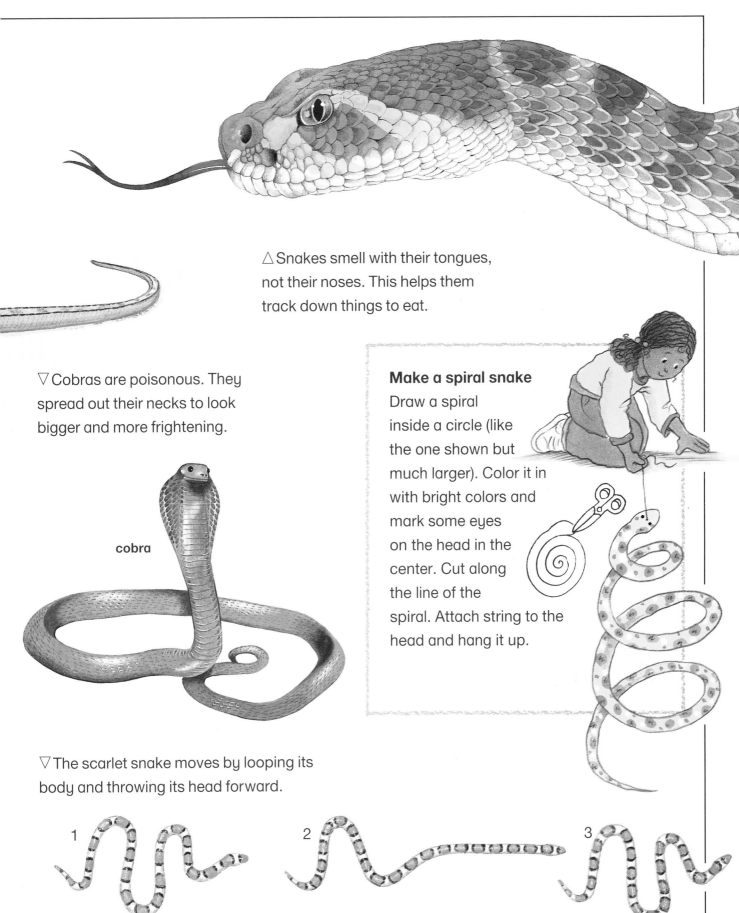

△ Snakes smell with their tongues, not their noses. This helps them track down things to eat.

▽ Cobras are poisonous. They spread out their necks to look bigger and more frightening.

cobra

Make a spiral snake
Draw a spiral inside a circle (like the one shown but much larger). Color it in with bright colors and mark some eyes on the head in the center. Cut along the line of the spiral. Attach string to the head and hang it up.

▽ The scarlet snake moves by looping its body and throwing its head forward.

1

2

3

Chameleons

The chameleon is a lizard that lives in trees. It grips the branches with its tail and toes. A chameleon catches insects by shooting out its sticky tongue and pulling them into its mouth.

△ Chameleons are usually green or brown, but they can change color to match their background. This is called camouflage, and it helps them to hide from their enemies.

△ Chameleons also turn dark when they are angry and pale when they are afraid.

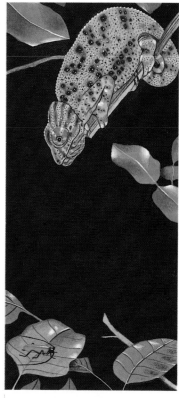

△ A chameleon's tongue is almost the same length as its body. It shoots out and in again very quickly.

Crocodiles

Crocodiles are large, fierce reptiles. Some are as big as twenty feet long. They live in rivers in hot countries, and are powerful swimmers. Crocodiles are good parents. They guard their eggs and look after the babies when they hatch.

△ When crocodiles are in water, they keep their eyes and nostrils above the surface so they can see and breathe.

Make snappy candy
Add food coloring to a large chunk of almond paste (bought or home-made). Roll into a sausage and flatten one end to make a tail. Make legs and stick on. Use frosting to make eyes and nose.

▽ With only their nostrils showing, crocodiles wait for animals that come to the river to drink. Then they seize their prey with their huge jaws.

Turtles

Turtles are reptiles that have a hard shell covering their bodies. Because their shells are heavy, turtles can only move slowly on land. A turtle that spends all its time on land is sometimes called a tortoise. When it is in danger it can pull its head and legs into its shell. Some turtles spend most of their time in the sea.

green turtle

Find the answers

What can turtles do when they are in danger?

Where do turtles lay eggs?

△ Turtles might move slowly on land, but in the water they are fast swimmers. Turtles eat jellyfish and other sea animals, and seaweed too.

◁ Sea turtles lay their eggs on land. The green turtle digs a hole on the beach. She lays lots of eggs, covers them with sand, and returns to the sea. The babies hatch and make for the sea. Many are eaten on the way by birds.

Make a turtle puppet

Make a hole on each side of a paper bowl. Stretch elastic through the holes and tie. Glue brown paper patches onto the bowl to make a shell. Stick eyes on the middle finger of a glove to make a head. Wear the glove and thread the shell over your hand.

The Hare and the Tortoise
(A story by Aesop)

Have you heard the story of a hare who made fun of a tortoise for being so slow? They had a race. The hare was so sure he would win he went to sleep on the way, but the tortoise kept plodding on and won the race.

▷Turtles eat leaves, fruit, and grass. They have no teeth. Turtles have a mouth like a beak with a hard bite.

giant tortoise

What is an amphibian?

An amphibian is an animal that lives both in water and on land. Frogs, toads, newts, and salamanders are amphibians. Amphibians lay their eggs in water, perhaps in a pond or stream. Amphibians cannot live in salt water, so there are none in the sea.

Find the answers

Where do tadpoles live?

What is an amphibian?

Is a newt an amphibian?

great crested newt

▷Newts and salamanders are amphibians. Unlike frogs or toads, they do not lose their tails when they grow up.

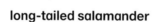
long-tailed salamander

alpine salamander

frogs and toads have two strong back legs for jumping and swimming

Word box
Amphibians are animals that spend part of their life in water and part on land.
Tadpoles turn into frogs or toads after losing their tails and developing legs.

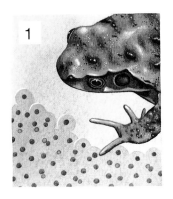 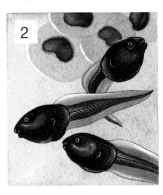 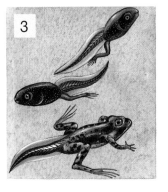 

△ Female frogs lay hundreds of small eggs in water. The eggs hatch into tadpoles, with long tails. To start with, tadpoles only eat plants.

△ The tadpoles get bigger and begin to grow legs. Their tails shrink, and after about four months, the baby frogs can leave the water.

amphibians have two eyes that can see all around them

▽ Male frogs and toads puff up their throats with air and let out a big, loud croak.

reed frog

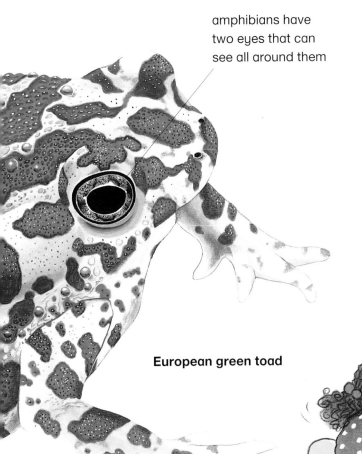

European green toad

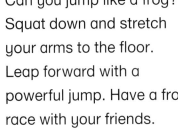

Frog jumping race
Can you jump like a frog? Squat down and stretch your arms to the floor. Leap forward with a powerful jump. Have a frog race with your friends.

What is a fish?

A fish spends its whole life in water. Some fish live in the sea, and some in rivers and lakes. Their bodies are usually covered with scales.

Like all animals, fish need oxygen to live. We get oxygen from air, but fish get it from water. Water enters the fish's mouth and passes over its gills, which take in the oxygen. The water then goes out through gill slits.

◁ Most fish lay eggs, often thousands at a time. The eggs have no shells, and many are eaten by other fish. Only a few hatch.

▽ The butterfly fish has a big spot like an eye to confuse its enemies.

herring

a tail helps most fish push through water

scale

The Little Mermaid

Hans Christian Andersen wrote a story about a mermaid. Mermaids are imaginary sea creatures. They are like humans, but have a fish's tail instead of legs.

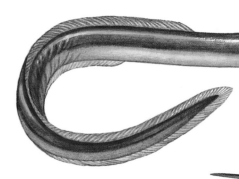

eel

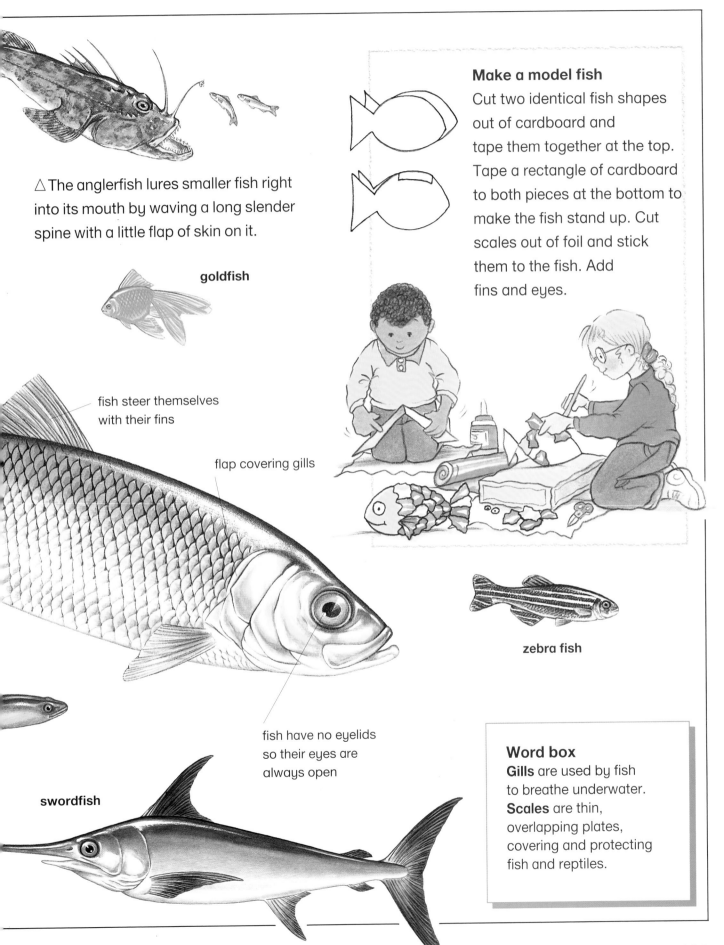

△ The anglerfish lures smaller fish right into its mouth by waving a long slender spine with a little flap of skin on it.

goldfish

fish steer themselves with their fins

flap covering gills

fish have no eyelids so their eyes are always open

swordfish

Make a model fish

Cut two identical fish shapes out of cardboard and tape them together at the top. Tape a rectangle of cardboard to both pieces at the bottom to make the fish stand up. Cut scales out of foil and stick them to the fish. Add fins and eyes.

zebra fish

Word box
Gills are used by fish to breathe underwater. **Scales** are thin, overlapping plates, covering and protecting fish and reptiles.

Sharks

Some fish feed on plants in the water, and some feed on other fish. Sharks eat animals of any kind. They are fast swimmers and fierce hunters. Sharks have a good sense of smell, which helps them find animals to eat. Unlike most other fish, sharks have to keep swimming all the time or they sink.

Find the answers

What do sharks eat?

What is a mermaid's purse?

How do sharks find animals to eat?

▷ Some sharks lay eggs in cases. These cases are called mermaids' purses.

mermaid's purse

▽ These two great white sharks are hunting a dolphin. Great whites are known as man-eaters because they sometimes attack people.

Salmon

Salmon have an amazing life. They hatch in rivers, and then swim down to the sea. When they are ready to breed, the adult salmon swim all the way back from the sea to the rivers where they were born.

start

Follow the salmon's journey to the river

Use your finger to find the right way for the salmon to get back to the river.

finish

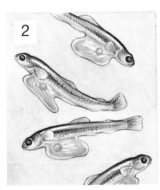

△ The female salmon lays her eggs in the river where she was born. When the eggs hatch, the babies are called fry.

▽ Adult salmon swim upstream to reach the place where they were born. They often have to leap up rushing waterfalls on the way.

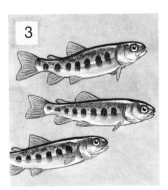

△ The young salmon live and grow in the river for over two years. When they are large enough, they swim down to the sea.

191

What is an insect?

Insects have six legs. Their bodies have a hard outer case called an exoskeleton. Every insect's body has three parts: a head, a thorax or middle, and an abdomen at the back.

Most insects can fly. Usually, insects have two pairs of wings. All flies, however, have only one pair of wings.

Insects are often brightly colored to warn other animals not to eat them because they taste nasty.

△ This ladybug has two pairs of wings. The front wings are hard, and they cover the delicate back wings when the ladybug is not flying.

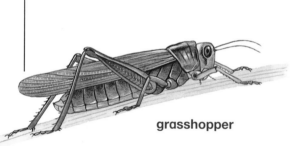

grasshopper

mayfly

housefly

an insect's legs and wings are attached to the thorax

Word box
Antennae are the two feelers on the heads of small creatures, such as insects.
Metamorphosis is the complete change that happens to some creatures' bodies before they become adults.

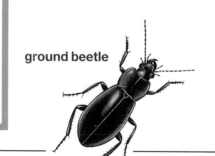

ground beetle

large blue butterfly

water strider

backswimmer

aphid

shield bug

insects have two eyes that can see all around them

antennae help insects to feel and smell things

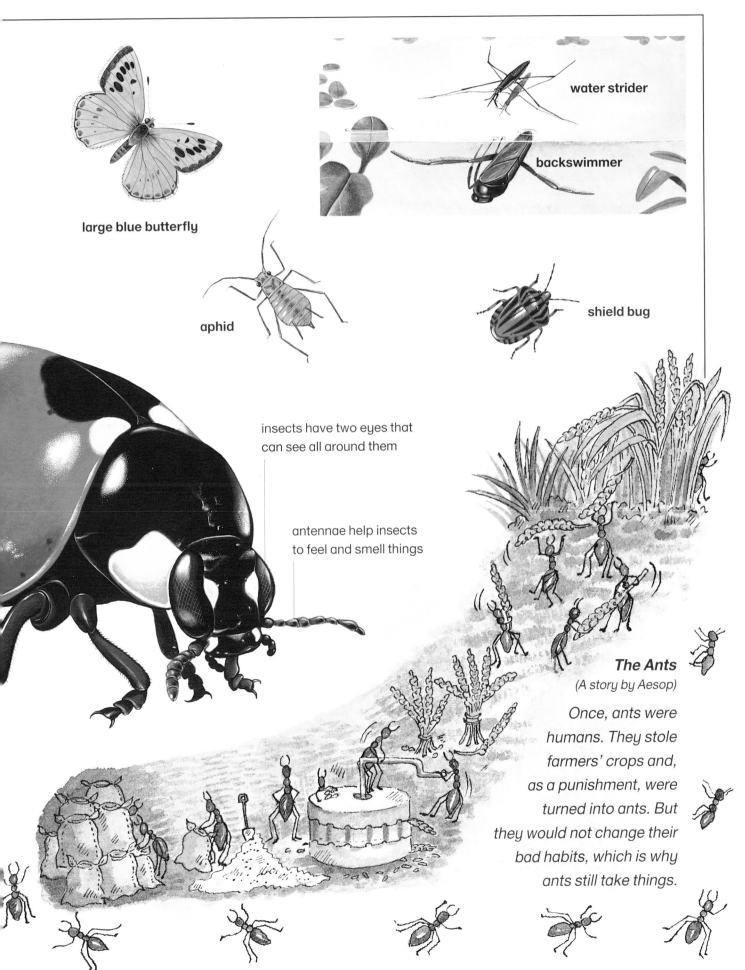

The Ants
(A story by Aesop)

Once, ants were humans. They stole farmers' crops and, as a punishment, were turned into ants. But they would not change their bad habits, which is why ants still take things.

Butterflies

Some of the most beautiful insects are butterflies. Their wings are covered with tiny, overlapping scales that give the wings their bright colors.

Butterflies, like many insects, go through several different stages before becoming adults. This change in their bodies is called metamorphosis.

△ The swallowtail butterfly lays eggs on a plant that her babies will be able to eat.

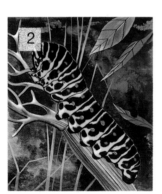
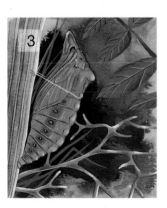
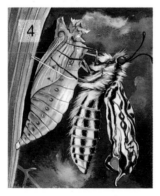

△ A caterpillar hatches out of each butterfly egg. Caterpillars eat a lot and grow quickly. The caterpillar turns into a chrysalis. Out of this crawls a beautiful butterfly.

Make butterfly prints

Fold a piece of paper in half.

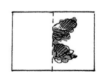 Open it up and put spots of paint on one side.

Refold and press down. Open out. When dry, paint a body and two antennae to complete a butterfly picture.

A wasps' nest

Some insects, such as wasps, live in large groups. There may be 8,000 wasps in just one nest. In each giant family, the wasps work together and depend on each other to survive.

In spring, the queen wasp builds the nest. She scrapes wood from trees, chews it up and mixes it with her saliva to make each cell or room in the nest.

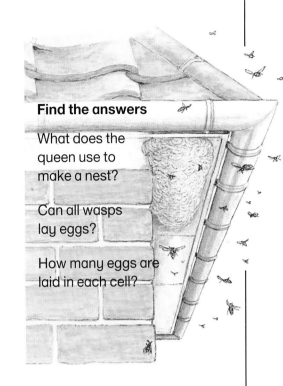

Find the answers

What does the queen use to make a nest?

Can all wasps lay eggs?

How many eggs are laid in each cell?

The queen wasp lays one egg in each of the cells she has made. The eggs hatch into grubs and are fed on insects. The grubs grow into adults and leave the cells.

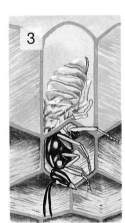

△ When the new adults hatch, most of them take over the nest building and find food for the queen and her next batch of grubs. These are called workers. Only the queen wasp lays eggs.

Mollusks

Mollusks are animals with soft bodies. Many are protected by a hard shell. Those with shells either have one shell or two shells hinged together. Many mollusks live in water. Land mollusks are covered with slime to keep their bodies moist.

octopus

garden snail

queen conch

△The octopus is a mollusk without a shell. It has eight long arms to catch animals to eat.

sea slug

△Many mollusks can pull their bodies back inside their shells to protect themselves.

scallop

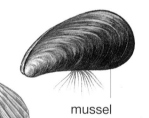

mussel

◁Mollusks with two shells live in water. They filter tiny bits of food from the water.

Word box
Mollusks have soft bodies and they usually have hard shells made of chalk.
Crustaceans have close-fitting hard cases that form their skeletons. These cases need to be shed as the animal grows.

Make a shell creature
Collect lots of different shells. Glue them together to make creatures. Draw on eyes.

Crustaceans

The animals here are called crustaceans. They all have a tough, crusty covering, or case. They have to shed this as they grow bigger. Many crustaceans have long antennae to help them find their way around. Crabs, lobsters, and shrimps are crustaceans.

lobster

hermit crab

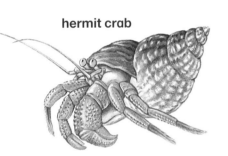

▷Lobsters and crabs have huge claws for protecting themselves, and for picking up food.

antenna

△The hermit crab lives inside an old shell. As it grows, it must move to a bigger shell.

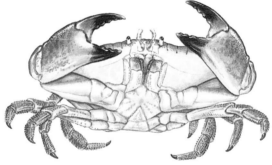

shore crab

◁Crabs and lobsters have ten legs and scuttle over the seabed. Some are good swimmers too.

◁Shrimps have ten legs for walking, and more for swimming.

shrimp

▽Crabs move by walking sideways.

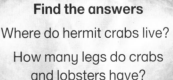

Find the answers
Where do hermit crabs live?
How many legs do crabs and lobsters have?

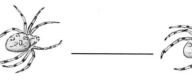

Spiders

Spiders are animals with eight legs. Most spiders catch their food by building webs of silk. Insects get caught in the silk and the spider eats them. As they grow bigger, spiders grow new skins and shed their old ones.

most spiders have two rows of four eyes, which makes eight eyes altogether

spiders pull threads of silk from tiny spinnerets

house spider

Make a pompom spider
Wind yarn around two disks of cardboard with large holes in the middle. Then push four long pipe cleaners through the middle to make legs. Cut the yarn around the outside and tie the pompom securely between the disks. Remove the cardboard and fluff up. Bend the pipe cleaners to look like legs and stick on eyes.

△ Many spiders can walk up walls because their feet have hairy pads for extra grip. A spider does not get stuck in its own web because it walks only on the spokes of the web and these are not sticky.

A garden spider's web

△ First the spider spins a bridge thread.

△ Then it adds spokes.

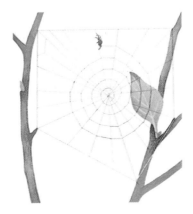

△ It finishes with a spiral of silk.

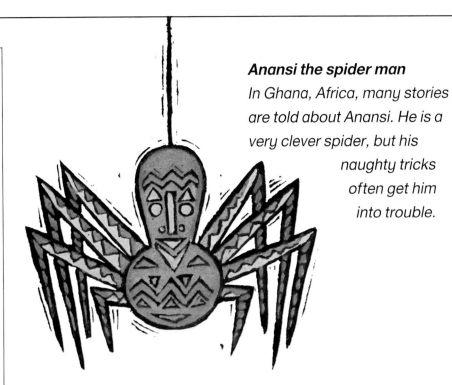

Anansi the spider man
In Ghana, Africa, many stories are told about Anansi. He is a very clever spider, but his naughty tricks often get him into trouble.

Find the answers

How many legs does a spider have?

How can a spider walk up walls?

△ When a fly is caught in a web, the spider can feel it along the threads. The spider bites the fly with poisonous fangs, wraps it in silk, and keeps it to eat later.

Worms

Earthworms are strange-looking animals. They do not have eyes, ears, or legs. They spend their lives under the ground, tunneling. Tiny bristles help them grip as they wriggle along. At night, earthworms come up to look for dead leaves. They pull the leaves down into their burrows to eat in safety.

Find the answers

What do worms eat?

What are worm casts?

Do worms have eyes?

Make a worm friend

Cut off a leg from an old pair of panty hose. Fill it with scrunched up newspaper, old stockings, or bits of material. Tie a knot in the end. Stick on eyes, nose, and wool hair.

▽ Earthworms swallow soil while tunneling. They eat dead plants and animal remains in the soil. The leftovers are pushed up above ground, making small heaps called worm casts.

worm cast

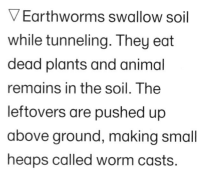

Plants

Plants everywhere

The amazing world of plants is all around us. There are plants everywhere. They are of every size, shape, and color. Like people, plants live in many different places, including some unexpected ones. Some plants can even survive in places where people cannot.

△ Some plants grow in the high mountains.

Do not eat strange plants. Always wash your hands after touching plants.

△ Plants grow in the center of big cities.

△ Many plants are found by the seashore.

Word box
Environments are the surroundings in which life exists.
Adaptation is what happens when plants and animals change slowly to fit in with a changed environment.

△ In the countryside, plants are everywhere.

202

▷People can live in many places. They dress and feed themselves according to where they live. Plants are like that too. They can adapt to different conditions.

Andes mountains

Sahara

Amazon rain forest

△Glacier buttercups live high up in the Alps. They can survive the very cold weather. People would find it difficult to live in these conditions.

△The yucca lives in the hot Arizona desert, where there is very little rain.

△Some types of plant grow on the stems and branches of other plants.

◁There are many different seaweeds that grow under the water.

Plants can adapt

Many plants live in very difficult
environments, or surroundings.
Over millions of years, they
change very slowly to suit these
environments. The changes are
called adaptations. There are
plants adapted to all kinds of
conditions. Different plants can live
in places that are very dry, very wet,
very hot, or very cold.

Find the answers

Where does the saguaro
cactus store water?

How does the mimosa
plant protect itself
against animals?

▽ The saguaro cactus stores
water in its thick stems.
This helps it to live in
the dry Arizona
desert.

△ The water crowfoot grows
in streams and ponds.

△ Some grasses grow
in clumps to hold water.

▽ The mimosa plant folds its leaves to protect it against cold nights and hot days. It also closes its leaves if it is touched by an animal.

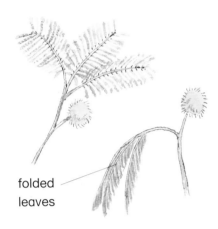

folded leaves

scale

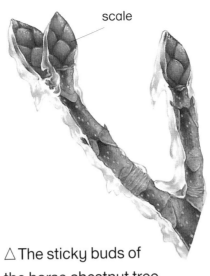

△ The sticky buds of the horse chestnut tree are covered in scales. The scales are there to protect the buds from cold winter winds.

▷ Brightly colored bellflowers grow between the rocks of a wall. They do not need soil to grow in.

▷ Some plants just perch on other plants.

◁ The swollen trunk of the African baobab tree shows where it stores water.

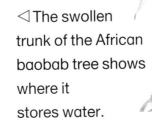

▽ Climbers are long, straggly plants. They clamber up trees or other plants to reach the sunlight.

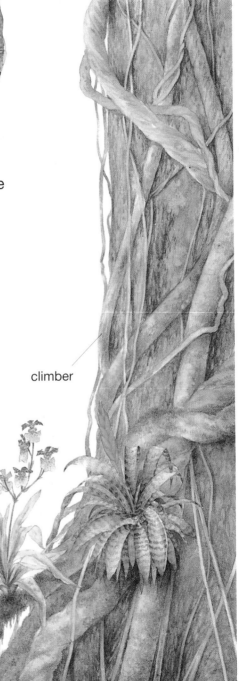

climber

205

Smart plants

Some plants have weapons to protect themselves. They have stings, thorns, or poisonous chemicals to try to stop animals from harming them.

Many plants need insects to help them produce new plants. They attract insects with smells, or by the way they look.

△ The bee orchid looks like a bee to attract real bees.

△ The stapelia has a smell like rotting meat that attracts flies.

Sleeping Beauty
(A story by Charles Perrault)

A bad fairy made a beautiful princess fall asleep with a spell. Then a hedge of roses grew up around her castle. The thorns stopped people from reaching her.

Do not pick or touch toadstools. Many of them are poisonous.

△ The nettle has hairs that sting.

△ Holly scratches.

△ A cactus also scratches.

△ Rose thorns prick.

△ The fly agaric fungus is poisonous.

Water plants

Water plants grow in rivers, pools, and lakes. Usually, their roots are in the mud on the bottom. Their stems grow up to the top of the water where the leaves and flowers open out. There are many different types of water plant. Some have flat leaves that float on the water. Others have tall, narrow leaves.

Find the answers

How big can Amazon water lily leaves grow?

Where do you find water plants?

Where do reeds grow?

▽ Underwater plants often have fine leaves. These let the water flow past easily.

▽ Water lilies have flat leaves called lily pads. The Amazon water lily has leaves up to $6\frac{1}{2}$ feet across. Tall reeds grow at the edge of the water.

reeds

lily pad

Fold a water flower
Take a square of paper. Fold each corner to the center. Repeat. Turn over. Fold corners to center.

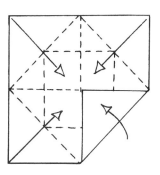

Hold the center firmly and lift up the folded corners. Push them into petals. Fold out the four flaps below for leaves.

Plants are alive

Plants are living things. They need food to give them energy. Plants make their own food by taking in water from the soil through their roots. The water travels up the stem to the leaves. The leaves contain a green coloring called chlorophyll. With sunlight, chlorophyll helps change the water into food.

▽ Plants need water to live. They take it in through their roots. The water travels through their stems to the veins in their leaves.

vein

stem

root

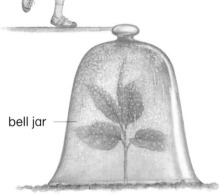

bell jar

△ People sweat, and so do plants. Some of the water soaked up by the roots is given off by the leaves. You can see this if you place a plant inside a bell jar.

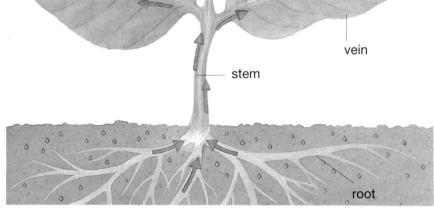

Make a potato maze
Make a hole in the end of an old shoebox. Stick cardboard inside to make a maze, as shown. Put a sprouting potato at the end of the maze. Put the lid on. Leave in a light place. See a shoot grow out of the hole, toward the light.

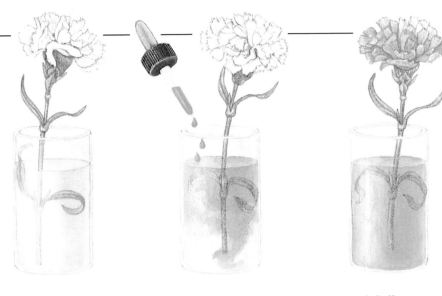

white flower **add coloring** **pink flower**

◁ Here is a way to show that water travels right through a plant. Put a white flower in water. Add some red food coloring to the water. The flower will soak up the colored water. After a few hours it will turn pink. The water has moved up the stem and into the leaves and petals.

△ A potted plant needs light, air, soil, and water to survive.

△ Cut flowers survive in just water, but only for a few days.

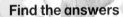

Find the answers

What do potted plants need to live?

How do plants soak up water?

△ Plants wither and die if they are left in the dark.

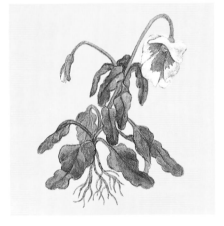

△ Plants dry out and die if they are uprooted from the soil.

Word box
Chlorophyll is a green coloring found in the leaves of plants. It uses sunlight to make food for plants.
Veins are the tiny tubes in the leaves of plants.

209

Making new plants

Flowers make the seeds that grow into new plants. Each flower has male parts, called stamens, and female parts, called carpels. The stamens produce grains called pollen. For a plant to make seeds, pollen must reach the carpels. This is called pollination. It happens in several different ways.

▽ Look closely at the center of a sunflower. You will see that it is made up of many small flowers. Each has a carpel.

carpel

cuckoopint

▷ Insects climb down to the sweet liquid at the bottom of the cuckoopint plant. On the way, pollen from the stamens sticks to them. If this pollen rubs off onto the carpel, pollination occurs.

stamen

carpel

nectar

fuchsia

lily

stamens

◁ The stamens of the fuchsia and the lily are easy to see. They are on long stalks. Insects visit the flowers because they like their color and smell.

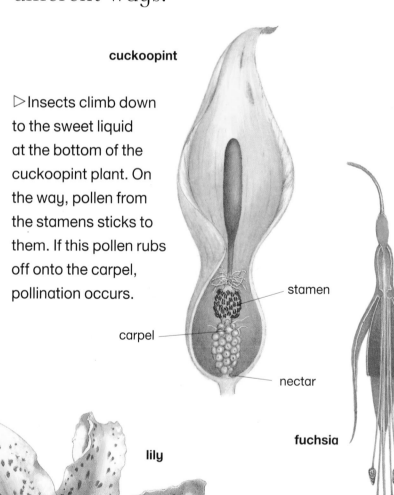

◁ Pine trees make pollen in little yellow male cones. The wind blows the pollen from the male cones on one tree to the female cones on another.

cone

stamen

carpel

leaf

inner petal

stamen

outer petals

carpel

△ Sometimes pollen travels from the stamens to the carpels of the same flower. This is called self-pollination.

▽ This rose is pollinated by a bee. Pollen sticks to the bee's furry body on one flower. Then it brushes off on another flower.

Make a flower
Trace the shapes onto very thin, colored cardboard. Cut out five inner petals, the outer petals, five stamens, one carpel, two leaves. Poke a flexible straw through the outer petals. Push the petal ends into the straw, then the carpel and stamens. Tape on leaves.

211

From flower to fruit

Inside the carpels there are little eggs called ovules. When pollen reaches an ovule, a seed starts to grow. Then a fruit grows around the seed. This is to protect the seed as it grows. Some fruits have one seed inside a hard pit. Other fruits, such as oranges, have several seeds in their juicy pulp.

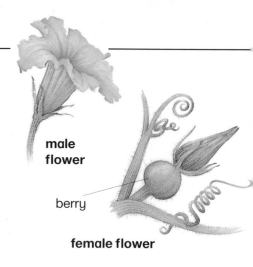

male flower

berry

female flower

△ The pumpkin plant has male and female flowers. After pollination, each female flower grows a fruit called a berry.

▷ Rose hips are the fruits of the wild rose. They contain a lot of small seeds. As soon as the fruit starts to grow, the petals of the wild rose drop off. The rose hips turn from green to red.

rose hip

▽ The berry grows into a big orange pumpkin. The pumpkin has thick, juicy flesh. In the center of the pumpkin there are lots of small seeds.

pumpkin

pear

△ After pollination, tiny fruits grow underneath the pear flowers. The petals drop off and the fruits begin to swell.

△ The fruits grow bigger. Some drop off. Others become ripe pears. Inside are small seeds.

Henny Penny
(An English folk tale)

A nut fell on Henny Penny's head. She thought it was the sky falling down. She told the other birds and they went to warn the king. But on the way, they met cunning Foxy-Loxy. He tricked them by saying his den was a shortcut to the palace. Then he ate them all.

sloes

peach

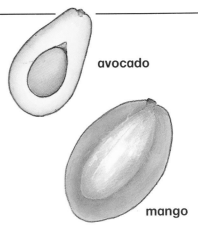
avocado

mango

▷These are all fruits with pits. They have only one large seed inside.

blueberries

passion fruit

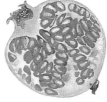
pomegranate

kiwi fruit

△ These are fruits with a lot of small seeds inside them.

Make a dried seed picture
Use dried peas, lentils, sunflower seeds, and lima beans.

Do not use red kidney beans. They are poisonous before they are cooked.

Draw a simple picture on a piece of paper. Glue on different colored seeds. You could make a face, a bird, or an animal.

▷These are nuts. They are seeds with a hard shell around them.

◁ The poppy holds its seeds inside a case with a lid. It has lots of tiny seeds.

Ready for a journey

Seeds need to reach the ground to grow into new plants. They travel in different ways. Some fall straight to earth. Others are carried by wind, or water, or by birds and other animals. Once the seeds are buried in soil and watered, they begin to swell. A plant begins to grow out of the seed. The root grows first and then a shoot. This is called germination.

▷ When birds eat fruit, they spit out the seeds or swallow them. Some seeds reach the ground in the bird droppings.

△ Dandelion seeds are scattered by the wind.

▽ Honesty seeds are flung out when the pods burst open.

◁ Some fruits have tiny hooks and spines. They stick to the coats of animals. Sometimes they are carried a long way.

Jack and the beanstalk
(An English folk tale)

Jack planted a magic bean. It grew into a huge beanstalk. He climbed to the top and found the castle of a wicked giant. He took some gold. Then he took a hen that laid golden eggs. The giant found out and chased him down the beanstalk. Jack chopped the stalk with an ax. The giant fell down dead.

△ Fava beans are good to eat. The beans from the pod are seeds and can also be used to grow new plants.

△ The gardener puts the beans in the soil and covers them. Then the soil is watered.

△ Soon little bean plants appear. The plants will grow quickly with sun and water.

Grow string beans

Soak string bean seeds in water overnight. Take a glass jar and cut a piece of blotting paper to fit around the inside. Crumple paper towels in the middle. Push beans between the blotting paper and the side of the jar. Water the towel just enough to keep the blotting paper damp. Put the jar in a warm, dark place. When roots and shoots appear, put the jar upright by a sunny window.

▽ When a bean germinates, a small root appears first. It grows downward. Then a leafy shoot appears. It pushes upward toward the light. More leaves and flowers appear above the soil.

leaf

shoot

root

The seasons

There are four seasons. They are spring, summer, fall, and winter. The weather changes, and this affects the way plants grow. Leaves, flowers, and fruit come and go as the seasons change. Not all parts of the world have four seasons. Some places have only one or two.

△ Many plants lose their leaves in the cold of winter.

△ In spring, it gets warmer and new leaves start to grow.

△ In summer, trees are in full leaf. The weather is warm.

△ The tomato seed is sown at the end of winter.

△ During the spring, a young plant grows.

△ In summer, the plant flowers. Then small fruits appear.

short rainy season

The Secret Garden
(A story by Frances Hodgson Burnett)

Two children find a secret garden. In winter, they work hard to clear and plant it. In spring, the flowers look beautiful.

△ In the fall, it gets cooler. The leaves turn brown.

△ In the fall, the fruits ripen and are picked.

△ In the tropical rain forests near the equator, it stays hot and wet all year round. These rain forests are always green. There is only one season here.

△ In the desert, there is a long dry season and a short rainy season. When the rain comes, some plants sprout, flower, and make seeds very quickly.

Make a cactus

Take a rectangle of corrugated paper or thin cardboard. Bend it around to form a tube. Glue the sides together. Paint it green. Fill a flowerpot with sand and stand the cactus in it. Cut some paper flowers from colored paper. Glue them on the cactus. Put small rocks on the sand.

217

Plants without seeds

Not all plants grow from seeds. Plants such as potatoes, cassavas, and irises grow new plants from special underground stems. Many plants grow from bulbs. These store food in winter and then grow into new plants the next year.

Grow a potato
Put a sprouting potato in a bucket of damp soil. Put the bucket in a warm, dark place. When the potato sends out a shoot, bring it into the light. Water it and see how it grows.

▽ The tulip grows a new plant from a bulb. The bulb is at the bottom of the stem.

▽ The iris grows new plants from its underground stem. The stem is called a rhizome.

▽ The cassava plant grows from underground stems called tubers.

▽ The strawberry plant sends out long stems called runners. The runners take root to make new plants.

tulip

iris

strawberry

cassava

bulb

rhizome

runner

tuber

The age of plants

Plants do not all live for the same length of time. Some plants live for just a few months or even weeks. After they have produced flowers, seeds, and fruit, they die. They are called annuals. Other plants live for several years. They are called perennials.

▽ Flowers like these are annual plants. They will live for only one year.

△ In the Australian desert, Sturt's desert pea seeds live under the sand for up to ten years. As soon as it rains, they grow and flower very quickly.

dragon tree

△ These flowers are perennial plants. They will flower again and again.

yew

bristlecone pine

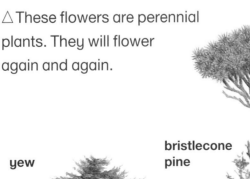

▷ The dragon tree, the bristlecone pine, and the yew are all perennial plants that live a long time. They may live for thousands of years.

Studying plants

Plants come in all shapes and sizes. They can be very small, such as the tiny duckweed, or very big, such as a huge tree. Many plants have flowers, but some do not. Some do not even have leaves. People who study plants are called botanists. They think that there are about 350,000 species, or different kinds, of plants. Botanists divide these into groups, depending on how they look and grow.

▽ The tree, the duckweed, the ferns, and the daffodils are all types of plant. But they are very different.

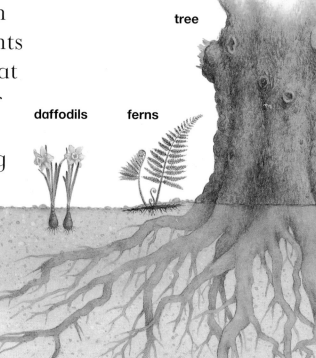

tree

daffodils   ferns

duckweed

Ask a grown-up before touching a new plant. Always wash your hands afterward. Some plants are poisonous.

Word box
Botany is the study of all kinds of plant life.
Species are made up of animals or plants that are the same and can produce more of the same kind.

Flowering plants

There is a big group of plants called flowering plants. It includes trees, shrubs, and climbers, as well as flowers.

◁ Many flowering plants have soft stems.

▽ Trees are flowering plants with thick, woody trunks.

trunk

▷ Climbers have long, twisting stems.

△ Shrubs are smaller than most trees.

Nonflowering plants

Algae, fungi, and lichens are all plants that do not have flowers. So are mosses and ferns. Instead of seeds, these plants have spores. Conifers have cones instead of flowers.

△ Algae live in all kinds of water.

△ Fungi have no chlorophyll.

△ Lichen is a strange plant made up of an alga and a fungus.

◁ Some botanists study plants in the rain forest. They often discover new species.

△ Conifers are trees that have cones.

moss

spore

fern

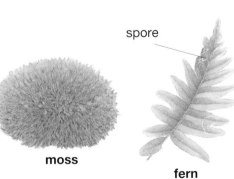

△ Mosses and ferns make new plants with spores.

Flowers

The shapes of flowers vary. Some flowers have petals that are all the same size and shape. Others have petals that are different sizes and shapes. The way flowers grow on plants also varies. Some flowers cluster at the top of a stem. Others grow all along the stem.

Thumbelina
(A story by Hans Christian Andersen)

Thumbelina was the size of a thumb. She was small enough to sleep inside a flower and ride on a swallow's back.

▷The bellflower and St. John's wort have petals that are all the same. Flowers like this are called regular flowers.

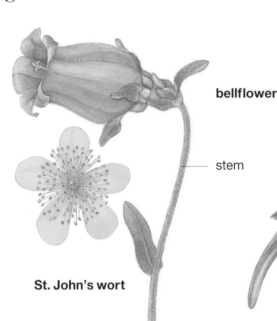

bellflower

stem

St. John's wort

◁The toadflax has petals of different shapes and sizes. This is what is called an irregular flower.

▽The dahlia head has a lot of small flowers that are packed tightly together.

◁The wild celery has flowers that all grow from the same point at the top of its stem.

▷Lily of the valley has little bells arranged along its stem.

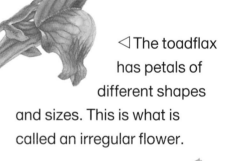

▷These flowering plants have leaves with veins in parallel lines. That means that the veins all run straight from one end of the leaf to the other.

oat

amaryllis

orchid

vein

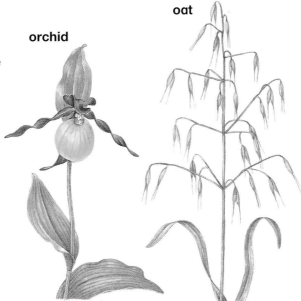

▷These flowering plants have leaves with veins that branch out from a middle vein.

eryngo

spurge

speedwell

vein

Make a Hawaiian garland

Draw the shape of a flower like the one below onto cardboard. Use it as a pattern to cut out lots of flowers from brightly colored paper.

Thread yarn through the center of each flower with a darning needle. Then tie both ends of the yarn together.

Trees and shrubs

There are two main sorts of trees and shrubs. Some shed their leaves in the fall and grow new leaves in spring. They are called deciduous. Others grow new leaves all year round. They are called evergreens. Many evergreens are trees called conifers, with seeds in cones.

Buddha and the bo tree
An old story tells how Buddha sat under a bo tree to think. A bo tree is a kind of fig tree. Buddha had an idea that changed his life. He became a great teacher.

▽ These trees are all conifers. Most conifers are evergreen. They have narrow leaves called needles that are not hurt by bad weather. Their cones contain winged seeds.

cone

Nootka cypress

△ This is a gingko tree. These trees are related to conifers. They are very ancient.

larch

spruce

weeping sequoia

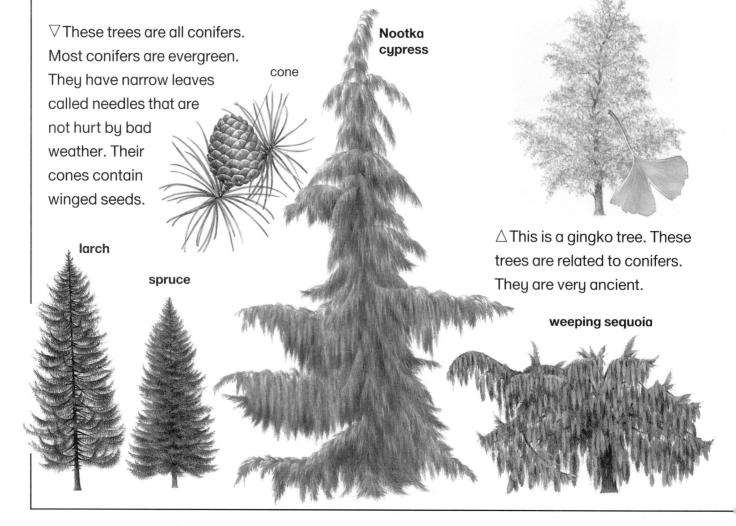

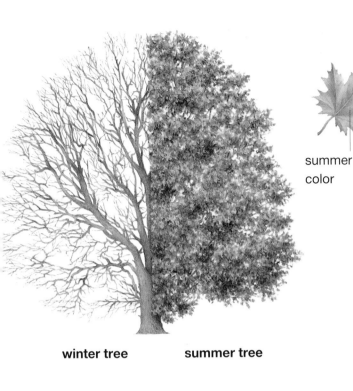

summer color fall color

winter tree **summer tree**

passion flower

▽ Most trees and shrubs grow flowers. The magnolia, the rhododendron, and the passion flower all have beautiful blossoms.

magnolia

rhododendron

△ Deciduous trees have no leaves in winter. In summer they are leafy and green. Their leaves change color before they drop off in the fall.

Make a twig tree

Find a small branch with lots of twigs. Decorate a flowerpot with colored paper. Fix the branch in the pot with modeling clay. Glue on tissue paper leaves and flowers.

▷ Every year, a new ring of wood grows under the bark. You can count the rings to tell how old the tree is.

bark

new growth rings

heartwood

Find the answers

What are the leaves of conifers called?

When do deciduous trees lose their leaves?

225

Other plants

Fungi, algae, lichens, mosses, and ferns are all plants that do not flower. They have tiny spores instead of seeds. Fungi have no leaves, stems, or roots. Most algae are water plants. Lichens are small plants that live for a very long time and will only grow where the air is not too polluted. Mosses grow in damp places. Ferns often grow in woods.

△ The chanterelle is a bright yellow fungus that grows in some woodlands.

Elves and fairy rings

In fairy tales, elves and fairies live in toadstools, or sit on them. This is why the rings of little toadstools you sometimes see on the grass are called fairy rings.

Do not pick or even touch fungi.

△ It is easy to see why this rare type of fungus is called a cage fungus.

△ Puffballs contain millions of spores. They look like puffs of smoke when they burst.

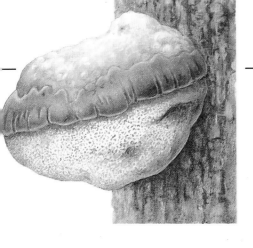

△ The beefsteak fungus grows on trees. This type of fungus is called a bracket fungus.

△ The morel has a dark brown, wrinkled cap. The cap is the top part of a fungus.

△ The mold on old food is tiny fungi. The medicine penicillin comes from mold.

▽ Many algae form long, green, slimy strands in ponds. They look like this under a microscope.

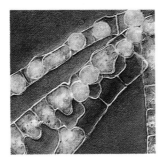

△ Seaweeds are types of algae. Some seaweeds are more than 10 feet long.

▽ Moss grows in damp places. It is made up of tiny stems and leaves. It looks like this under a microscope.

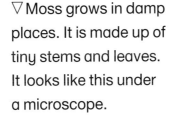

△ Lichens grow very slowly on walls, trees, and rocks. Some types can live for as long as 4,000 years.

▷ Fern leaves are tightly coiled when they are young. After they unfold, little brown spores fall out.

spore

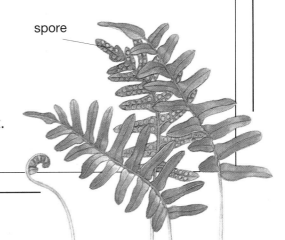

Weird and wonderful

Some plants are very strange. They grow in odd shapes. Some are brightly colored and beautiful. Others are ugly. There are plants shaped like rocks, bottles, and pipes. Some plants have their roots above ground. There are even plants that feed on insects. Some trees live for thousands of years and grow to an enormous size.

▽ The flowers of the canna are enclosed in large, colorful leaves. These leaves are called bracts. They are bright red and have sharp points.

canna

bract

▷ The flower of the Dutchman's pipe has a pouch that smells of rotting fish to attract flies. It looks like an old-fashioned Dutch pipe.

Dutchman's pipe

◁ The pitcher plant feeds on insects. It has vase-shaped leaves. Insects fall down their slippery sides and drown in the liquid inside.

▷ The leaves of plants called living-stones look like rocks. This is so that animals do not eat them. Except for their bright flowers, they blend with the rocks around them.

◁ The giant sequoia is one of the biggest and oldest trees in the world. One giant sequoia in California is thought to be more than 3,000 years old. It has been named General Sherman.

▽ The root of the mandrake can look a bit like the legs of a human body.

△ The bottle tree has a trunk shaped like a bottle. This stores water in the desert.

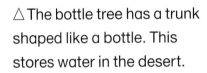

Mandrakes

Long ago, people thought that mandrakes were magical plants. They believed that the roots screamed if you pulled them up.

▽ Some roots of the swamp cypress come up above the surface of the wet soil.

◁ Look how small a ten-year-old child looks next to this huge giant sequoia.

Vegetables

Vegetables taste good and they provide us with vitamins and minerals that keep us healthy. We can eat raw and cooked vegetables. Parts of vegetables that are eaten include their roots, leaves, stems, pods, and seeds.

You **cannot** eat all plants. Many are poisonous.

lettuce

carrot

potato

cauliflower

spinach

green bean

△ We eat lettuce leaves and carrot roots.

△ We eat potato tubers and cauliflower flowers.

△ We eat green bean pods and spinach leaves.

Word box
Vitamins are natural chemicals found in fruit, vegetables, and other foods.
Grains are small, hard seeds. They are usually ground into flour to make bread and pasta.

The enormous turnip
(A Russian folk tale)

An old man planted some turnip seeds. One grew into the biggest turnip he had ever seen. He could not pull it up on his own. It took the whole family, the dog, the cat, and a little mouse to move it.

Cereals and oils

Cereals are types of grasses grown for their seeds or grains. Some grains are ground into flour to make bread, pasta, cookies, and cakes. Others are used in breakfast cereals. Farmers also feed grains to their animals.

The fruits and seeds of a number of different plants provide vegetable oils. These contain some of the vitamins we need. We use a lot of vegetable oils in our cooking.

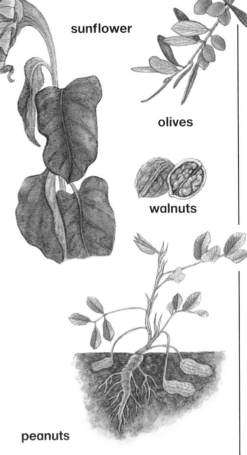

sunflower

olives

walnuts

peanuts

▽ Wheat and corn are both cereals. Wheat is made into flour for bread. Cornflakes are made from corn.

▽ Rice and millet are also cereals. Rice grains are usually eaten whole. Millet can be crushed into a porridge.

△ Olives, walnuts, sunflower seeds, and peanuts are all used to make vegetable oils.

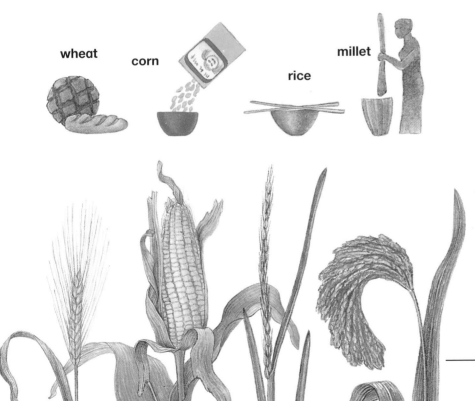

wheat

corn

rice

millet

Find the answers

Where do vegetable oils come from?

What are cornflakes made from?

What is made from olives?

Fruits, nuts, and sugars

Fruit is tasty to eat. It is also good for you. There are many different types of fruit. They grow all over the world. Fruits are sweet because they have a type of sugar in them.

The sugar we buy in stores is different—it comes from sugarcane or sugar beet.

Write a secret message
Write a secret message in fresh lemon juice. When it dries, ask a grown-up to iron the paper. Now you can see what you have written!

◁ Apples are fruit. They have thin skin and juicy flesh with small seeds inside.

▽ The prickly pear is the fruit of a type of cactus. It is good to eat, but it is difficult to pick.

▽ Oranges are good for you. Their juice is delicious to drink.

◁ Bananas grow in big bunches on tall trees. They turn from green to yellow as they ripen. Bananas grow in hot countries.

△ Some of our sugar comes from the crushed root of the sugar beet plant.

▽ Hard shells keep nuts fresh for a long time. So we can eat nuts throughout the winter.

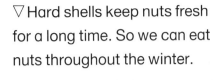

△ Sugarcane is grown in hot countries. Sugar comes from the juice in its stems.

▽ Sugar is used to make food taste sweeter. Candy has a lot of sugar in it. Too much sugar is bad for your teeth.

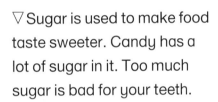

△ Most fruit can be eaten raw. It is also good to eat cooked in jams, cakes, and desserts.

△ Fruits can be dried. They shrink, and then taste even sweeter. Dried summer fruits are eaten all year.

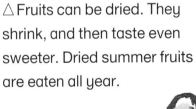

△ Bees gather a sweet juice called nectar from flowers and turn it into honey.

Winnie the Pooh
(A story by A. A. Milne)

Winnie the Pooh was a cuddly bear. He had all sorts of adventures because of his love for honey. The more honey he had, the happier he was.

233

Herbs and spices

We use herbs and spices to add flavor to food. Sometimes they are freshly cut, and sometimes they are dried. Some of these plants can also be used to make herbal teas. We use the leaves of plants as herbs and their fruits, stems, flowers, and roots as spices. Some herbs and spices are very hot and others are mild and sweet.

Make gingerbread

You need:
½ cup soft brown sugar
6 tbsp. margarine
2 tbsp. molasses
2 cups flour
2 tsp. ginger
licorice

Ask an adult to melt margarine, sugar, and molasses in a pan over a low heat. Stir in flour and ginger. Mix and roll out to ¼ inch thick.
Cut out people shapes. Bake for 10 to 15 minutes at 350°F.
Add licorice rope for hair.

mint   basil

coriander   bay leaf

Can you find?
1 peppers
2 cinnamon
3 ginger
4 nutmeg
5 cloves
6 peppercorns
7 turmeric
8 saffron
9 licorice ropes

△ These plants are all common herbs. They are used to flavor food in many different parts of the world.

▽ Vanilla is a sweet spice. It comes from the seed pod of an orchid.

Drinks from plants

The juice squeezed from many fruits makes delicious drinks. We can also mix fruit and milk or ice cream in a blender, to make a milkshake. Hot drinks such as coffee, tea, and hot chocolate are also made from plants.

Always ask a grown-up before you make juice from a strange fruit.

▷ Here are some fruits that can be used to make drinks. We drink the juice of fruits such as oranges, grapefruits, lemons, pineapples, apples, and grapes.

◁ Chocolate is made from the fruits or pods of the cacao tree. Inside them are seeds called cacao beans.

▷ The cacao beans inside the pod are taken out. They are dried and roasted.

◁ Then the beans are crushed to produce cocoa powder. This is used to make chocolate to eat or to drink.

△ Tea is made from the leaves of tea plants.

△ Coffee is made from the beans of the coffee plant.

Find the answers

What is made from the fruits of the cacao tree?

Does coffee come from beans or leaves?

Houseplants

Many plants are easy to grow indoors as long as they have soil, air, light, and water. Plants can be grown in the house all year round. Even in winter, we can have flowers in the home. We can also grow garden plants such as herbs or bulbs indoors. Houseplants usually have beautiful flowers or leaves. Most are easy to care for too.

△ The Japanese make beautiful miniature gardens with bonsai trees.

bonsai tree

▽ Bulbs can be grown in a pot of bulb fiber or soil. They are germinated in the dark, then brought into the light.

hyacinth

narcissus

daffodil

△ Parsley is a herb. You can sow the seeds in pots and grow them on a windowsill.

△ If it is kept in a light, warm spot, the parsley will not be harmed by frost.

▷ Orchids can be grown in a terrarium.

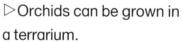

bulb

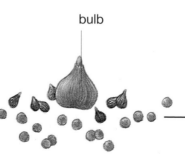

palm

begonia

cactus

Make a cress head
Watercress seeds are fun to grow like this. Put damp cotton balls in a clean eggshell. Sprinkle the seeds inside and draw a face outside. The seeds grow to look like hair.

▽ A terrace is a good place for big plants. But some plants will need protection in winter.

△ There are many kinds of houseplant. Here are some different types.

Word box
Greenhouses are warm buildings made of glass. They protect delicate plants from cold and wind. **Bonsai** is the Japanese art of growing dwarf trees and shrubs in pots.

Caring for plants

Plants need care, especially if they are grown in pots. They need water, air, and light. Sometimes they need to be protected from harmful bugs, insects, and fungi. If a plant is healthy, we can often use parts of it to grow new plants. This is called propagation.

trellis

leaf cutting

△ The leaves of some plants will produce a new plant if they are placed in soil. This is called a leaf cutting.

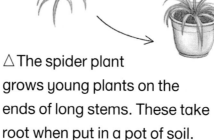

△ The spider plant grows young plants on the ends of long stems. These take root when put in a pot of soil.

△ In spring, an ivy stem left in a jar of water will grow roots. Then it can be planted.

△ Some plants produce baby plants from their roots. These can be grown as new plants.

△ The stems of some plants form clumps. These are easy to divide. Then they can be planted in separate pots. Each part of the plant will grow as big as the old plant.

hanging basket

Ways to grow plants

Plants can be made to grow in different ways. A climbing plant can be grown up a trellis. This is a type of wooden frame. Trailing plants look pretty in a hanging basket.

△ Pebbles in the bottom of the plant pot let water drain away. This keeps the roots from rotting.

△ Mealybugs are insects that attack the cactus. Sprays can be used to kill them.

△ Blackspot is a type of fungus that damages the leaves of roses.

△ Plants still need water if you are away. A cord carries water from a bottle to the plant.

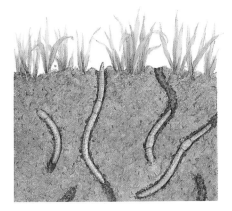

△ Some small creatures help plants grow. Worms make tunnels that let air into the soil.

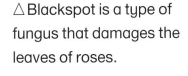
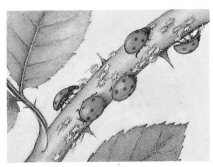

△ Ladybugs eat small insects called aphids that are harmful to some plants.

△ If the air is too hot or dry, it is often a good idea to spray the leaves with water.

Plants for decoration

Plants and flowers can be used to decorate our homes. People often make flower arrangements from fresh flowers and leaves.

There are also ways to make plants last longer. Flowers and leaves can be dried or pressed.

Many plants smell nice. Our rooms can be scented with dried petals or herbs.

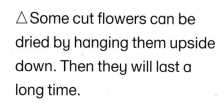

△ Some cut flowers can be dried by hanging them upside down. Then they will last a long time.

▽ Making beautiful flower arrangements is an art. We can use fresh flowers, dried flowers, and interesting grasses and leaves.

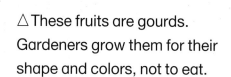

△ These fruits are gourds. Gardeners grow them for their shape and colors, not to eat.

Press flowers

Dry flowers by pressing them. You will need books and blotting paper. Put the flowers between two sheets of blotting paper. Put the paper in a book. Put heavy books on top. Leave for a month. Use the flowers to decorate a card or bookmark.

Plants for protection

In times gone by, people thought that the scent of herbs and other plants could keep away disease. They carried scented balls called pomanders. These were often oranges stuck with cloves. They also believed that some plants could protect them against evil spirits. Garlic was supposed to keep away vampires!

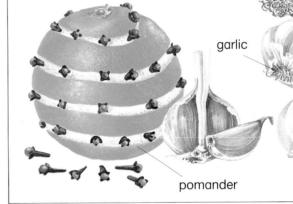

garlic

pomander

Jack-o'-lanterns

People make jack-o'-lanterns from pumpkins. They cut off the top and hollow out the inside. Then they cut a face in the pumpkin and put a lighted candle inside.

▽ Scented plants can be dried and used to make our houses smell nice. Here are some well-known ones.

cinnamon

lavender

citrus peel

damask rose

orris root

241

Plants for life

Plants are a vital part of life. They take sunlight and turn it into food. Animals eat plants. Many animals are then eaten by other animals. Without the sun, plants could not live. Without plants, animals could not live.

Plants also give shelter. Many creatures use plants as their habitat, or home.

bamboo

△ The panda depends on bamboo because it is almost the only food that it eats.

▽ Plants need sunlight to grow. Animals need plants to eat. Animal droppings and the remains of dead plants and animals are taken into the soil by insects and worms. The soil provides food for the new plants that grow in it. This is called a food chain.

Some seeds are **poisonous**.

Grow a seed
Plant a melon, apple, or orange seed in a pot. Then water it. Cut the bottom off a clear plastic bottle and use it to cover the pot. Put the pot in a dark place.

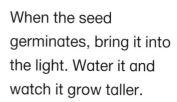

When the seed germinates, bring it into the light. Water it and watch it grow taller.

Word box
Habitats are the natural surroundings in which plants and animals live. **Pollution** causes damage to our environment. It can kill living things.

eucalyptus

△ The koala
needs the
eucalyptus tree
because it eats its leaves.
If pollution kills the trees, the koalas
will die out.

Can you find?

1 owl
2 buzzard
3 magpie
4 woodpecker
5 squirrel
6 fungi
7 butterfly
8 moth
9 ivy

Plants in danger

Many plants are in danger. Pollution, fires, new roads, and buildings can damage the places where plants live. Huge areas of forest are cleared for farming each year. Some plants are in danger of becoming extinct. That means they may disappear forever.

△ When a fire breaks out, firefighting aircraft spray water and chemicals over the forest to put out the flames.

▽ These plants are so rare that they are in danger of becoming extinct.

slipper orchid

rafflesia

African violet

△ Many forests are being destroyed to provide timber and make room for farmland.

The future of plants

All over the world, botanists are studying plants and their habitats. They try to learn more about plants, so that they can protect them and find new ways of using them for food and medicine. Scientists are trying to develop new plants that can survive in places where it is difficult to grow enough food.

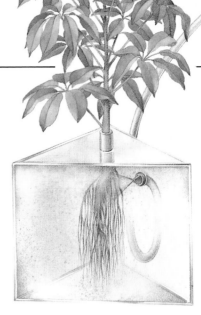

△ Scientists can now grow plants without soil. A mixture of water and fertilizer is sprayed onto their roots.

New sorts of wheat

Scientists have developed new sorts of wheat that can resist pests and diseases and produce more grain. This means more people can be fed in places where food is scarce.

◁ A carrot with lots of vitamin A is being created for people living in countries where they cannot grow enough food containing vitamin A.

▽ This expedition is studying plants in the rain forest. It may find new and useful plants.

Useful plants

Long ago, people found out that plants are useful. Some plants have been grown for food and other uses for thousands of years. Many medicines and health products are made from plants. So are beauty products. All sorts of plants are useful to us, from small flowers to large trees.

△ Lotions made with arnica help to soothe bruises.

△ Lime blossoms are used to make a relaxing lime tea.

◁ Farmers have grown vines for about 5,000 years. Their grapes are used to make wine.

▷ The papyrus plant is a kind of reed. It grows by the water in warm countries. Papyrus was used to make paper in Egypt 4,500 years ago.

◁ Corn was grown in Mexico 4,000 years ago. Farmers still grow it for food today.

Make your own dyes
You can make natural dyes from plants. Use beets or blackberries for red, and onion skins for yellow.

Put what you are using to make the dye in an old handkerchief. Tie it securely and put it in a pan of water.

△ Lemon balm can be used to make a relaxing drink.

△ Dandelion juice can be used to treat warts.

Add a teaspoon of salt to the water. Ask an adult to boil the water until the dye comes out. Then put a white T-shirt in the pan and leave for an hour. Your T-shirt will now be the same color as the dye.

annatto berry

△ Indians in the Amazon forests use plant dyes to protect their skin from insects. Annatto berries make a red dye.

△ The strong stems of the bamboo are used to build fences and houses.

△ Baskets are woven from willow branches.

△ Stems of the rattan palm are used to make furniture.

Word box
Dye is a substance you can use to change the color of things.
Lotion is a liquid that you put on the skin.

247

Plants for ideas

Plants give people good ideas. Many useful inventions in houses, clothes, transportation, and other areas of life have come from people looking at plants.

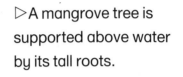

▷ A mangrove tree is supported above water by its tall roots.

◁ Stilt houses copy mangrove trees. The houses are built on stilts above water.

▽ Burdock was the model for Velcro fastenings. Its burrs have tiny hooked spines.

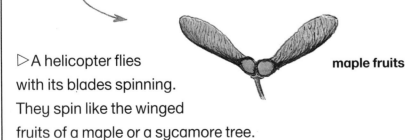

maple fruits

Velcro —

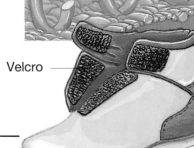

▷ A helicopter flies with its blades spinning. They spin like the winged fruits of a maple or a sycamore tree.

When Dinosaurs Lived

Meeting dinosaurs

Dinosaurs lived on Earth millions of years ago. Then they became extinct, which means they died out forever. They were extinct long before people lived, so no one has ever seen a live dinosaur.

We know a great deal about dinosaurs because people have found fossils of their bones and teeth. Often the bones make up whole skeletons which can be put on show in museums.

▷This skeleton belonged to one of the fiercest dinosaurs of all, Tyrannosaurus rex. Scientists studied the different bones and found out about how Tyrannosaurus lived.

a long tail helped this enormous dinosaur to balance

Word box
Fossils are the remains of animals and plants that lived long ago. They are usually found hardened in rock.
Paleontologists are people who study fossils.

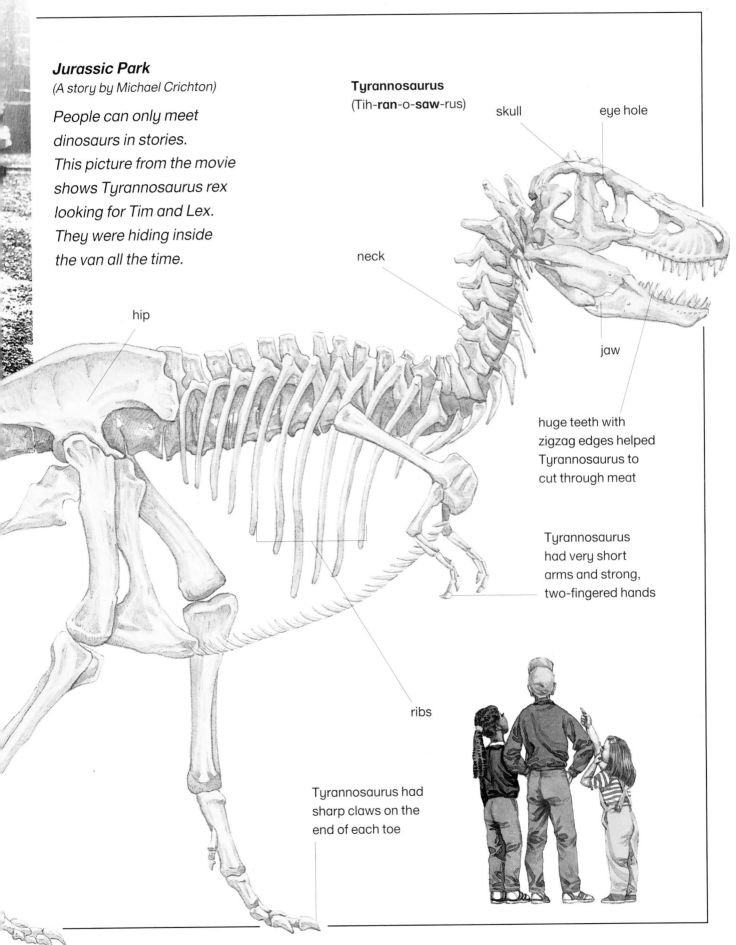

Jurassic Park
(A story by Michael Crichton)

People can only meet dinosaurs in stories. This picture from the movie shows Tyrannosaurus rex looking for Tim and Lex. They were hiding inside the van all the time.

Tyrannosaurus
(Tih-**ran**-o-**saw**-rus)

skull

eye hole

neck

jaw

hip

huge teeth with zigzag edges helped Tyrannosaurus to cut through meat

Tyrannosaurus had very short arms and strong, two-fingered hands

ribs

Tyrannosaurus had sharp claws on the end of each toe

Dinosaur ideas

We know about dinosaurs from the clues they left behind. People have found fossils of dinosaur bones, teeth, footprints, skin prints, eggs, and nests. They all help scientists figure out what dinosaurs might have looked like and how they might have lived.

People are still finding these clues. As new discoveries are made, ideas change.

▽ Teeth and claws tell us what dinosaurs ate. We can tell how fast a dinosaur ran from its footprints. Sometimes baby dinosaur skeletons are found inside fossilized eggs.

tooth

eggs

leg bones

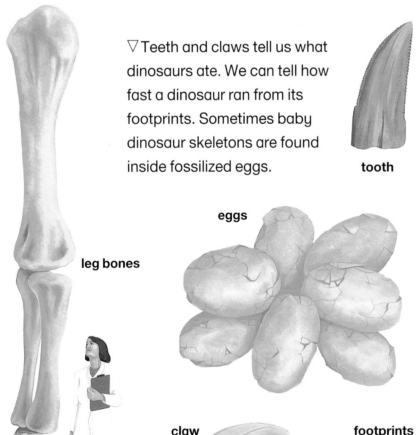

Land Before Time
(A story by Judy Freudberg and Tony Geiss)

A cartoon has been made about this small dinosaur, Littlefoot. He was separated from his family and set out on a dangerous journey to the Great Valley.

claw

footprints

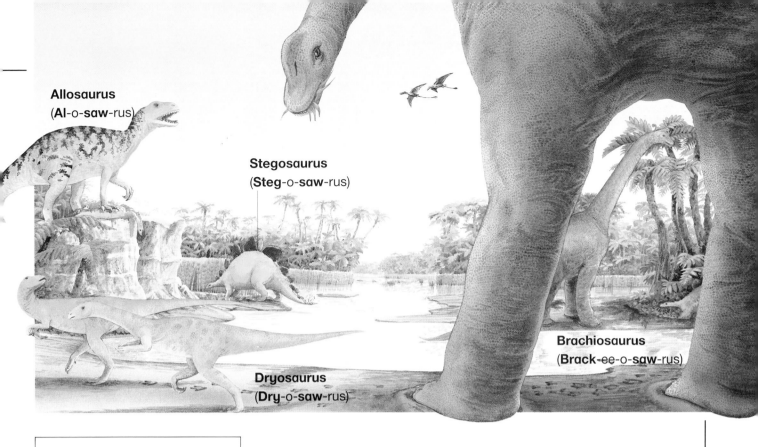

Allosaurus
(**Al**-o-**saw**-rus)

Stegosaurus
(**Steg**-o-**saw**-rus)

Dryosaurus
(**Dry**-o-**saw**-rus)

Brachiosaurus
(**Brack**-ee-o-**saw**-rus)

Iguanodon
(Ig-**wan**-o-**don**)
model, 1853

In 1853, people thought
Iguanodon had a horn
on its nose. Now we
know the horn was a
spike on its thumb.

model, now

△ From the clues they left
behind, we can guess that this
is what dinosaurs might have
looked like in North America,
150 million years ago.

▽ Scientists known as
paleontologists study
dinosaur fossils. They fit the
bones together and work out
what dinosaurs looked like.

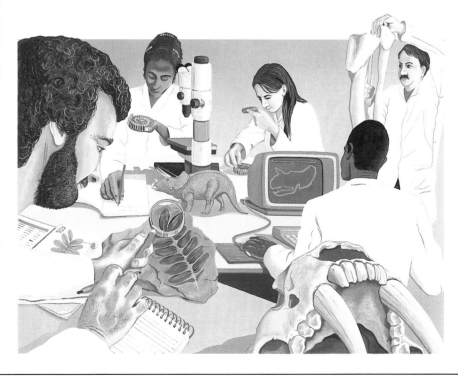

253

Different dinosaurs

Dinosaurs were all different shapes and sizes. Some were huge. Others were the size of a turkey. Some plodded on all fours. Others walked and ran on their back legs. There were fierce meat-eaters and gentle plant-eaters. Scientists believe that dinosaurs were reptiles, so they all had scaly skin and laid eggs.

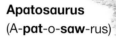

Apatosaurus
(A-**pat**-o-**saw**-rus)

Apatosaurus prints
Some Apatosaurus footprints were found in Mexico. Before this, scientists thought that Apatosaurus had been too heavy to live on land and must have needed water to support its great weight.

Coelophysis
(**See**-lo-**fie**-sis)

△ Coelophysis was one of the first dinosaurs to have lived. It was about the size of a ten-year-old child.

▽ Diplodocus was one of the longest dinosaurs. It had a tiny skull compared to its huge body.

Word box
Reptiles are cold-blooded animals that use heat from the sun to keep warm. They lay eggs.
Camouflage is a way of hiding. Animals use their shape and color to blend in with their surroundings.

▽ Compsognathus is the smallest known dinosaur. It had sharp little teeth and could run very fast to catch lizards to eat.

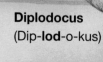

Diplodocus
(Dip-**lod**-o-kus)

Compsognathus
(Komp-**sog**-nath-us)

Make a dough dinosaur

Make dough using the recipe and instructions at the beginning of this book. Add some food coloring. Mold the dough into your favorite dinosaur shapes. Roll out a thick sausage of dough for the larger dinosaurs' necks.

▽ Some of the largest dinosaurs, such as Seismosaurus and Brachiosaurus, were plant-eaters. Seismosaurus was the biggest dinosaur. Its name means earthshaker. Tyrannosaurus rex was the biggest meat-eater ever. If it were alive today, it could peer into upstairs windows!

Seismosaurus
(**Size**-mo-**saw**-rus)

Brachiosaurus

Tyrannosaurus

Sorting dinosaurs

Scientists use dinosaurs' hipbones to sort them into two groups. If the hipbone points forward, it is a lizard hip. If it points backward, it is a bird hip.

Skin prints show that dinosaurs had different kinds of skin. Some had big, knobby plates and others had small, smooth scales. We can only guess what color their skin was. Maybe they were the same color as modern reptiles.

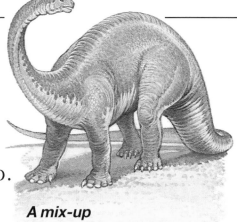

A mix-up
A Camarasaurus's head was put on the first Apatosaurus fossil found. Scientists called the dinosaur Brontosaurus. This was a mistake. We now know that this mixed-up Brontosaurus never existed.

Protoceratops
is a bird hip

▽ Protoceratops is a bird hip, because its hip points back. Compsognathus's hip points forward, so it is a lizard hip.

Compsognathus
is a lizard hip

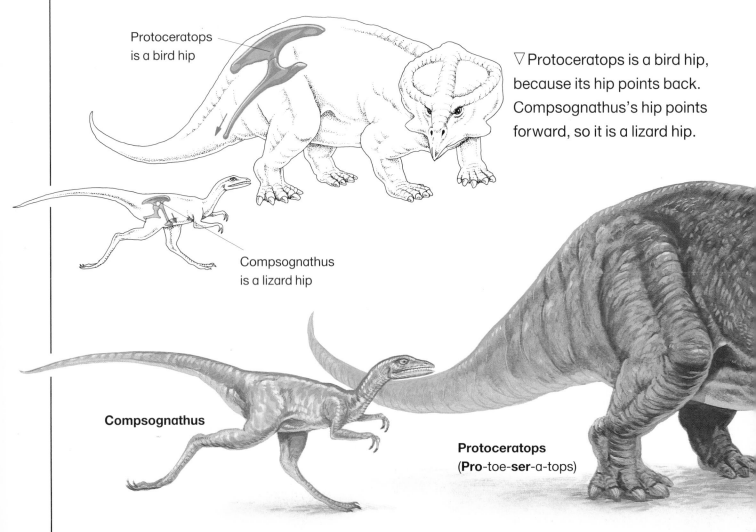

Compsognathus

Protoceratops
(**Pro**-toe-**ser**-a-tops)

▷ Fossilized skin prints do not show us what color dinosaurs were. Perhaps they were different colors for different reasons, just like reptiles today.

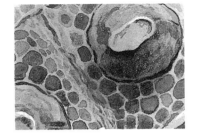

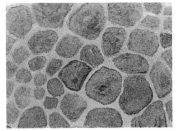

coral snake

Ankylosaurus
(**Ang**-kill-o-**saw**-rus)

Diplodocus

desert snake

△ Coral snakes have bright stripes to warn off meat-eaters. Their poison can kill. Desert snakes are a dull color. They can hide in the sand.

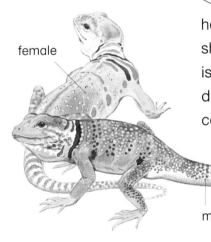

female

male

◁ The modern collared lizards have different markings to show which is male and which is female. Perhaps male dinosaurs had different colorings from females.

▷ Young alligators are striped. Their stripes camouflage, or hide them, among the grasses.

▽ Adult alligators are a different color. They are camouflaged when they lie in muddy rivers.

baby alligator

adult alligator

Where dinosaurs lived

Millions of years ago, the continents were joined together in a single land. Dinosaurs lived all over this land. We know this because bones have been found on every continent. Many different dinosaur bones have been dug up. This map shows the world today and some of the places where fossils have been found.

▽ Tyrannosaurus rex is one of the largest dinosaurs. Its bones have been found in Asia as well as North America.

▽ Hypsilophodon bones are found as far apart as Antarctica, Australia, and Europe. Can you find these places on the map?

NORTH
AMERICA

SOU
AMER

△ When all the continents were joined together as one land it was known as Pangaea. The world looked very different from today.

Hypsilophodon
(Hip-see-loff-o-don)

▷ Staurikosaurus was found in South America. It was one of the oldest dinosaurs to be discovered.

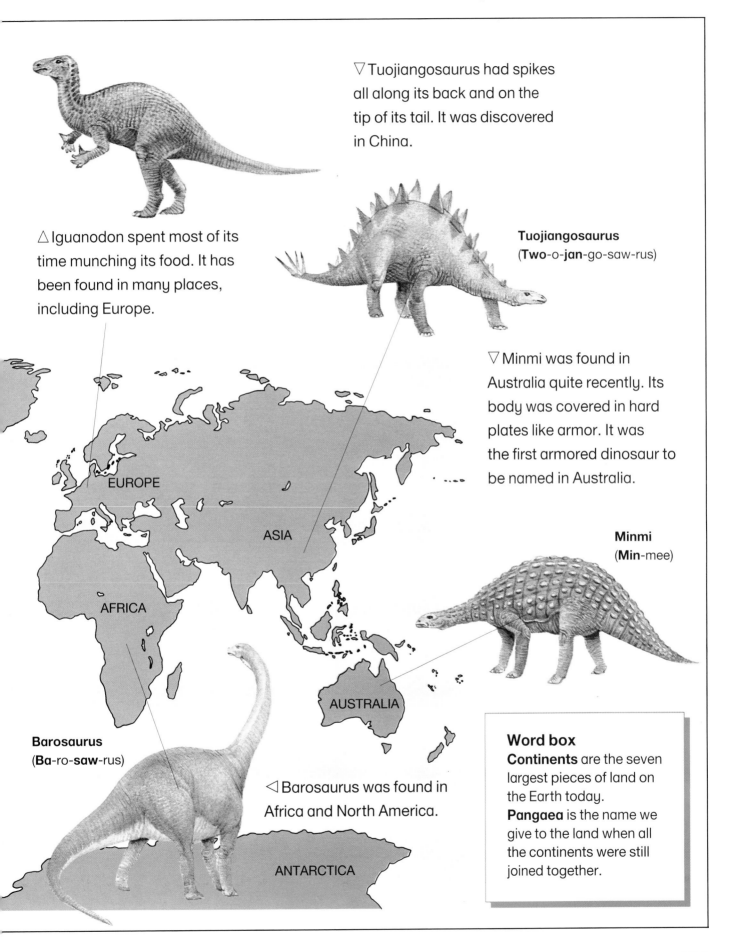

▽ Tuojiangosaurus had spikes all along its back and on the tip of its tail. It was discovered in China.

△ Iguanodon spent most of its time munching its food. It has been found in many places, including Europe.

Tuojiangosaurus
(**Two**-o-**jan**-go-saw-rus)

▽ Minmi was found in Australia quite recently. Its body was covered in hard plates like armor. It was the first armored dinosaur to be named in Australia.

Minmi
(**Min**-mee)

EUROPE

ASIA

AFRICA

AUSTRALIA

Barosaurus
(**Ba**-ro-**saw**-rus)

◁ Barosaurus was found in Africa and North America.

ANTARCTICA

Word box
Continents are the seven largest pieces of land on the Earth today.
Pangaea is the name we give to the land when all the continents were still joined together.

Dinosaur families

Dinosaurs laid eggs, as modern reptiles do. We know that they did this because of fossil nests containing eggs found in North America. Some of these nests were found close together. Perhaps mothers looked after their babies in groups for safety. Bones of Maiasaura adults, young, and babies have been found in one place. This could mean that family groups lived together.

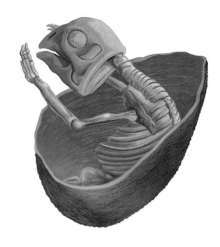

△ Fossils of dinosaur eggs are very hard to find. This model shows what a dinosaur baby might have looked like inside.

Maiasaura (My-a-**saw**-ra)

△ A Maiasaura mother scraped the ground to make a big nest in which to lay her hard-shelled eggs.

△ She laid up to 30 eggs in the nest, in neat circles. Their narrow ends pointed inward.

△ Then Maiasaura covered her eggs with leaves, ferns, and some soil. This hid the eggs and kept them warm.

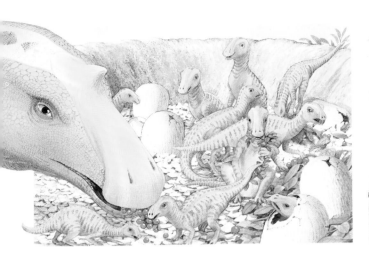

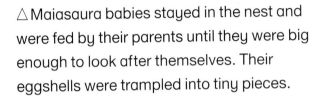

△ Maiasaura babies stayed in the nest and were fed by their parents until they were big enough to look after themselves. Their eggshells were trampled into tiny pieces.

△ Others left their nest to search for food soon after they hatched. We think Hypsilophodon babies left the nest quickly, because their eggshells were not as badly damaged.

Hatching egg game

Draw an egg shape on cardboard. Cut it out and use it to draw 20 egg shapes. Draw a baby dinosaur on each one and cut them out. Make two boards with 10 egg shapes drawn on both. Each player places 10 eggs on their board, blank side up.

Take it in turns to throw the die. Turn over the same number of eggs as the number shown on the die. The winner turns over, or hatches, all their eggs first.

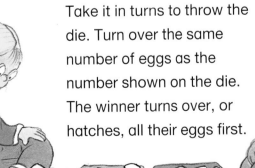

△ Other Maiasaura built their nests nearby. They all helped to keep watch, to stop other dinosaurs from stealing eggs.

261

Dinosaur lives

Some dinosaurs grew up and lived in large groups called herds. The dinosaurs in the herd protected one another. No one is exactly sure how long dinosaurs lived. Scientists think that some reached an amazing age of 200 years old, but many died from injury or disease before that.

Draw a zigzag scene
Draw two pictures the same size. One has a dinosaur alone, the other has the dinosaur with the rest of its herd.

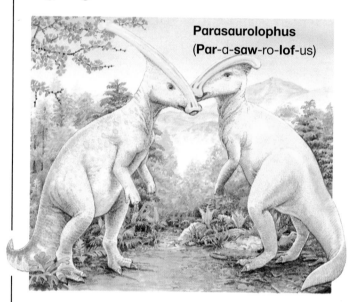

Parasaurolophus
(**Par**-a-**saw**-ro-**lof**-us)

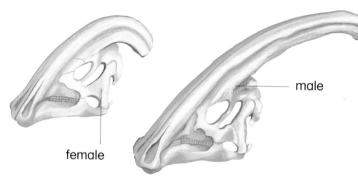

male

female

◁ Skulls show that the male Parasaurolophus had a longer crest than the female. Male dinosaurs may have used their crests and horns for showing off to the females.

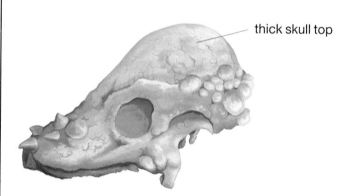

thick skull top

▷ Pachycephalosaurus had a thick skull top. The males probably crashed heads in fights to win a female, just as stags use antlers today.

Pachycephalosaurus
(**Pak**-ee-**kef**-a-lo-**saw**-rus)

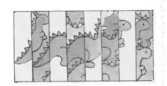

Fold pictures into zigzag pleats. Cut folds to make strips. Paste strips alternately onto a piece of paper. Fold into a zigzag pleat.

Look from one side, then the other. What can you see?

Corythosaurus

Corythosaurus had hollow pipes inside their head domes. Some people think they used these to make loud sounds that could warn other herd members of danger.

▽ A fierce Tyrannosaurus is attacking this herd of Triceratops. The babies and the weaker animals huddle together in the middle. The big males stand around the herd to protect them. They point their horns outward, ready to fight.

Corythosaurus
(**Ko-ree**-tho-**saw**-rus)

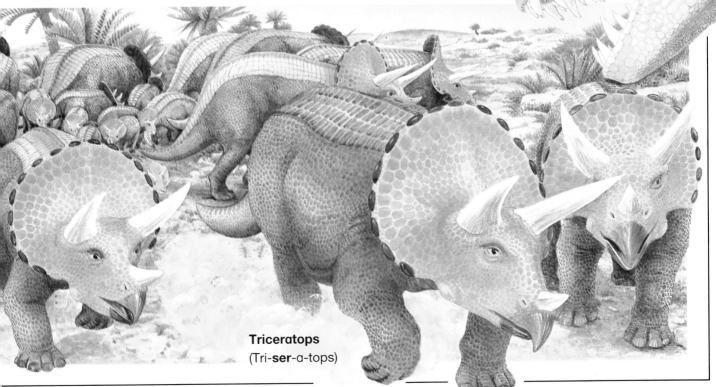

Triceratops
(Tri-**ser**-a-tops)

On the move

Dinosaurs may have swum to cross a river, but they spent their time eating, sleeping, and raising their young on dry land. Fossil footprints show how dinosaurs moved. From these we can tell whether a dinosaur was traveling alone or in a herd. We can also tell how fast they traveled. These footprints are found worldwide.

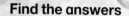

Find the answers

Who left behind three-toed prints?

How do we know some dinosaurs traveled in herds?

◁ Iguanodon usually walked on all fours, but rose on its back legs to move faster.

▷ Megalosaurus left huge, three-toed footprints. They show that it always went around on its back legs.

Iguanodon

Megalosaurus
(**Meg**-a-lo-**saw**-rus)

Struthiomimus
(**Strooth**-ee-o-**mime**-us)

▷ By looking at the length of its legs and footprints, we know that Struthiomimus ran as fast as a racehorse. The faster an animal runs, the bigger the spaces between its footprints, or tracks.

△ Many plant-eating dinosaurs traveled long distances in herds of up to a hundred animals, looking for grazing places. Some tracks seem to show that the young animals walked in the middle of the herd, safe from attack.

▷ These Apatosaurus prints were all made at the same time. This proves that some dinosaurs moved in herds.

Dinosaur race

Cut out cardboard dinosaur shapes like the one shown here. Make a hole in each one's head. Tie string to an equal number of chairs at the far end of a room. Thread the dinosaurs onto the string and move the string up and down to race them.

Looking for food

Some dinosaurs were herbivores. That means they ate only plants. Others were carnivores. They ate meat. The many known kinds of herbivore fed on leaves, cones, and roots. Often the carnivores, with their large, strong jaws and sharp teeth, would attack and eat these peaceful animals.

▽ Edmontosaurus was a plant-eating dinosaur. It had hundreds of teeth in a huge jaw, which helped it eat tough leaves and roots.

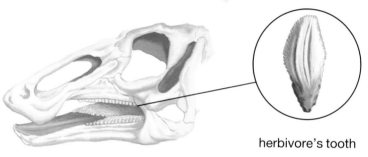

herbivore's tooth

Edmontosaurus
(**Ed**-mont-o-**saw**-rus)

△ Edmontosaurus's skull had a bony beak at the front, for nipping bits off a plant. Its teeth were worn down by all the chewing, so new teeth were always growing.

▽ Some herbivores swallowed rocks, just as birds swallow grit, to help grind up and digest the food in their stomachs.

Make dinosaur plant food

Roll up a newspaper tightly. Secure the middle and bottom with rubber bands. Make four cuts as far as the first band. Pull the middle of the roll out, to make a plant for a dinosaur.

Coelophysis the cannibal

Scientists found a baby Coelophysis inside an adult of the same kind. So some dinosaurs were cannibals, which means they ate each other!

Tyrannosaurus

▽ Carnivores' teeth were different from the herbivores'. The edges were like tiny saws, so they could tear flesh.

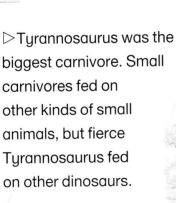

carnivore's tooth

▷ Tyrannosaurus was the biggest carnivore. Small carnivores fed on other kinds of small animals, but fierce Tyrannosaurus fed on other dinosaurs.

Hunting and defending

Some herbivores could move very fast. They could often outrun their enemies. Other dinosaurs moved more slowly and had body weapons. Tough armored plates, sharp spikes, and horns helped protect them from their enemies.

Carnivores were always looking for a tasty meal, so herbivores had to be able to escape quickly or fight.

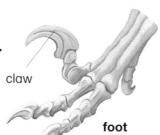

hand

claw

foot

△ Deinonychus had long fingers to grip flesh and a terrible slashing claw on its back feet that could rip and tear.

▽ Deinonychus was only the size of a human adult, so it had to hunt in packs to catch larger dinosaurs. The pack would corner the animal, bring it to the ground, and kill it.

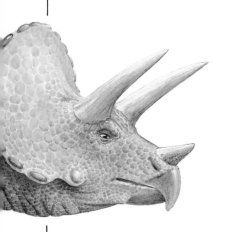

◁ Triceratops had three horns for fighting off a carnivore. Also, a large bony shield protected its neck. Some attackers were put off by such strong protection.

▽ Ankylosaurus had bony armor over its back and head, and a hard club on the end of its tail. So it was able to defend itself.

club

▷Even the giant Diplodocus needed to defend itself. Diplodocus could lash its long tail like a whip to keep the carnivores away.

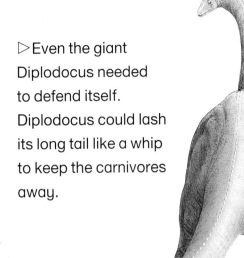

Make an Ankylosaurus
Cut out a cardboard Ankylosaurus shape like the one shown here. Cut up an egg carton and glue on the cups. Add scrunched up tissue paper and bottle caps. Paint it brightly.

▽Iguanodon had two sharp thumb spikes. A nasty stab from one of those would often be enough to scare off enemies.

Deinonychus
(**Dine**-o-**nike**-us)

Noisy dinosaurs

Dinosaurs made all kinds of noises. One particular group, the duck-billed dinosaurs, were very noisy. They honked and hooted through their noses. Perhaps this was to attract a mate or warn an enemy.

crest

▷Parasaurolophus was a duck-billed dinosaur. It had hollow breathing tubes inside its amazing crest. So when it breathed out hard, Parasaurolophus tooted like a trumpet or a trombone.

stretchy skin

◁Edmontosaurus, another duck-bill, had some stretchy skin on top of its broad nose. This could fill with air and vibrate to make sounds. A modern frog croaks with a stretchy pouch in its throat. But Edmontosaurus was much bigger and much louder than any frog.

Smart or stupid?

It was thought that dinosaurs were stupid because their skulls had such a small space for their brain. Experts wonder how such large animals survived for so long. Perhaps they were smarter than we think.

Find the answers

Which dinosaur had a brain that was little bigger than a walnut?

Did carnivores or herbivores need a bigger brain?

Stenonychosaurus
(**Sten**-o-**nike**-o-**saw**-rus)

◁ Stenonychosaurus was a fast little carnivore. It had big eyes and a good sense of smell for finding small animals to eat. Hunters, such as Stenonychosaurus, needed a bigger brain than herbivores.

▷ Stegosaurus was as heavy as an elephant. But it had a brain no bigger than the size of a walnut. Perhaps Stegosaurus did not need a big brain. After all, it was big, which made it safe from most attackers. So it could spend most of the day grazing slowly.

walnut

brain

Hot or cold?

Today, reptiles are cold-blooded. Dinosaurs were reptiles, so were they cold-blooded? Scientists are not sure.

Cold-blooded animals cannot heat their bodies. If the air is warm, they are warm and active. If the air is cold, they are cold and sluggish. Warm-blooded animals stay warm because their bodies do make heat.

△ Modern lizards laze in the sun to warm their bodies. If they get too hot they cool off in the shade.

◁ Perhaps Stegosaurus was cold-blooded and used the spiny plates on its back to soak up the sun's heat in the early morning.

▷ Small, active dinosaurs, such as Deinonychus, were probably warm-blooded, so had no need to heat their bodies before they could search for breakfast.

Deinonychus

▽ When the sun came up, Tyrannosaurus probably grunted and stretched as its body felt the warmth.

▽ This huge animal must have used its tiny arms to help it balance as it tried to pull itself upward.

▽ First it straightened its back legs. Then it pushed its head back and swung itself upright.

Diplodocus

▽ When the sun went down, dinosaurs probably slept. It was then safe for warm-blooded mammals to come out of their burrows to hunt for insects and fruit.

◁ Large dinosaurs, such as Diplodocus, were so massive that they only lost heat very slowly and could easily stay warm all the time.

273

What is evolution?

The Earth is very, very old. The first plants and animals were tiny cells in the sea. Bigger plants and animals slowly developed from these cells. This is called evolution. Dinosaurs first appeared 230 million years ago. They became extinct, which means they died out, 65 million years ago.

the first living things appeared in the sea 3.5 billion years ago

the first land animals lived 395 million years ago

the first reptiles lived on land 345 million years ago

▽ Imagine the age of the Earth as one day and one night on a clock. It is midnight now. Humans appeared at one minute to midnight. Dinosaurs arrived just before eleven.

all the dinosaurs became extinct 65 million years ago

the first humans lived two million years ago

◁ The Earth was formed
4.6 billion years ago. But
for millions of years there was
no life of any sort on Earth.

ERA	STARTED
Archeozoic	4 billion years ago
Proterozoic	2.5 billion years ago
Paleozoic	570 million years ago
Mesozoic	245 million years ago
Cenozoic	65 million years ago

the first fish lived in the sea
500 million years ago, when
there was no life on land

the first plants grew
on land 435 million
years ago

the first dinosaurs lived
230 million years ago

the first birds appeared
145 million years ago

today humans share the
Earth with many animals
and evolution is still going on

Word box
Evolution is how life
on Earth has developed
from the tiny cells of
millions of years ago.
Extinct means that
all of a certain animal
or plant group has
died out forever.

The first animals

The first plants and animals lived in the sea. To begin with, most of them were so tiny that they could only be seen with a microscope. Fish were the first animals with bones. Other bony animals, including dinosaurs and humans, developed on land.

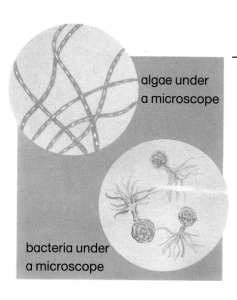

algae under a microscope

bacteria under a microscope

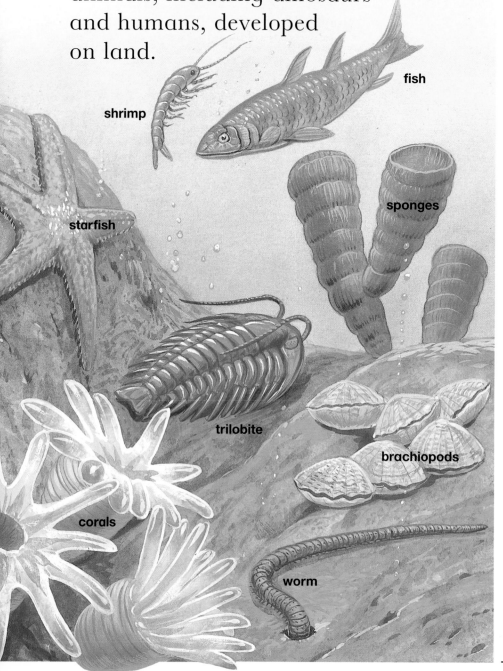

shrimp

fish

starfish

sponges

trilobite

brachiopods

corals

worm

jellyfish

△ The earliest plants and animals looked like the tiny algae and bacteria that we find living in the seas and on land today. Jellyfish and shellfish came after these.

◁ Trilobites are extinct now. We know what they, and other kinds of animals, looked like 600 million years ago, from the fossils they left behind.

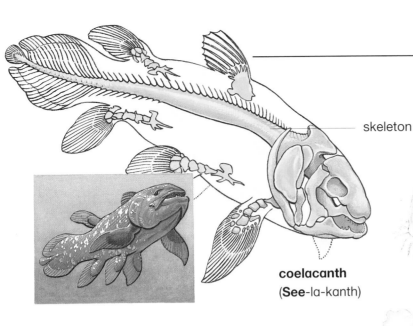

skeleton

coelacanth
(**See**-la-kanth)

Find the answers

Which were the first
animals with bones?

Are there any
Trilobites alive today?

△ The first coelacanths lived more than 300 million years ago. They were thought to be extinct until one was caught in 1938. There are still coelacanths in some seas today.

**Match animals
and fossils**
Look at the pictures carefully. Which fossil matches which animal?

ammonite

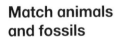

fish

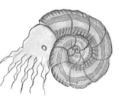

trilobite

1

2

3

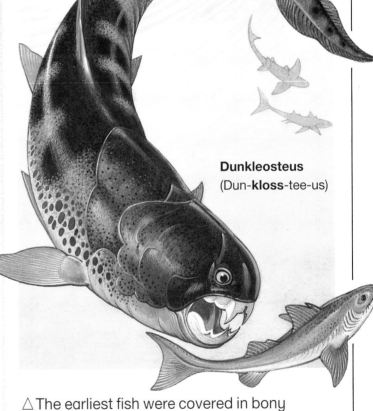

Dunkleosteus
(Dun-**kloss**-tee-us)

△ The earliest fish were covered in bony armor that helped to protect them. Dunkleosteus was a giant carnivore with large, frightening teeth.

Onto the land

About 380 million years ago, some fish moved onto land. These new animals became amphibians. They lived on the land but had to go back to the water to lay their eggs. After the amphibians came the reptiles. These animals could lay their eggs on the land. Dinosaurs were reptiles.

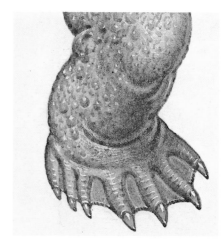

△ The first land animals had feet that looked like fins.

◁ Ichthyostega was one of the first amphibians. It had seven toes on each of its back feet to help it walk. A short neck and strong ribcage helped support it.

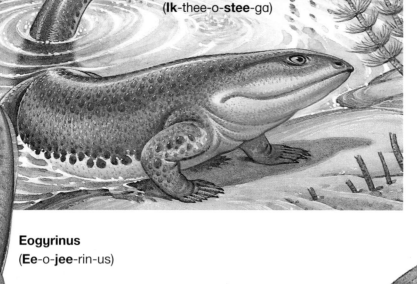

Ichthyostega
(**Ik**-thee-o-**stee**-ga)

Eogyrinus
(**Ee**-o-**jee**-rin-us)

▽ The amphibians could live on land and in fresh water but not in salty seas. Eogyrinus fed on fish in the lakes.

Diplocaulus
(**Dip**-lo-**kaw**-lus)

△ Diplocaulus had an odd head that helped it swim. Perhaps it also stopped other animals from swallowing it.

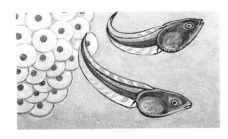

△ Amphibians laid their eggs in water during the dinosaur age, just as they do today. The eggs were soft like Jell-O, and hatched into tiny, swimming tadpoles.

△ Reptiles lay their eggs on dry land. Inside the hard eggshell, the baby feeds on the yolk until it is big enough to hatch.

Hylonomus
(**Hie**-lo-**nome**-us)

△ Hylonomus was one of the first reptiles. It lived in Canada 300 million years ago. It looked like a modern lizard.

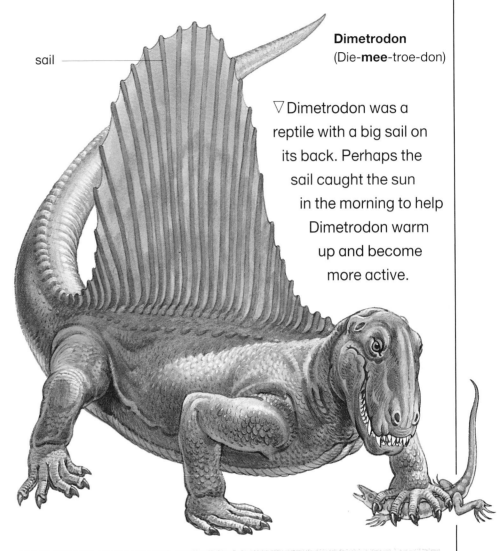

sail

Dimetrodon
(Die-**mee**-troe-don)

▽ Dimetrodon was a reptile with a big sail on its back. Perhaps the sail caught the sun in the morning to help Dimetrodon warm up and become more active.

Make an amphibian wheel

Cut out a circle of cardboard. Draw two lines to make four sections. Draw one stage of an amphibian's life in each.

Place circle under the cardboard. Join with a paper fastener. Turn wheel to see the amphibian grow up.

Cut out a square of cardboard that is a little bigger than the circle. Cut a triangle out of one side of the cardboard, as shown.

279

Back to the sea

Some reptiles went back into the sea to find their food. These sea reptiles lived at the same time as the dinosaurs. Some of them, such as Nothosaurus, could live on the land and in the sea. They may have had webbed feet, like paddles, to push through the water. But these could also have been used for waddling on shore. Some reptiles, such as Ichthyosaurus, may have hunted in packs for seafood.

△ Ichthyosaurus could not leave the sea to lay eggs on the land. So it gave birth to its babies underwater.

Child finds giant fish!
At the age of twelve, almost 200 years ago, Mary Anning found a whole Ichthyosaurus fossil in the rocks on a beach. At the time, people thought it was a giant fish.

▽ Nothosaurus may have hunted for its food in the sea and rested on the land, just as seals do today.

Nothosaurus
(**No**-tho-**saw**-rus)

Ichthyosaurus
(**Ik**-thee-o-**saw**-rus)

mother's skeleton

baby's skeleton

△ Ichthyosaurus gave birth to live babies. A skeleton of one has been found that has a baby coming out tail first.

Ammonite
(**Am**-mon-ite)

▽ Many sea reptiles ate Ammonites. An Ammonite had long arms called tentacles. It could squirt a cloud of dark ink which sometimes helped it escape.

Placodont
(**Plak**-o-dont)

◁ The sea was full of food for the sea reptiles. Placodonts crushed oysters and other hard-shelled animals with their large teeth.

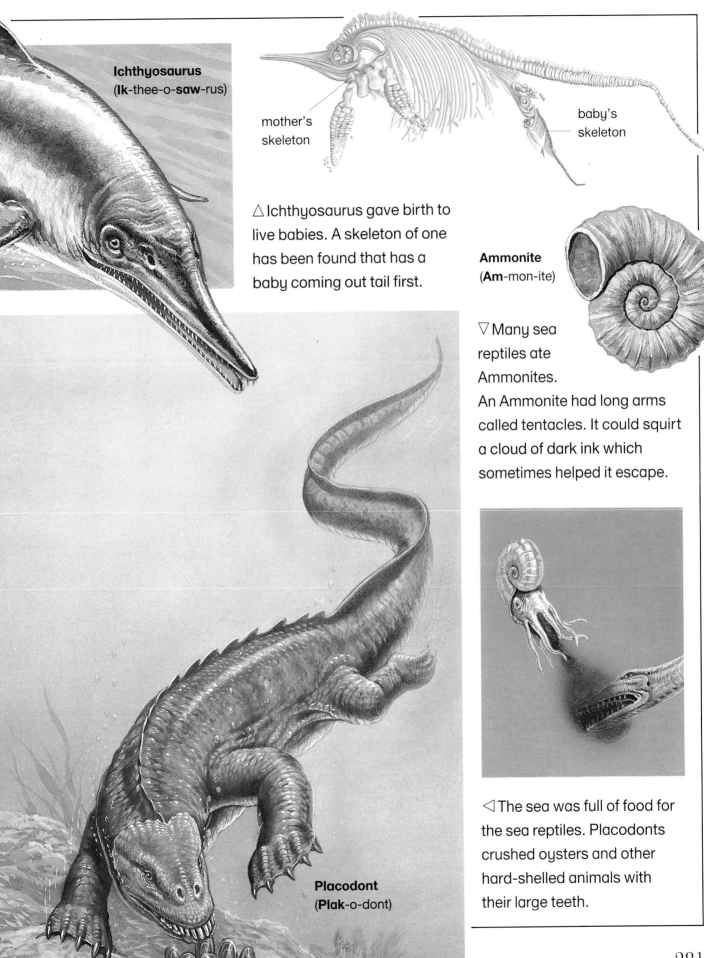

Giant reptiles

As far as we know, no dinosaurs actually lived in the sea. But their cousins, the giant sea reptiles, did. Like the dinosaurs, they breathed air and needed to reach the surface to take in oxygen.

Many ancient land and sea reptiles died out, but snakes, lizards, crocodiles, and turtles are still around today. Scientists study today's reptiles to find out more about their early relatives.

Kronosaurus
(**Krone**-o-**saw**-rus)

△ Kronosaurus belonged to a group of sea reptiles called pliosaurs. All pliosaurs had huge heads, short necks, and very long tails. Kronosaurus's skull was the size of a big car.

Tanystropheus
(**Tan**-ee-**stro**-fee-us)

▽ Some of the sea reptiles had the best of both worlds. A baby Tanystropheus caught insects on land. But when fully grown, it could catch fish from the sea. It used its amazing long neck to reach deep into the water. Each of the 12 bones in its neck was up to a foot long!

Deinosuchus
(**Dine**-o-**sook**-us)

▽ The first crocodiles lived over 200 million years ago. Deinosuchus was a huge monster that lived in the swamps. It was bigger than any crocodile alive today. The biggest measured 55 feet from nose to tail.

Edward Cope

Othniel Marsh

Elasmosaurus
(Ee-**laz**-mo-**saw**-rus)

Heads and tails

An American scientist, Edward Cope, made a model of Elasmosaurus. But it was wrong. In 1870, Othniel Marsh showed that Cope had put its head at the tail end!

Archelon
(**Ar**-kee-lon)

▷ Archelon was a monster turtle, 13 feet long. It swam in the seas that covered part of North America 100 million years ago. Its big paddles made it a fast and strong swimmer.

Into the air

Some reptiles took to the air 250 million years ago. At first, they were gliders. Their wings kept them up in the air as they leaped from tree to tree. The first true flying reptiles were the pterosaurs. Each wing was a thin sheet of skin stretched along the arm and one very long finger. Pterosaurs were warm-blooded. Their bodies and wings were covered with short fur, like bats today.

△ The largest pterosaurs were more like small planes than birds in size. The biggest was Quetzalcoatlus. It had wings that measured 40 feet from tip to tip.

Rhamphorhynchus
(**Ram**-fo-**rink**-us)

▷ Most pterosaurs ate fish. Rhamphorhynchus scooped fish out of the sea and swallowed them whole.

◁ Coelurosauravus was one of the first gliding reptiles. Its wings grew from the sides, held up on long ribs.

Coelurosauravus
(**See**-loo-ro-**saw**-rah-vus)

Dimorphodon
(Die-**morf**-o-don)

▷ Dimorphodon might have clung to clifftops and branches when it rested. Its clawed fingers and toes helped it hang on.

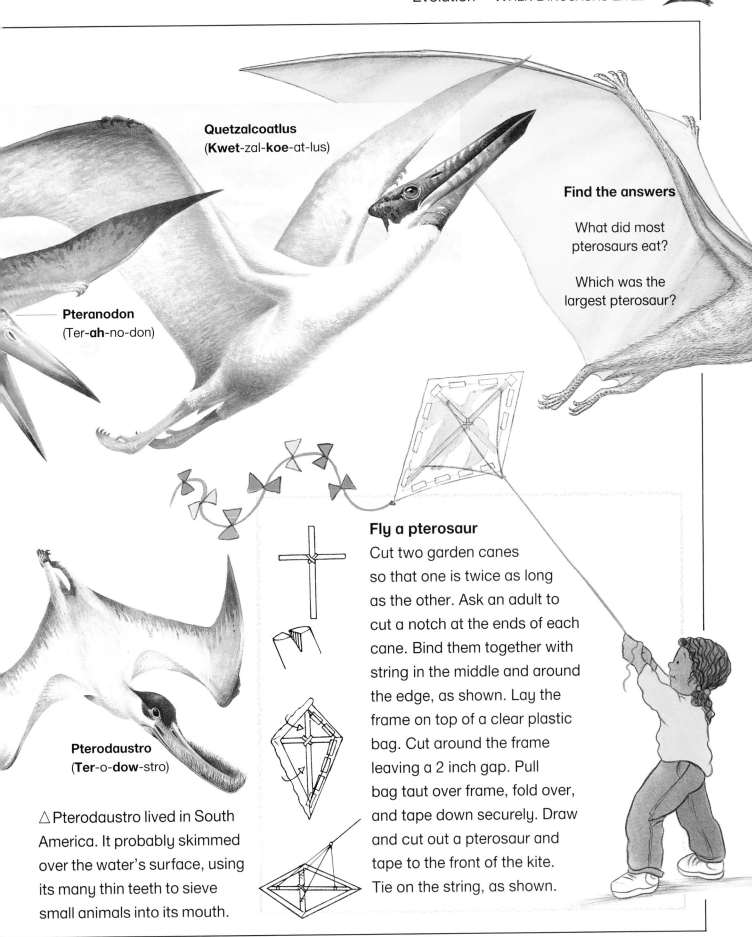

Quetzalcoatlus
(**Kwet**-zal-**koe**-at-lus)

Pteranodon
(Ter-**ah**-no-don)

Find the answers

What did most
pterosaurs eat?

Which was the
largest pterosaur?

Pterodaustro
(**Ter**-o-**dow**-stro)

△ Pterodaustro lived in South
America. It probably skimmed
over the water's surface, using
its many thin teeth to sieve
small animals into its mouth.

Fly a pterosaur
Cut two garden canes
so that one is twice as long
as the other. Ask an adult to
cut a notch at the ends of each
cane. Bind them together with
string in the middle and around
the edge, as shown. Lay the
frame on top of a clear plastic
bag. Cut around the frame
leaving a 2 inch gap. Pull
bag taut over frame, fold over,
and tape down securely. Draw
and cut out a pterosaur and
tape to the front of the kite.
Tie on the string, as shown.

285

The first birds

In 1860, the fossil of a feather was found in a quarry in Germany. One year later, a whole skeleton was found. It had feathers on its wings and tail. It was 150 million years old, so it had lived at the time of the dinosaurs. This first bird was given the name Archaeopteryx, which means ancient wing.

▷ The first birds had claws on their wings.

Eoraptor
(Ee-o-**rap**-tor)

◁ Reptiles may have learned to fly as they leaped from tree to tree. When Archaeopteryx chased insects it may have flapped its wings to soar off the ground.

roadrunner

△ Many scientists think that dinosaurs were the ancestors of modern birds. For example, Archaeopteryx is similar to Eoraptor, which is the oldest dinosaur we know. Roadrunners, which are modern birds, have a similar shape to Archaeopteryx, too.

Archaeopteryx
(**Ark**-ee-**op**-ter-ix)

286

Find the answers

Where was the first fossil feather found?

What does Archaeopteryx mean?

Did the first birds have teeth?

▽ Archaeopteryx had claws on its wings. Today, young hoatzins use claws on the front of each wing to grip branches.

hoatzin

modern seagull

Ichthyornis
(**Ik**-thee-**or**-nis)

Modern birds have no teeth, but the first birds did. Ichthyornis was a seabird and may have lived like a gull.

Hesperornis could not fly and probably lived like a penguin. Instead of flying, it slid off a rock, swam into the sea, and dived down in search of fish.

Hesperornis
(**Hess**-per-**or**-niss)

287

Dinosaurs disappear

Dinosaurs roamed the world for 165 million years. This time is called the Mesozoic Era. No dinosaur bones are found from after this time. Dinosaurs became extinct, which means that they died out and disappeared forever. But why did they disappear?

	Triassic period

PALEOZOIC ERA

△ We divide time into sections, called eras. Dinosaurs lived during the Mesozoic Era. The Mesozoic Era is split into three periods: Triassic, Jurassic, and Cretaceous. Different dinosaurs lived in each period, but none lived after the Mesozoic Era.

▽ Not only the dinosaurs died out. Pterosaurs, ammonites, and the great sea reptiles also disappeared.

victims

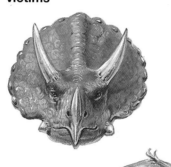

▽ A few types of animals survived. Insects, fish, frogs, birds, mammals, and some reptiles live today.

Word box
Mammals are warm-blooded animals with hair or fur. Baby mammals feed on milk from their mother's body.
Ice ages are times, long ago, when ice covered much more of the land than it does today.

survivors

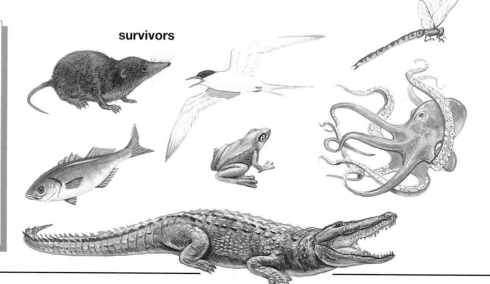

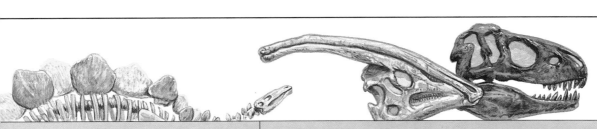

Jurassic period	Cretaceous period	

MESOZOIC ERA   **CENOZOIC ERA**

Why did they die?

Nobody knows exactly why the dinosaurs died.

▷ Perhaps they were too big. But the smaller ones disappeared as well.

◁ Perhaps dinosaurs were too stupid to survive. But if that were true, why did they survive for so long?

▷ Perhaps new plants poisoned them. But there were other plants to eat.

◁ Maybe mammals ate too many dinosaur eggs. But this would have killed the dinosaurs off earlier.

Some scientists believe dinosaurs were killed when a meteorite hit Earth. This made a huge dust cloud, blocking out the Sun. The dinosaurs may have died without the Sun's warmth.

Mammals rule

Mammals are warm-blooded animals. They have hair or fur. The first mammals lived side by side with dinosaurs, but they did not become extinct at the end of the Mesozoic Era. They have survived right up to today.

   After the dinosaurs, the mammals took over. The first mammals were small. Larger mammals developed later.

▽ Early mammals lived in forests where they fed on leaves and insects. Plesiadapis lived in the trees like a monkey. Hyracotherium was the first horse. The first big carnivore was Andrewsarchus.

Indricotherium
(In-dry-ko-thee-ree-um)

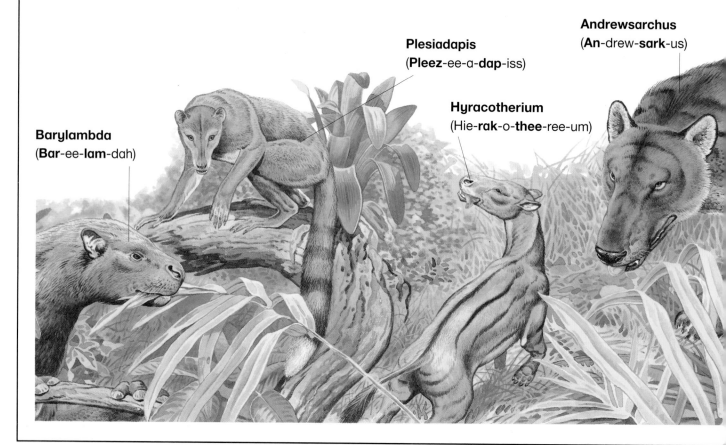

Barylambda
(Bar-ee-lam-dah)

Plesiadapis
(Pleez-ee-a-dap-iss)

Hyracotherium
(Hie-rak-o-thee-ree-um)

Andrewsarchus
(An-drew-sark-us)

◁ Indricotherium was the largest land mammal ever to have lived. It was the same weight as five of today's elephants put together.

Keeping warm experiment
Mammals' fur keeps them warm. To see how this works, fill two identical jars with warm water. Wrap one in a woolen cloth, such as a scarf, and leave the other as it is. After half an hour compare the temperatures of the water. The woolen cloth acts like a fur coat and keeps the water warmer.

▽ About 30 million years ago, the climate warmed up and grasslands appeared. Grass-eating mammals developed to take advantage of the food supply.

Gomphotherium
(**Gom**-fo-**thee**-ree-um)

Hoplophoneus
(**Hop**-lo-**fone**-ee-us)

Brontotherium
(**Bront**-o-**thee**-ree-um)

Archaeotherium
(**Ark**-ee-o-**thee**-ree-um)

Palaeolagus
(**Pal**-ee-o-**lag**-us)

Poebrotherium
(**Pee**-bro-**thee**-ree-um)

Cynodictis
(**Sine**-o-**dik**-tiss)

Ice age hunters

Several times during the last million years there have been ice ages. Slowly, the warm, dry grasslands gave way to snow and ice. Much of Europe and North America was covered with ice. Many animals grew thicker coats of fur to keep warm. Human beings appeared two million years ago, and hunted animals for food during the ice ages.

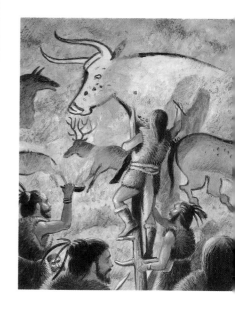

△ Ice age people painted pictures of animals they hunted on their cave walls.

▽ The long, thick fur of the woolly mammoth protected it against the cold. Smilodon hunted woolly bison by stabbing them with its huge front teeth.

Woolly mammoth

In Australia and New Zealand there was no ice age. Other animals, such as the Giant kangaroo and the Moa, lived in these warmer countries.

Moa, New Zealand

Giant kangaroo, Australia

Smilodon (Smile-o-don)

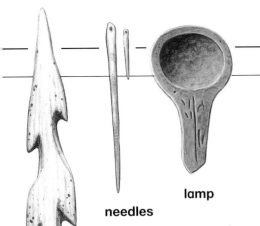

lamp

needles

spearhead

▷Human beings lived in small groups. They used animals' skins and bones to make clothes and tents. These kept out the cold.

◁Ice age people learned how to make fire. For light, they used stone lamps, which burned animal fat. They made tools out of rock and bone, which were used for hunting animals.

Make a woolly mammoth
Draw the outline of a woolly mammoth. Color in the tusks, toes, and eyes. For its fur coat, stick on pieces of reddish-brown yarn.

293

Discovering dinosaurs

We have known about dinosaurs for less than 200 years. Huge bones were found before that, but people thought they were the bones of dragons or giants.

Gradually, scientists realized that the bones were all that was left of animals that had died long ago. The bones had gradually turned to stone and become fossils.

△ Some fossils show us more than bones. This spider got trapped in sticky resin on a tree. As the resin hardened, it turned into amber and preserved the whole spider.

△ Animals such as Diplodocus died 150 million years ago.

△ Its flesh rotted away and it was buried in layers of sand and mud.

△ The mud and sand slowly became rock. The bones became fossils.

△ Much, much later a lucky discovery is made and the fossil is carefully removed.

Word box
Laboratories are special buildings where paleontologists can study fossils.
Microscopes are instruments that help scientists look at objects more closely.

▷ This woolly mammoth was frozen solid thousands of years ago in icy Russia. The ice preserved the mammoth's flesh and woolly coat.

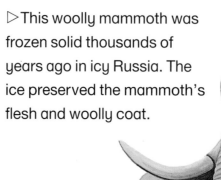

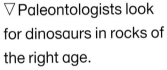

Be a paleontologist
Draw some dinosaur shapes on cardboard. Cut them out, then cut each into five pieces. Bury the pieces in a tray of dry sand. Using a brush, uncover the pieces and put the dinosaurs back together.

Find the answers

What is amber?

Why are maps drawn of bone sites?

What are bones covered with to protect them?

▽ Paleontologists look for dinosaurs in rocks of the right age.

bulldozers dig into the rock

small brushes are used to clean the fossils

maps are drawn to show where the fossils lie

the fossils are covered with plaster to protect them

the fossils are numbered and taken away for study

295

Building a dinosaur

Dinosaur bones are taken to a laboratory to be studied. Scientists carefully work on the bones to clean and protect them. This may take years to do. If enough bones are found, a whole dinosaur is put together. This is like fitting together a huge and complicated jigsaw puzzle.

Build a model dinosaur
Draw large outlines of the dinosaur's body and legs onto stiff cardboard, using the shapes shown as a guide. Cut them out and color in. Cut slits in body and legs, as shown. Put the model together by pushing leg slits into body slits.

△ Scientists remove the protective plaster cases with saws.

△ The bones are cleaned under a microscope.

△ The bones are put on a frame, to make a whole skeleton.

△ A model is made to show what the dinosaur looked like.

▷ Then, the dinosaur is ready for people to come and view it.

My Body

One person, one body

Adults and babies, boys and girls are all human beings. Their bodies are made the same way, but they are all different. No two human beings look exactly the same. People who belong to the same family are more alike than other people. Twins are most alike.

◁ In a family, people often look alike. Children and their parents may have hair and eyes that are the same color.

▽ This is a family tree. It shows three generations of the same family. A generation is people of about the same age.

Word box
Human beings are the vast, worldwide family of men, women, and children.
Generations are humans of about the same age. Grandparents are one generation, parents the next, and children the next.

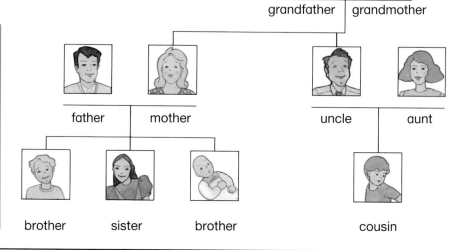

grandfather | grandmother

father | mother

uncle | aunt

brother | sister | brother

cousin

Here I am!

◁ There are human beings almost everywhere on Earth. They are of many sizes, shapes, and colors. Human bodies all work in the same way, but they are all different. No one else is exactly the same as you.

Tweedledum and Tweedledee

Tweedledum and Tweedledee are characters in Lewis Carroll's story Through the Looking Glass. *They were identical twins who looked so alike that Alice could not tell them apart.*

△ The color of our hair and skin, the shape of our eyes, ears, nose, and chin all make us look different from one another. The shapes of our faces make us different too.

299

A body for living

The body is like a clever machine that can do lots of things. It can laugh, cry, talk, run, think, work, and play. The body has adapted, or changed, to live in different places. But there are times when our bodies cannot adapt. We need special equipment under the sea, in the sky, and in outer space.

▽ There are so many things that the human body can do. What are the people doing in this park?

Make a moving body

Draw two arms, two legs, and a body shape onto cardboard. Color them in and cut the parts out. Add yarn for hair. Use a hole punch to make holes in the body joints, as shown. Join the body parts together with fasteners.

punched hole

△ Clothes help the body stay warm in cold places. The more clothes you wear, the warmer you are.

△ In hot countries, you do not need warm clothes. But you still need to cover your body, to protect it from the Sun.

Can you find?

1 hang glider
2 swimmer
3 scuba diver
4 space shuttle
5 submarine
6 mountain

▷ When we play some sports, we wear special clothes such as a helmet and pads to protect our bodies.

Body parts

The human body is made up of different parts. At the top is a head, with hair on it. The head is on a neck. Below that is a torso. This is the middle part of the body. We have two arms and two legs that are joined to the torso. Arms and legs are also called limbs. These parts of the body help it do different things.

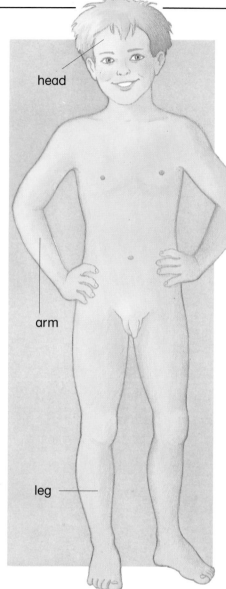

head

arm

leg

boy

Superman

Superman is a story character. He is very strong and can fly faster than any aircraft. He has X-ray vision, which means he can see through anything. He uses his special powers to help others in the world.

Word box
Torso is the main part of the human body, to which the head, arms, and legs are attached.
Limbs are the arms and legs of human beings and other animals.

△ Hair protects our head. It helps keep it warm in winter and stops it from burning in the summer Sun.

▽ We have feet at the bottom of our legs. Our feet are flat so that we can stand on them and walk upright.

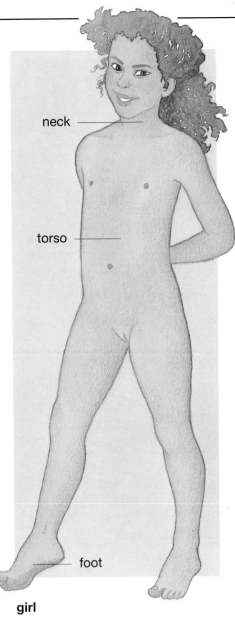

neck

torso

foot

girl

▷ Our head is on our neck. The neck bends and turns. This means that our head can move up and down and from side to side.

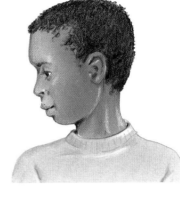

◁ Our neck, arms, and legs are attached to our torso. This is the largest part of the body. It can twist, turn, and bend in the middle.

▷ We move on our legs. They are long and strong. Legs let us stand upright and walk, run, and jump.

▽ Our arms can bend and stretch. We use them to reach for things. Our hands can hold things.

"Simon Says" game
One person is Simon. Simon faces the other players and says, "Simon says pat your head" (or similar). The rest copy. If Simon says, "Pat your toes" without "Simon says" first, the rest stand still. Anyone who moves is out. The last person left is Simon next time.

The skin

Skin covers the whole body. It keeps the parts inside us safe. Skin is tough, but it can also be hurt. It can be burned, cut, or bruised. If skin is broken, it will bleed. Skin is not always the same color. A brown coloring, called melanin, helps protect the skin from sunlight. Black skin has more melanin than white skin.

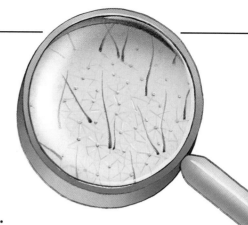

△ When you look at skin under a magnifying glass, it is not smooth. It has bumps on it and small holes. Hairs grow through these holes.

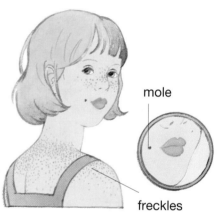

mole

freckles

△ Freckles and moles are patches of extra melanin on the skin. Freckles can come and go, but moles stay.

△ Skin may be burned by the sun. It turns red, then peels off. Sunscreen creams can protect skin.

▷ Sometimes our skin changes color. We may turn white if we are frightened and red if we are embarrassed.

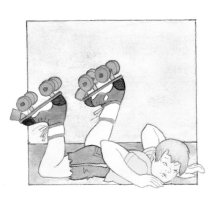

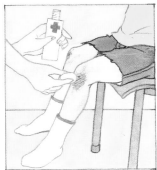

△ If you fall down, you sometimes break your skin, or scrape it. Scraped skin bleeds.

△ The scrape can be cleaned with a disinfectant to get rid of dirt and germs.

▽ A bandage keeps the wound clean. The blood dries up and new skin grows.

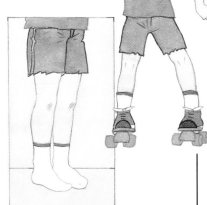

▽ Marks appear on our skin when it is hurt in any way. These marks have different names, depending on what caused them. They look different too.

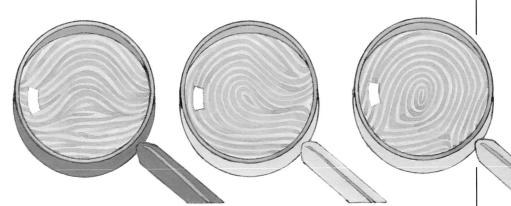

△ Every person in the world has their own special fingerprint pattern.

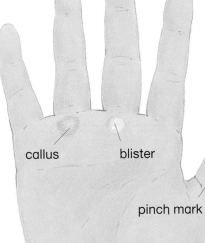

callus

blister

pinch mark

bruise

Make fingerprints

Lightly rub a thin coating of lipstick onto your fingertip. Press the fingertip on a piece of paper. It will leave a print. Do the same for your friends. Now look at the prints through a magnifying glass and see how different they are.

Hair and nails

We have hair all over our bodies, except for our palms and the soles of our feet. A lot of this hair is too fine to see easily. Hair grows thickest on our heads.

Nails protect our toes and fingertips. Our hair and nails are both made from a substance called keratin.

Rapunzel
(A story by the Brothers Grimm)

A witch shut Rapunzel in a tower. A prince climbed up her long hair to rescue her.

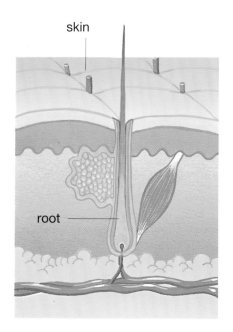

skin / root

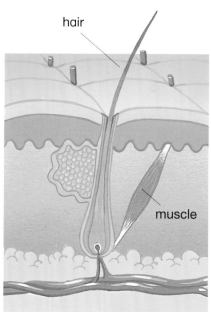

hair / muscle

◁ You see only part of the hair. The rest is under the skin and is called the root. When you are cold, a little muscle pulls the hair upright.

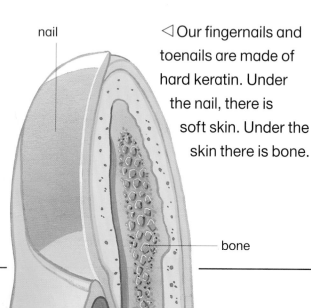

nail / bone

◁ Our fingernails and toenails are made of hard keratin. Under the nail, there is soft skin. Under the skin there is bone.

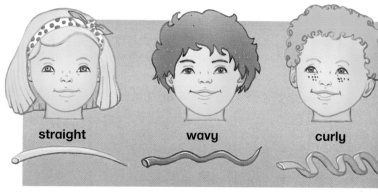

straight   **wavy**   **curly**

△ Some hair grows straight, some grows wavy, and some grows curly. It comes in lots of different colors, too.

Muscles

Our muscles are under our skin. We use muscles whenever we move. Muscles are joined to our bones. They move by becoming shorter or longer. Muscles move every part of the body, not just the bones. Our face muscles move our mouths. Our chest muscles help us breathe.

△ The muscles in our face help us smile, frown, wink, and chew. When we smile, we may use 15 different muscles.

△ Muscles grow bigger and stronger with exercise and training. Athletes and people who play sports often have strong muscles.

▷ We have more than 650 muscles. There are muscles in every part of our body.

Find the answers

How many muscles do we use when we smile?

What makes muscles grow strong?

Bones and joints

There are more than 200 bones in your body. Together, they form the skeleton. Bones support the body and give it shape. They also protect the soft organs inside the body. The places where the bones meet are called joints. Bones are very strong, but they can break.

Find the answers

What is the tip of your nose made of?

Name four joints.

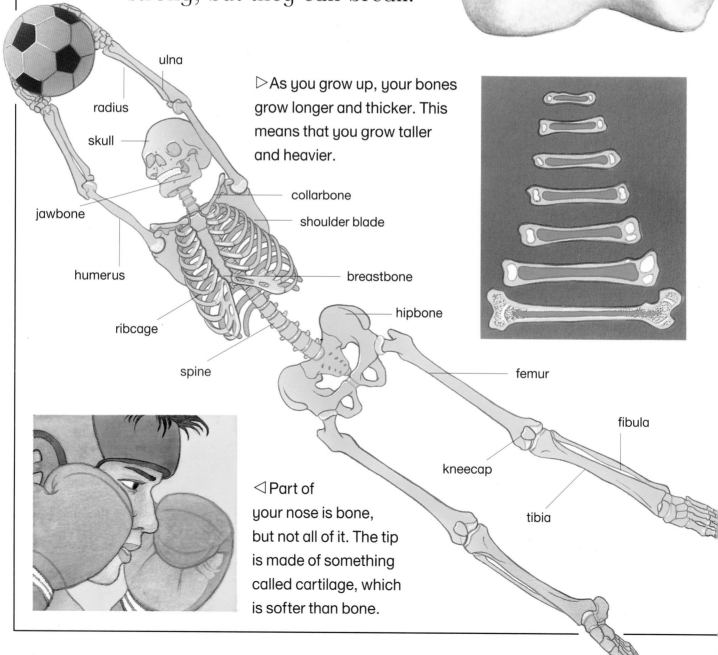

ulna

radius

skull

jawbone

humerus

ribcage

spine

▷ As you grow up, your bones grow longer and thicker. This means that you grow taller and heavier.

collarbone

shoulder blade

breastbone

hipbone

femur

fibula

kneecap

tibia

◁ Part of your nose is bone, but not all of it. The tip is made of something called cartilage, which is softer than bone.

308

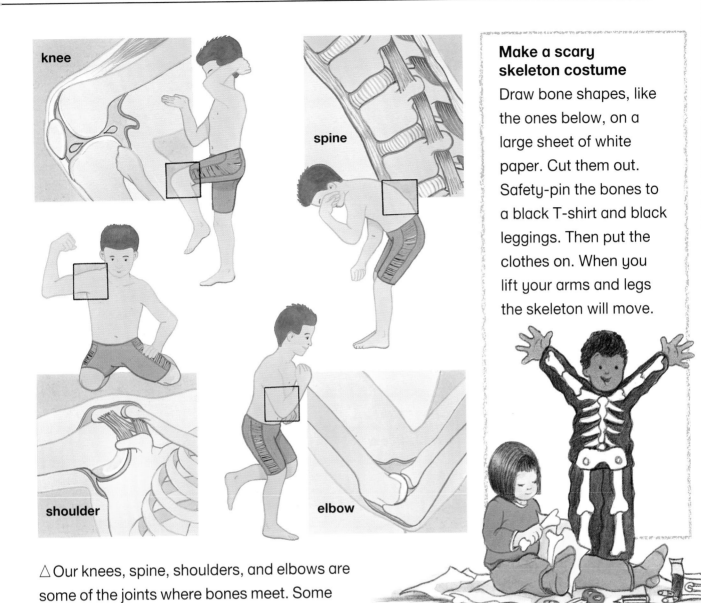

knee

spine

shoulder

elbow

Make a scary skeleton costume

Draw bone shapes, like the ones below, on a large sheet of white paper. Cut them out. Safety-pin the bones to a black T-shirt and black leggings. Then put the clothes on. When you lift your arms and legs the skeleton will move.

△ Our knees, spine, shoulders, and elbows are some of the joints where bones meet. Some bones fit together, others slide over each other.

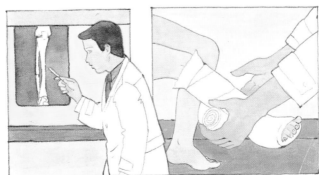

△ Bones may break in a fall. A broken bone is called a fracture.

△ A doctor X-rays the bone to see the break.

△ Plaster holds the bone straight while it grows back together again.

309

Body organs

There are soft parts called organs inside your body. They are protected by the bones and skin. The organs include the brain, lungs, liver, heart, pancreas, kidneys, stomach, and intestines. Each of the organs has a special job to do. The brain tells all the other organs what to do. Together, they help the body to work properly.

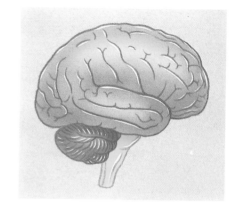

△ The brain is very important because it tells your body how to work. It controls all the other organs.

▷ The brain is in the head. Other organs are in the torso, the main part of the body. They are all different shapes, but they fit together very neatly.

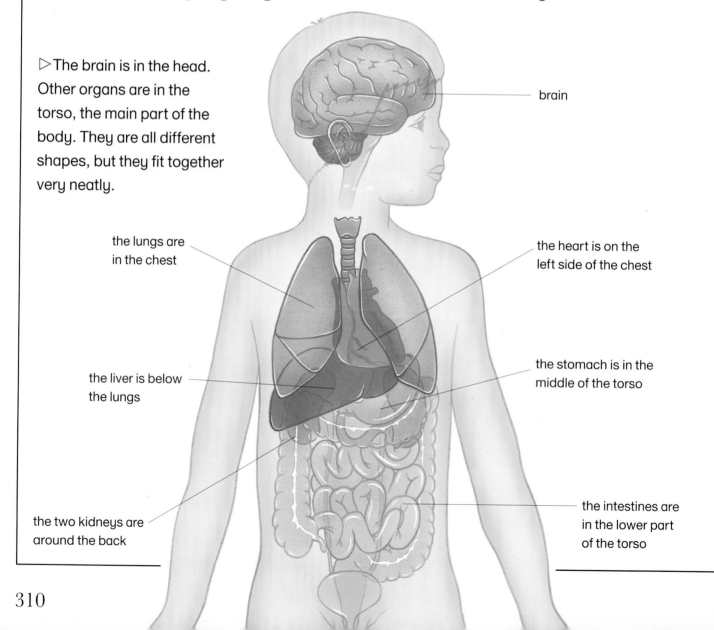

brain

the lungs are in the chest

the heart is on the left side of the chest

the liver is below the lungs

the stomach is in the middle of the torso

the two kidneys are around the back

the intestines are in the lower part of the torso

310

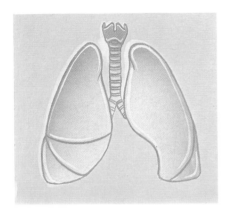

△ We breathe with our lungs. They take air into the body.

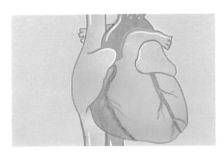

△ The heart pumps blood around the body.

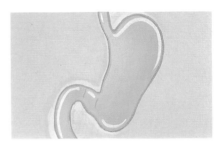

△ The food we eat goes down into the stomach. It turns the food into a pulp before it goes into the intestines.

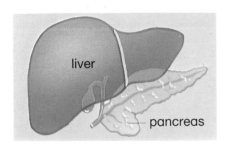

liver

pancreas

△ Fluids from the liver and pancreas help us to digest food.

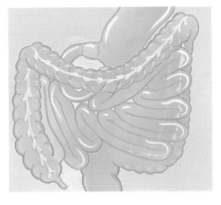

△ The intestines pass liquid food into the blood.

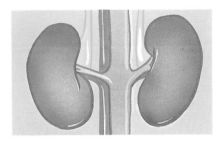

△ Two kidneys help to get rid of the waste from our blood and produce urine from it.

The Wizard of Oz
(A story by L. Frank Baum)

In The Wizard of Oz, *Dorothy meets some characters who have organs missing. Tin Man has no heart and Scarecrow has no brain. In this picture from the movie, you can see Dorothy and Scarecrow on the yellow brick road. They all travel along the yellow brick road in search of the Wizard, who they hope will help them.*

How are we made?

The body is made of lots of tiny living parts called cells. Before we are born we all begin as one cell inside our mother's body. A baby grows in a place called the uterus. Genes are parts of the cell that tell it how to grow. Every baby has genes from both the mother's and father's cells.

△ Every baby is made by a man and a woman. They are called its parents.

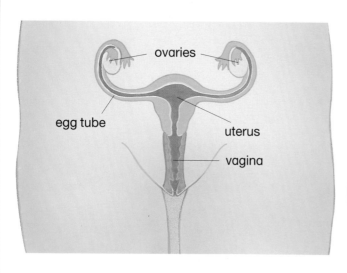

△ These are the organs that a woman has to make a baby. The ovaries produce eggs.

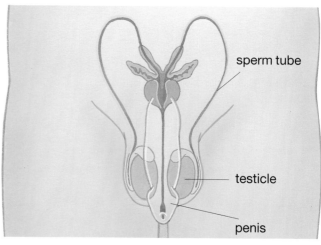

△ These are the organs that a man has to make a baby. The testicles produce sperm.

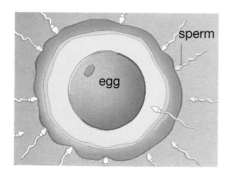

△ A sperm enters an egg. This makes the baby's first cell.

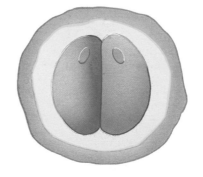

△ The egg splits into two cells. It will then split into four.

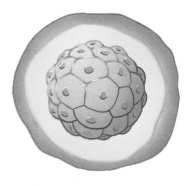

△ It goes on splitting and grows bigger and bigger.

▷A doctor or a specially trained nurse checks that the baby is growing properly in its mother's uterus. A scanning machine shows the baby inside her.

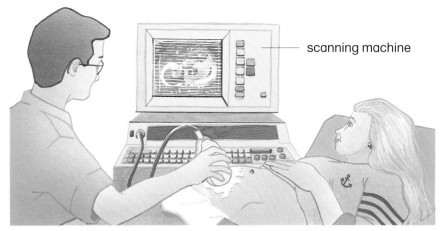

scanning machine

◁Sometimes a mother has two babies from one egg. They are identical twins. Identical twins are two boys or two girls who look just like each other.

▷A mother may also have twins from two eggs. These twins are not identical. The children do not grow up to look alike.

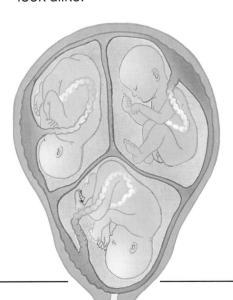

◁Sometimes a mother may have three, four, five, or six babies. This is very rare. It is called a multiple birth.

Word box
Cells are tiny living parts that make up our bodies. **Genes** are the instructions in cells that decide how living things will develop. **Uterus** is the place inside the mother where a baby grows until it is born.

313

Nine months for a baby

The baby grows in a bag of warm liquid in the mother's uterus. It gets all the food and oxygen it needs from its mother's body, through a tube called the umbilical cord. After nine months, the baby is born. The mother may give birth in a hospital.

▽ When a baby is about three months old it looks like this. This is a life-size picture.

 a sperm enters an egg to make the first cell of the baby

 at one month, the baby is no bigger than a pea

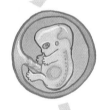 at three months, the baby is just over 2 inches long

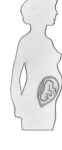

 at four months, the baby can move around

at six months, the baby can hear sounds

at seven months, it opens its eyes and kicks strongly

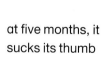

 at five months, it sucks its thumb

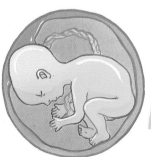

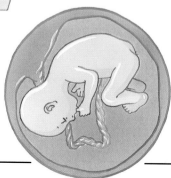

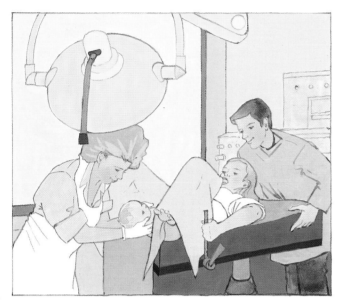

◁ When the baby is ready to be born, the mother may go to the hospital to give birth. Her muscles help to push the baby out. Usually the baby comes out head first.

△ The doctor or nurse helps the baby to come out. The baby takes its first breath and cries. It does not need the umbilical cord after it is born, because it can get food and air from outside. So the cord is cut off.

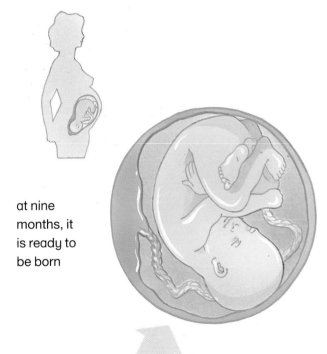

at nine months, it is ready to be born

at eight months, it can taste things

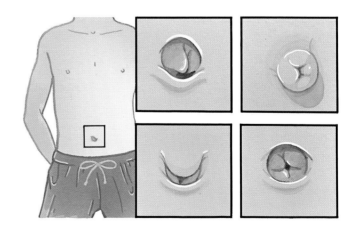

△ When the umbilical cord is cut, it leaves a scar. This becomes our navel, or belly button. Belly buttons can be several different shapes, depending on how the cord was cut.

Growing up

It takes a long time for a baby to grow up. As it grows, it changes. Human beings keep changing all their lives. A new baby cannot look after itself, but it learns quickly. It becomes a child, then a teenager, then an adult. Adults may work and have children of their own. Then they become older. Their bodies start to get tired, and they do less.

Peter Pan
(A story by J.M. Barrie)

Peter Pan was not like other boys. He could fly and never grew any older.

◁ New babies need a lot of care and love. At first, they sleep a lot and cry when they are hungry.

▽ As babies grow, they do more and more things by themselves. First they crawl, then they walk.

△ Babies grow into children. They learn quickly, especially through play.

△Children go to
school. They study,
play games,
and make friends
with other children.

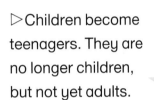

▷Children become
teenagers. They are
no longer children,
but not yet adults.

▷Teenagers grow
into adult men and
women. They can
start work. There
are lots of different
jobs for them to do.
They can also start
a family.

▷When they grow
older, people retire,
or stop work. Now
they have time to
relax and do things
that they enjoy.

Seeing

The senses help us know what is happening around us. Seeing, hearing, smelling, tasting, and touching are all senses.

We see with our eyes. First, light enters our eyes. It sends messages to the brain, which then tells us what we see.

Our eyes are protected by eyelids and cleaned by tears.

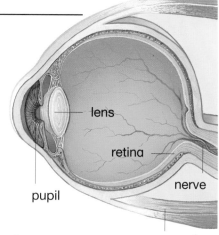

△ The pupil is the black circle in the center of our eyes. It takes in light. Behind it are the lens, retina, and nerves.

▷ The eye has muscles attached to it, so it can move up and down and side to side.

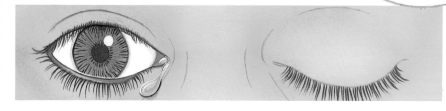

◁ Every time we blink, our eyelids spread tears over our eyes to keep them clean.

◁ In bright light, we need dark glasses to protect our eyes from the glare.

The Emperor's New Clothes
(A story by Hans Christian Andersen)

The Emperor was tricked into wearing no clothes. He was told his new clothes were made out of special cloth that fools could not see. Really, no one could see the clothes.

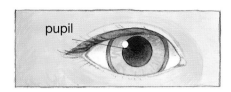

pupil

△ When it is dark, our pupils grow larger. They do this to let in more light. This is to help us see better.

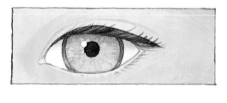

△ In daylight, the light is bright. Our pupils do not need to let in so much light, so they become smaller.

▷ Not everyone can see well. Sometimes we need help to make our sight better. That is why a lot of people wear glasses or contact lenses. These improve the eyesight.

glasses

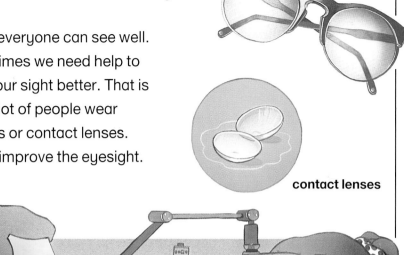

contact lenses

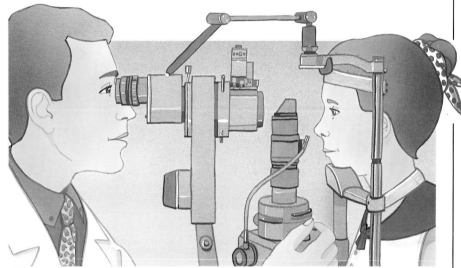

▽ Some people cannot see at all. They are blind. Some blind people have Seeing Eye dogs to help them find their way.

△ Optometrists look after people's eyes. They have special instruments to find out if anything is wrong. They can see through the pupil to the retina at the back of the eye.

Word box
Senses are the way we see, hear, smell, taste, and touch the world around us.
Nerves carry messages to and fro between the brain and the different parts of the body.

Smelling

We use our noses to breathe and to smell. Smells float in the air. We smell things when we breathe in air through our noses. Smells are invisible, but our noses send messages to the brain, which tells us what they are.

Smells come from many different things around us. Some smells are nice, some are not. Our sense of smell also helps our sense of taste.

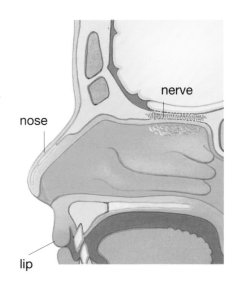

nerve

nose

lip

△ When a smell reaches the back of our nose, nerves tell the brain about it.

◁ There are some special doctors who look after people's noses, ears, and throats only.

◁ If our nose is blocked and we cannot smell things, it is hard to taste them.

Can you find?

1 cheese
2 flower
3 soap

4 car exhaust
   fumes
5 perfume

Find the answers

What do we use the nose for?

Why can you not see smells?

1
2
3
5
4

Tasting

We taste things with our tongues. There are thousands of little bumps all over the tongue called taste buds. Inside them are nerves that send messages to the brain about what we are eating. There are four main types of taste: sweet, salty, bitter, and sour. Each is tasted by different parts of the tongue and mouth. The tongue is also able to feel heat, cold, and pain.

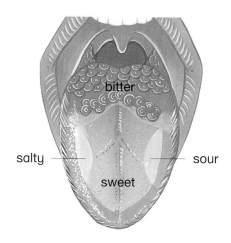

△ Different parts of the tongue are good at picking up different tastes. There are taste buds at the front, back, and sides of the tongue.

△ The front of the tongue tastes sweet things mainly.

△ The sides taste salty things.

△ The sides also taste sour things.

△ The back tastes bitter things mainly.

Try tasting without smelling
Put water in four cups. Add salt to one, lemon juice to another, and sugar to another. Leave plain water in the fourth. Ask a friend to hold their nose and taste them. Without smell, the cups of water should all taste the same.

Hearing

We hear sounds all the time. They tell us about the world around us. Sounds are vibrations in the air. We cannot see them. We hear sounds through our ears.

We can only see a part of the ear, the part that is outside the head. The rest of the ear is inside the head.

Some people cannot hear very well. People who cannot hear are deaf.

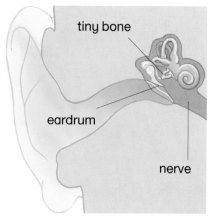

△ Sounds make the eardrum move. This makes three tiny bones move. A nerve carries the message to the brain.

▽ There are many different types of sound. Construction workers wear earmuffs to protect their ears from very loud sounds.

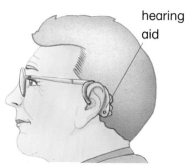

◁ A hearing aid helps people who cannot hear very well. It is a small machine that goes into the ear and makes sounds louder.

Helen Keller

Helen Keller could not hear, speak, or see. She learned to listen to people by placing her fingers on their lips and throat and feeling the vibrations that their voice made.

Touching

When we touch things, we can feel them. We can feel heat, cold, pain, softness, hardness, and sharpness. Nerves just under the surface of the skin help us to feel things. They send messages to the brain about what we touch. We can feel best with the tips of our fingers because that is the place where we have the most nerves.

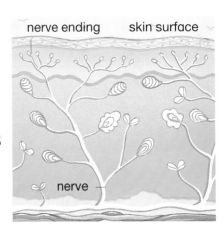

△ Tiny nerves in the skin send the brain messages about the things we touch. Nerves end just under the skin surface.

△ When we hold a drink of hot cocoa we can feel the heat through the cup.

▽ This blind person can read and write Braille, by using her sense of touch.

△ Pianists use their sense of touch to control sound. They can play softly or loudly depending on the pressure.

△ If we touch a thorn we feel a sharp prick on our fingers.

Feely game

Put some objects in a bag. They should all feel different. Ask your friends to put their hands in the bag and feel them. They must guess what the objects are by touch alone.

323

Breathing

We need air that contains oxygen to stay alive. The lungs take oxygen from the air we inhale, or breathe in. They also exhale, or breathe out, used air. Blood takes the oxygen from the lungs and carries it to the rest of the body.

The lungs work very hard. Every day we take about 23,000 breaths!

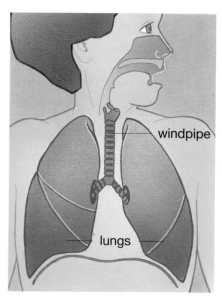

windpipe

lungs

△ When you inhale, or breathe in, air goes down the windpipe into the lungs. Blood in the lungs collects oxygen and takes it around the body.

△ Exercising in fresh mountain air is good for us. The air is cleaner than in the cities where there are often fumes from traffic and factories.

Word box
Inhale is what we do when we breathe in. The lungs become bigger and the air rushes in.
Exhale is what we do when we breathe out. The lungs become smaller, pushing the air out again.

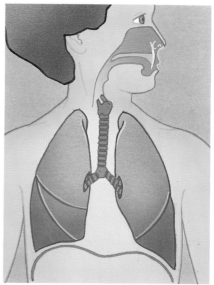

△ Blood also carries used air back to the lungs. When you exhale, or breathe out, your lungs push used air back out through your nose or mouth.

The three little pigs
(An English folk tale)

Three little pigs each built a home. The first built a house of straw. The second built one of twigs. The third used bricks. A wicked wolf blew down the first two houses. But his lungs and breath were not strong enough to blow down the brick house.

◁ It is impossible to stay underwater without a snorkel or air tank, because there is no air to breathe. Most of us need to breathe at least 20 times a minute.

Blow soccer game
Make two goalposts with straws, using modeling clay as shown. Place one at each end of a table. Make a scrunched-up paper ball. Each player chooses a home goal. The idea is to blow the ball into the other player's goal. Each goal scored earns one point. Play for five minutes. The winner is the one with the most points.

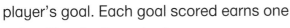

△ People who have asthma may use an inhaler to help them breathe. Their air passages are narrower than usual. This causes noisy breathing or wheezing. The inhaler puffs or squirts a drug that makes their air passages wider, so they can breathe more easily.

Talking

We can talk, shout, laugh, and sing. The sounds come out of our mouths. They are made by vocal cords in our throats. We move our tongue, lips, and jaws to form words.

Sometimes we do not need words to show how we feel. We use our bodies instead. Our faces, hands, and the way we move all give messages to other people.

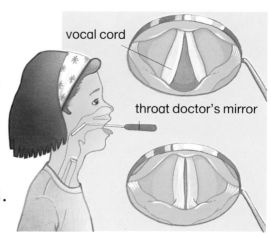

vocal cord

throat doctor's mirror

△ Our vocal cords are two stretchy flaps. The air that we breathe out moves them. This makes sounds.

▷ The way people stand and move, the movements of their hands, and the looks on their faces all show how they feel. This is called body language.

Can you find?

1 happy

2 sad

3 playful

4 silly

5 teasing

6 angry

7 tired

8 proud

9 worried

▷The harder we breathe out, the louder our voice is. We can feel our throat move when we are singing.

◁Some people cannot speak. They use their hands to make sign language instead.

△Singing is one way that we use our voices. Their sounds make music. Most people can sing, but some are better than others.

Guess how they feel

You can often tell how people feel by the expressions, or looks, on their faces. Look at the faces below. Try and decide what these people are feeling by the way they look. Ask your friends what they think.

Blood supply

Blood flows around the body through thin tubes called veins and arteries. It carries oxygen from the air we breathe in and nutrition from food that we eat. It also helps to fight germs. The heart is a hollow muscle that pumps blood each time it beats. It must be strong enough to send blood to every cell in the body.

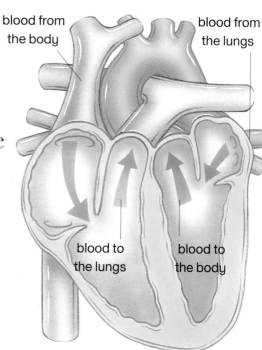

blood from the body

blood from the lungs

blood to the lungs

blood to the body

heart

△ One side of the heart receives blood from the body and sends it to the lungs to collect oxygen. The other side receives blood carrying oxygen back from the lungs. This is then pumped around the body.

artery

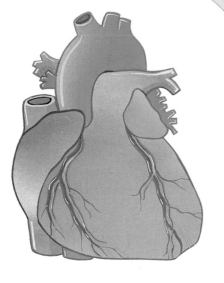

◁ The heart beats about 70 times each minute.

vein

Make a stethoscope

A doctor uses a stethoscope to listen to patients' heartbeats. To make your own stethoscope, push a piece of tubing over the end of a funnel, as shown. Hold the funnel to your patient's chest and put the tubing near your ear. You will be able to hear their heartbeat.

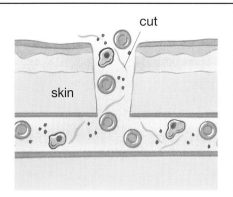

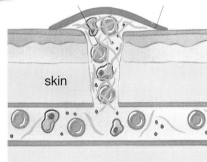

△ When you cut yourself, the white cells attack any germs that get in, and platelets rush to plug the cut blood vessels.

▷ Blood contains red cells, white cells, and platelets in a liquid called plasma. Red cells carry oxygen and white cells help fight germs. Platelets help the blood to clot.

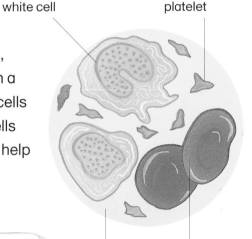

white cell

platelet

plasma

red cell

△ A sticky clot is formed. This hardens into a scab that protects the wound.

Find the answers

What does a scab do?

How many times does the heart beat a minute?

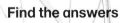

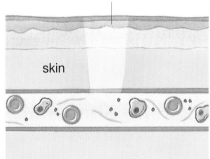

△ As the wound heals, new skin grows underneath. This is pink when the scab drops off.

The nervous system

Nerves all through our bodies take messages from our senses to the brain. This is called the nervous system. The brain is the most important part of the body because it tells it how to work. It helps us to feel things and to think, learn, and remember. Part of the brain also helps us to balance.

▽ Your brain helps you think and concentrate.

▽ Your brain helps you move at different speeds.

▽ It helps you learn how to swim.

▽ It helps you keep your balance.

▽ It helps you walk and talk.

Play the memory game

Ask a friend to put ten objects on a tray. There could be a watch, a cup, a pen, a coin, a book, and so on. Look at the tray for one minute, then cover it up. Write down all the things you saw. Can you remember every single one?

brain

spinal cord

nerve

▷Messages from our senses pass through the nerves to the spinal cord. This is a thick bundle of nerves down the middle of our backs. It carries signals to the brain. Then the brain sends messages along other nerves that tell the body what to do.

△Sometimes the nervous system reacts very quickly. This happens when you are in danger of hurting yourself.

△When you touch something sharp, your hand will jerk away. You do not have to think about it. This is called a reflex action.

◁When you learn something, the brain stores it so that you can remember it another time. This is called memory.

Eating for energy

We eat food because it gives our bodies energy. People eat many different kinds of food, but our bodies use everything in the same way. When you swallow food, it moves down a tube into the stomach and then into the intestines. On the way, the nutrition is taken out of the food. This is called digestion.

The Magic Porridge Pot
(A story by the Brothers Grimm)

A lady gave a tired, hungry girl a magic pot and told her magic words to make the pot cook delicious, nourishing porridge. But when the girl's mother used the magic pot she forgot how to stop it. The porridge flooded the whole village! When the girl stopped the pot, they had to eat their way into their home!

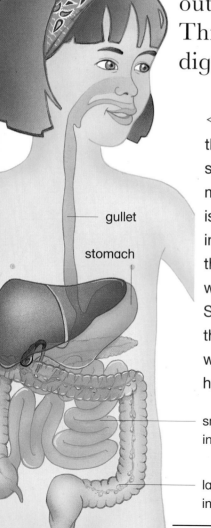

gullet

stomach

small
intestine

large
intestine

◁ Food goes down the gullet to the stomach, which mashes it up. Then it is squeezed along the intestines. It passes through the intestine walls into the blood. Solid fiber passes through as waste when all the goodness has been taken out.

△ In different parts of the world, people eat different types of food. All of it gives the body the energy it needs to live.

Getting rid of waste

As your body works, it makes waste products. The body has to get rid of them. It does this in several ways. We breathe out used air from our lungs. When we sweat we get rid of salt and other waste. We go to the bathroom to get rid of urine from our bladders and solid waste from our bowels.

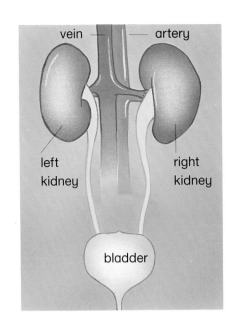

vein — artery

left kidney

right kidney

bladder

◁ We have to go to the bathroom to get rid of urine and solid waste. When our bowels are full, we get rid of solid waste. When our bladders are full, we get rid of urine.

△ Blood flows through the kidneys. The kidneys take water, salt, and other waste from the blood. This waste is turned into urine and stored in a pouch called the bladder.

▷ Sweat is a liquid that comes out of our skin. It gets rid of waste and cools us down.

Healthy eating

Your food should give your body what it needs to keep working. This is called nutrition. There are four main groups of food, called proteins, carbohydrates, fats, and fiber. Your body needs food from each group and water to drink. It also needs the vitamins in food.

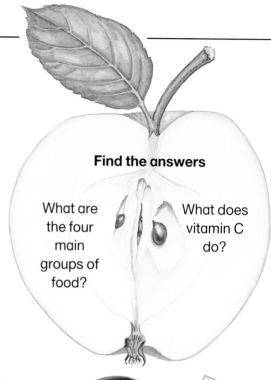

Find the answers

What are the four main groups of food?

What does vitamin C do?

△ Proteins such as meat, eggs, and fish help the body to stay strong.

△ Carbohydrates such as bread, pasta, and rice supply energy for the body.

△ Fats such as butter, milk, cheese, and oils store energy for the body to use later.

△ Vitamin B comes from these foods. It gives energy and healthy skin.

△ Vitamin A comes from these foods. It gives us good eyesight and healthy skin.

△ These fruits and vegetables give us a lot of fiber. They also give us vitamin C, which helps us recover from illness and injury.

△ Vitamin E comes from these foods. It helps the body's cells stay strong.

△ Vitamin D comes from these foods. It helps us grow properly.

△ Vitamin K comes from these foods. It stops us from bleeding too much if we get a cut.

Keep a food diary
Every day for a week, write down what you eat for breakfast, lunch, and dinner. Then look at the pictures on this page. Are you eating something from every food group each day? What sort of foods do you eat most?

	breakfast	lunch	dinner
Mon.			
Tues.			
Wed.			
Thurs.			
Fri.			
Sat.			
Sun.			

Word box
Nutrition is the process of eating and using the food for growth, energy, and keeping our body working. **Vitamins** are found in food. Our body needs them to stay healthy.

Teeth

We bite into food and chew it with our teeth so it is easier to swallow. Our teeth are different shapes and they do different things. Teeth are fixed into our jaws, but they can come loose. Children lose their first teeth and grow another, larger set. If we do not brush our teeth, they will rot, or decay.

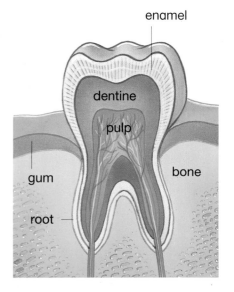

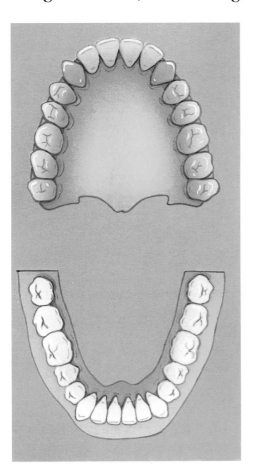

△ The sharp incisors at the front are for cutting food. Pointed canines at the sides tear it. Big molars at the back crush it.

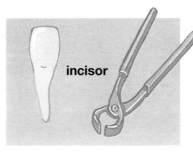

△ Incisors cut like pliers.

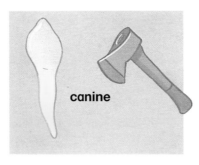

△ Canines cut like an ax.

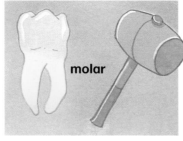

△ Molars crush like a hammer.

△ The outside of the tooth is a hard layer of enamel. This covers the dentine. Inside this is the pulp. Roots hold the tooth in place in the jawbone.

The Tooth Fairy

Some people say that if you lose a tooth, you should put it under your pillow. Then the Tooth Fairy will come and take it away. Sometimes the Tooth Fairy leaves money in exchange for the tooth.

▷When we are about six years old, our first teeth become loose and fall out. Larger teeth grow underneath.

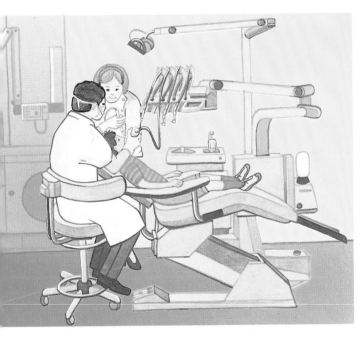

◁The dentist looks after our teeth. If he finds a decaying tooth, he removes the decay and fills the hole with a special mixture that hardens.

Make an eggshell decay

Ask an adult to hard boil an egg. Put it in a cup of malt vinegar. Leave it for a day, then see how much of the shell has been eaten away by the vinegar. This is what fizzy drinks and candy do to your teeth.

△Some people wear braces or a plate to make crooked teeth straight.

△Brush your teeth for three minutes.

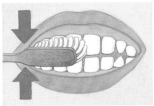

△Brush up and down the front of your teeth.

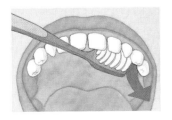

△Then brush up and down the back.

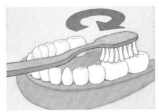

△Always brush with a circular movement.

337

Healthy life

If we want to be healthy, we should always look after our body. It needs to be kept clean. Our skin gets dirty, so we should wash regularly and change our clothes too.

Plenty of exercise is good for most people. Sports and games help our bodies to grow stronger and fitter.

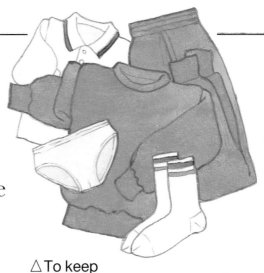

△ To keep clean, it helps to change our clothes when they are dirty, and put on clean ones.

△ Washing in soap and water helps get rid of germs.

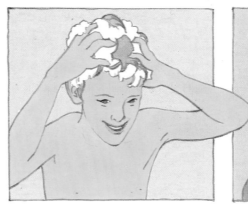

△ Washing our hair keeps it clean and shiny.

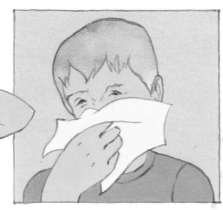

△ Blowing our nose gets rid of dirt and keeps it clean.

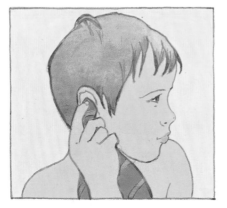

△ Clean your ears gently. Never use sharp objects.

△ Toenails must be cut, or they will grow too long.

Find the answers

Name two mountain sports and two water sports.

Why do we wash?

▷ In very high mountains there is nearly always snow. This means that in these places people can enjoy sledding and skiing for much of the year.

◁ Running is a very popular sport. It makes all the muscles in our bodies stronger. If we do it regularly, we will be fitter and will not get tired or out of breath.

▷ Water sports are activities that we do in the sea or in the swimming pool. Swimming and diving are water sports. We can also float in the water or do exercises.

◁ Whichever sport we choose, we have to follow the rules and concentrate to do well. When we play in a team, we should think of others, so that everybody has fun.

Sleep

We all need to sleep. Sleep allows the body to rest and gain strength after a busy day. Most children sleep for about twelve hours every night. Babies need even more sleep, because they are growing very quickly and this makes their bodies tired. Adults need less sleep, because they are no longer growing. If we do not have enough sleep, we may become grumpy.

Find the answers

How many hours of sleep do most children need?

What are frightening dreams called?

Why do we change position while we sleep?

△ While you are asleep, your body keeps working slowly. Slowing down helps it to rest a little and grow strong.

▷ You do not lie completely still all night, but change position many times. If you were to lie in one place, you would ache in the morning.

Sleeping Beauty

(A story by Charles Perrault)

A wicked witch cast a spell on Sleeping Beauty just after she was born. Years later, having pricked her finger, she and everyone in her castle fell asleep. One hundred years passed before a prince kissed her and broke the spell. They fell in love and got married.

△ While we are asleep, we have dreams. The stories in our dreams seem real while we are asleep. But we do not always remember them when we wake up. Often we dream about things we have seen or done the day before.

△ Nightmares are frightening dreams. Some nightmares are so frightening that they wake us up. But often nightmares can be useful, because they help sort out some of the fears and worries we have in real life.

When you are sick

When you are sick, you may have a high temperature, a cough, spots, or aches and pains. These are signs that your body is being attacked by germs. Germs are tiny living things that float in air and water. They can make you ill if they get inside your body. Doctors can give you vaccinations that fight germs and prevent you from getting sick.

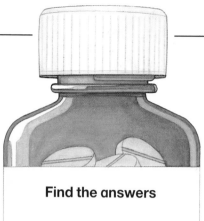

Find the answers

Why do you get hot if you are sick?

What does the doctor use to listen to your lungs?

▽ When your body is fighting off invading germs, it works harder. Your heart beats faster. It pumps more blood around your body. This makes you get hot and you may sweat. It is called having a temperature.

stethoscope

thermometer

△ The doctor examines you. She listens to your heart and lungs with a stethoscope, looks in your ears and throat, and asks you questions. The doctor may give you medicine to help fight the germs. Remember that you should only take medicines given to you by your doctor.

◁ Some diseases, such as chickenpox, are very easy to catch, but you usually catch them only once. After that, the body learns to protect itself against the disease.

▷ If you have already had chickenpox, you are safe to visit a friend who is sick with it. Your body recognizes the disease and can fight it, so you do not catch it again.

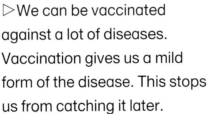

Play spotted faces

Draw two large faces on cardboard. Put 20 counters on each face. These are the spots. Take turns throwing a die. If you throw a six, take six spots off your face, and so on. The first with no spots left wins.

▷ We can be vaccinated against a lot of diseases. Vaccination gives us a mild form of the disease. This stops us from catching it later.

A happy life

Love and friendship and respect for each other make life happy for everyone. One way of showing these feelings is with our bodies. A hug, a kiss, a smile, a wave, or an outstretched hand are all things we can do that bring happiness.

Machines

What is a machine?

Machines are all around us in our daily lives. They help us do a job and can make all kinds of work easier. Machines can also do things for us that we cannot do ourselves.

Some machines are very simple. Did you know a pair of scissors is a machine? So is a corkscrew. Other machines, such as spacecraft and planes, are very complicated.

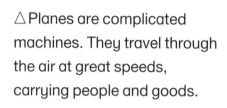

△ Planes are complicated machines. They travel through the air at great speeds, carrying people and goods.

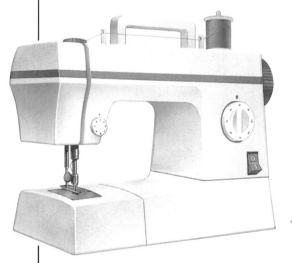

◁ Sewing machines mean that we can make or mend clothes quickly and easily.

△ Many machines are used in offices. Punching a hole in paper would take longer without a hole punch.

Word box
Levers lift and move big or heavy objects.
Pulleys are wheels used with ropes to lift things.
Cog wheels have teeth on their edges. Cog wheels fit and move together.

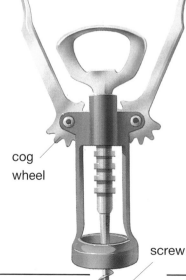

cog wheel

screw

◁ A corkscrew is a simple idea. It would be difficult to remove a cork from a bottle without one! This corkscrew works by using cog wheels.

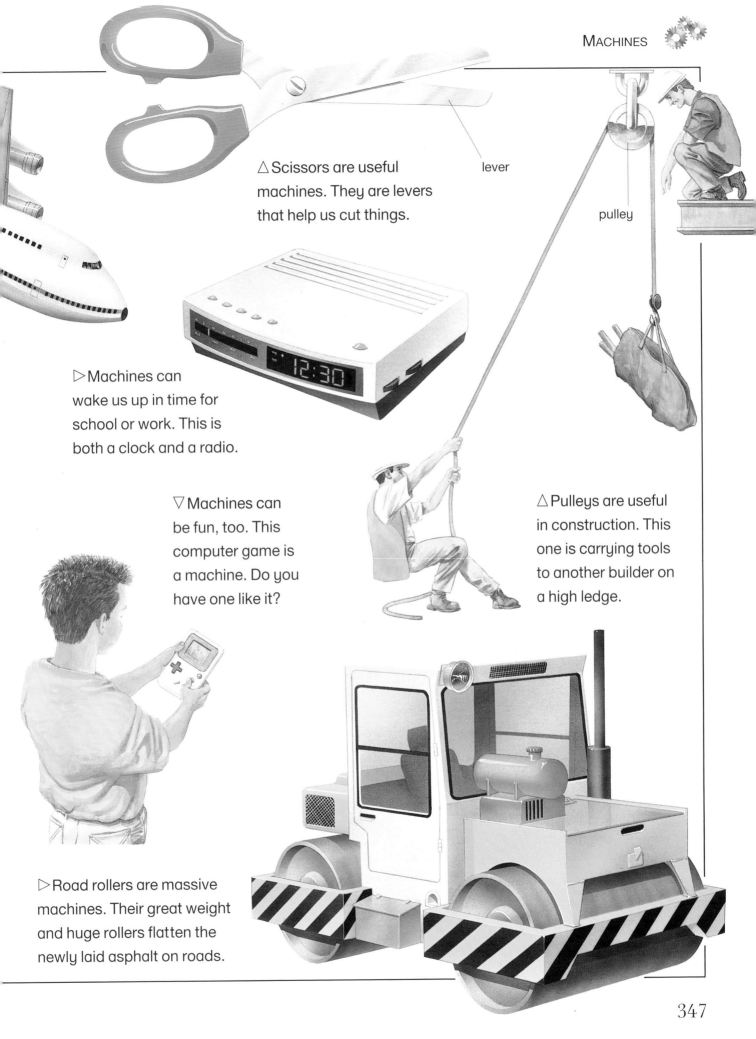

△ Scissors are useful machines. They are levers that help us cut things.

lever

pulley

▷ Machines can wake us up in time for school or work. This is both a clock and a radio.

12:30

▽ Machines can be fun, too. This computer game is a machine. Do you have one like it?

△ Pulleys are useful in construction. This one is carrying tools to another builder on a high ledge.

▷ Road rollers are massive machines. Their great weight and huge rollers flatten the newly laid asphalt on roads.

347

Wheels, pulleys, and levers

The first machines were invented thousands of years ago. Many of these simple machines are still used today. A lever makes it easier to move loads. A wheel and axle moves things along the ground. A pulley makes lifting easier. These simple machines are part of many complicated machines we use every day.

lever

load

effort

pivot

lever

pivot

lever

effort

load

◁ Levers lift and move loads. The lever balances on the pivot. Scales are levers. The pivot is between the two pans. When one pan rises, the other falls.

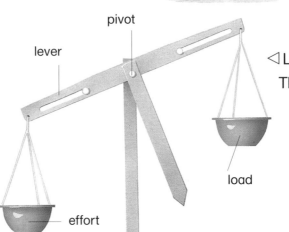

▷ Wheels are attached to axles. The axles turn the wheels. The wheel and axle on this tricycle help it roll smoothly along the ground.

wheel

axle

wheel and axle

axle

wheel

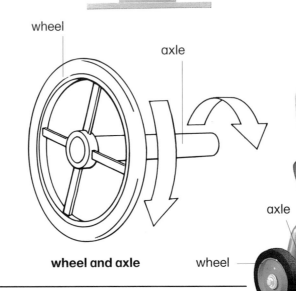

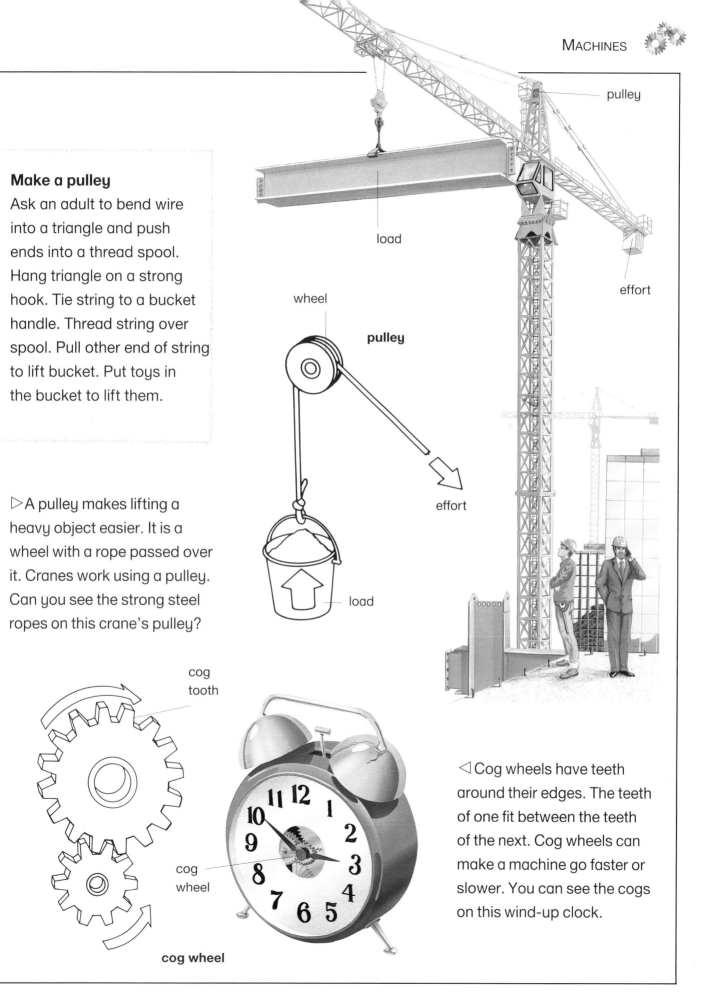

pulley

load

effort

Make a pulley

Ask an adult to bend wire into a triangle and push ends into a thread spool. Hang triangle on a strong hook. Tie string to a bucket handle. Thread string over spool. Pull other end of string to lift bucket. Put toys in the bucket to lift them.

wheel

pulley

effort

▷A pulley makes lifting a heavy object easier. It is a wheel with a rope passed over it. Cranes work using a pulley. Can you see the strong steel ropes on this crane's pulley?

load

cog tooth

cog wheel

cog wheel

◁Cog wheels have teeth around their edges. The teeth of one fit between the teeth of the next. Cog wheels can make a machine go faster or slower. You can see the cogs on this wind-up clock.

Cycles

A bicycle, or bike, is a cycle with two wheels. Other cycles have one wheel, and some have three. Bikes are used by children and grown-ups all over the world. In some cities, cycling is the most popular kind of transportation.

Bikes are fun, but you must make sure they are roadworthy. Cycling on roads can be dangerous if you are not careful.

△ A cycle-rickshaw has three wheels. In some Asian cities cycle-rickshaws are used as taxis.

▷ A unicycle is a cycle with only one wheel.

▽ Two people can ride a tandem bicycle.

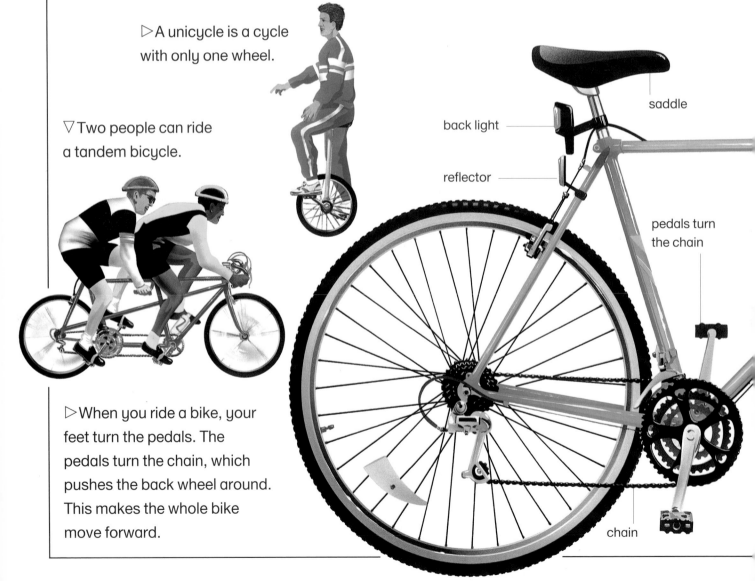

back light

reflector

saddle

pedals turn the chain

chain

▷ When you ride a bike, your feet turn the pedals. The pedals turn the chain, which pushes the back wheel around. This makes the whole bike move forward.

△A hole in a tire makes it flat. Air escapes from the hole, making the bike difficult to ride. To repair a flat tire, hold the tube under water and look for the air bubbles escaping.

△Brakes wear down and need checking.

△A bike's chain must be kept well oiled.

Can you find?

1 pump	5 repair kit
2 light	6 helmet
3 reflectors	7 bell
4 oil can	8 tool set

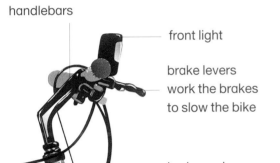

handlebars

front light

brake levers work the brakes to slow the bike

brake pads stop the wheel from turning

the valve cap is unscrewed to pump air into the tire

wheel

Word box
Brakes are the parts of a machine that slow it down or stop it moving.
Reflectors shine when light hits them. They do not make light.

Motorcycles

A motorcycle has two wheels, like a bicycle, but it has an engine to make it move. There are many different kinds of motorcycle. Some have small engines and go slowly. Others have large engines and go faster. The fastest motorcycles of all are used for racing. Racing motorcycles need special tires.

△ Mopeds have smaller engines than motorcycles, so are usually used for shorter trips.

▷ This bike is used in a sport called scrambling. It can ride over rough ground.

▽ This special motorcycle is called a chopper.

brake lights come on to let people behind the bike know when the driver is braking

seat

indicator

Find the answers

What are slicks?

What do brakes do?

▷ A motorcycle is powered by a gasoline engine. The engine drives a shaft, or a chain, that turns the back wheel. The back wheel pushes the motorcycle forward.

---

slicks are dry-weather tires

slicks skid in the wet

wet-weather tires can grip

△ Racers need two kinds of tire. In dry weather, smooth tires called slicks are used. Slicks are fast, but they skid in wet weather. Slower, grooved tires are used in the wet.

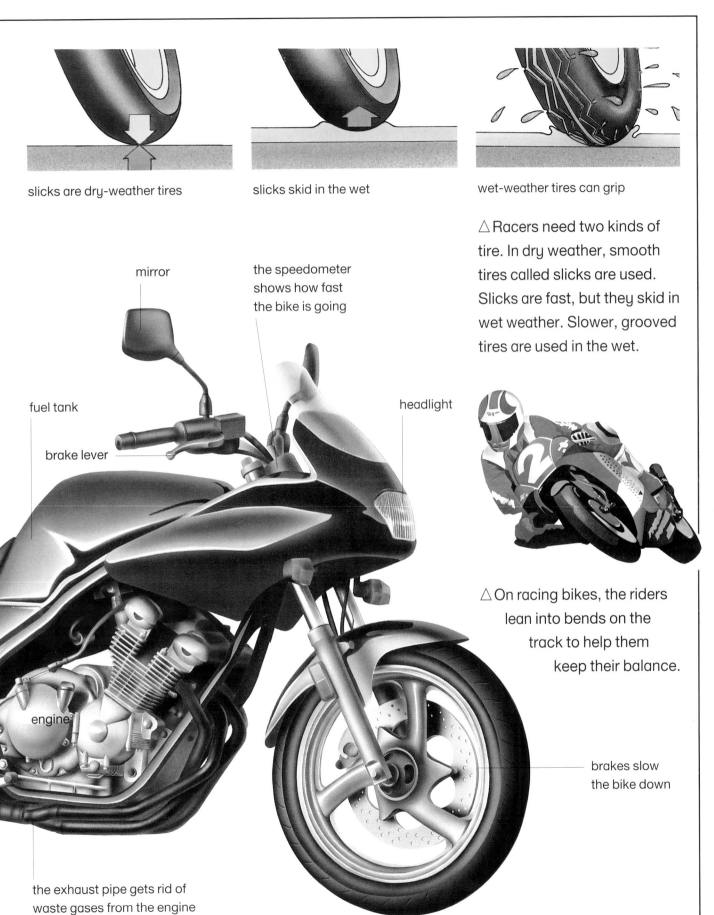

mirror

the speedometer shows how fast the bike is going

headlight

fuel tank

brake lever

engine

△ On racing bikes, the riders lean into bends on the track to help them keep their balance.

brakes slow the bike down

the exhaust pipe gets rid of waste gases from the engine

Cars

Cars come in many shapes and sizes. People use them for all kinds of different jobs. Most cars have gasoline engines, but some are powered by diesel. Cars are complicated machines with many moving parts. They need to be looked after or else they break down.

△ This car has lots of room to store baggage in. Its roof rack can be used for carrying extra loads.

▷Cars with powerful engines can tow heavy loads, such as this motor home.

▽A sports car has a long, low shape and a very powerful engine so that it can go fast.

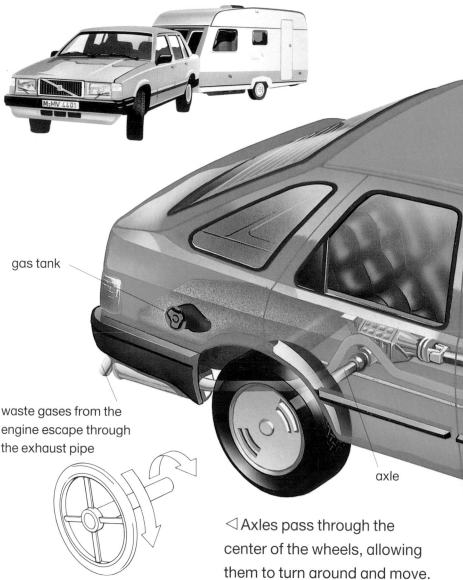

gas tank

waste gases from the engine escape through the exhaust pipe

axle

▷In this picture, you can see the engine under the hood. Can you find the steering wheel? Cars are made with the steering wheel either on the left or on the right. This one is on the left.

◁Axles pass through the center of the wheels, allowing them to turn around and move.

Chitty Chitty Bang Bang
(A story by Ian Fleming)

Chitty Chitty Bang Bang was a magical car. It could fly and float and do many other things. Colonel Caractacus Potts and his family had lots of adventures in it.

△ A car needs gasoline or diesel to run its engine.

△ Special machines with huge brushes can be used to wash cars.

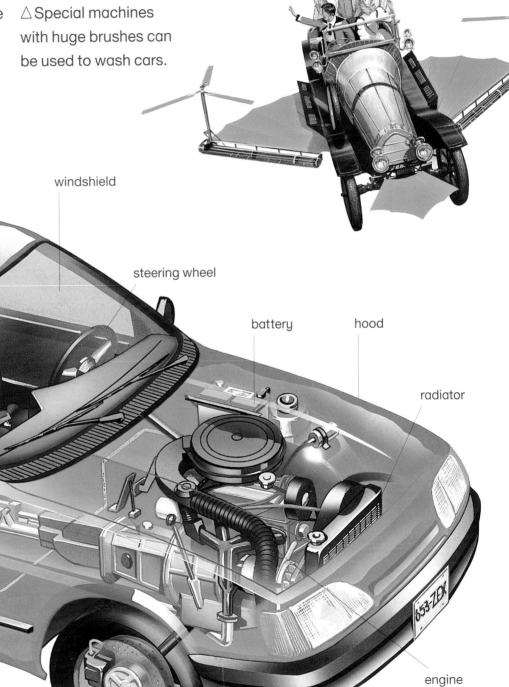

windshield

steering wheel

battery

hood

radiator

propeller shaft

engine

Trucks

Trucks carry all sorts of goods by road. Different trucks are used to carry different things. The huge container at the back is a trailer on wheels. It is pulled along by a tractor unit. The driver sits in a cab in the tractor unit.

◁ This logging truck has a crane to lift logs onto the trailer.

△ A car transporter carries new cars from the factory to the showroom.

△ A tanker carries all sorts of liquids in a strong tank.

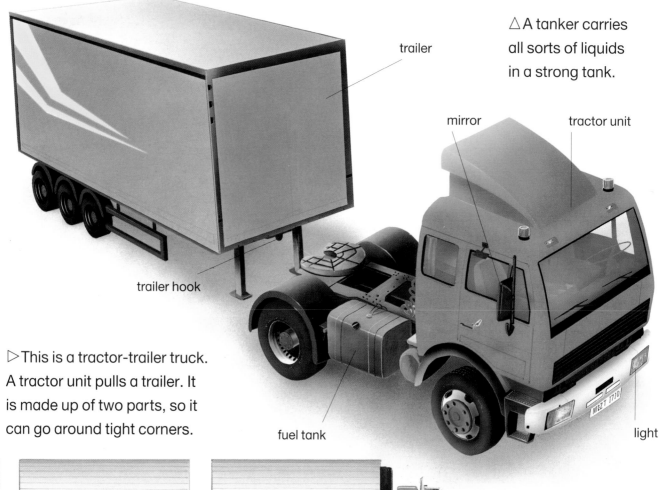

trailer

mirror

tractor unit

trailer hook

▷ This is a tractor-trailer truck. A tractor unit pulls a trailer. It is made up of two parts, so it can go around tight corners.

fuel tank

light

◁ A roadtrain is a truck that pulls three or more trailers.

Buses

Buses can carry many people. Some are used for short trips. Larger, more comfortable buses are usually used for traveling longer distances. Today, most buses have diesel engines.

▷This bus has a ladder for people to climb onto the roof.

◁A trolley bus uses electricity from wires above it to move.

△Some extra-long buses can bend to go around corners.

▷Greyhound buses are a cheap and easy way to travel. They run between many cities.

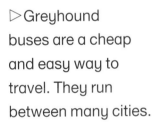

GREYHOUND

Make a toy bus
Ask an adult to pierce a hole near the bottom corners of a small box. Slot long pencils through for axles. Thread spools on the pencils to make wheels.

Push cardboard disks up to each spool so wheels and axles turn smoothly. Add modeling clay to each pencil to hold the wheels in place. Paint your bus, adding windows and passengers.

Trains

Trains are made up of cars pulled along by an engine. People travel in cars. Freight travels in flatcars or container cars. There are different trains for carrying different things. The first trains were powered by steam, but today almost all use electricity or diesel. Most trains have wheels that run on rails. Some trains travel underground and some travel above city streets.

△ Steam trains are still used on some railroads.

▷ The rack and pinion train uses three rails. Most trains use only two.

the pantograph is used to pick up electricity from an overhead wire

△ This is a modern diesel train. There are many diesel trains around the world.

engineer's cab

car

TGV

power car

△ The French TGV is the world's quickest passenger train. In French, TGV stands for High-Speed Train.

Make a play train

To make a play train that you and your friends can sit in, collect several large boxes. Glue two boxes together. Roll up some cardboard into tubes and stick on to make a smokestack and buffers. This is your engine. Glue on one box for each car. Paint the train brightly. Glue paper plates to each car for the wheels.

△ Subway trains carry people through tunnels under busy city streets.

△ A hanging monorail saves space in a busy city. It hangs high above the streets.

▽ Freight trains can be made up of as many as 150 different flatcars.

chemical car

container car

buffer

engine

flatcar

coal car

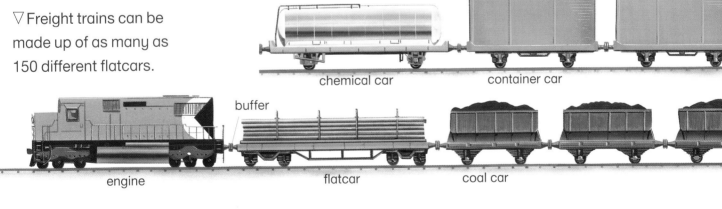

car carrier

Construction site

There are lots of machines to do the different jobs on the construction site. There are drills to bore giant holes deep in the ground, bulldozers to move earth, mixers to mix concrete, and cranes to lift heavy loads. The mobile crane can travel on roads like any truck, so it can be moved to wherever it is needed.

Make a crane

Ask an adult to make holes in a small box. Poke long pencils through the holes and glue in place. Add thread spools, cardboard circles, and modeling clay, as shown below.

Build a stand with more boxes, as shown.

Cut slits in a short straw, splay the ends, and glue to one spool. This is the handle. Tape end of string to one spool. Tie a small magnet to the other end of the string. Place string as shown below. You could use your crane to pick up paperclips.

△A tall crane is lifting building materials to the top of this skyscraper. How many machines can you see on the construction site?

pulley wheels wind the load up and down on wires

Word box
Skyscrapers are tall buildings with many floors.
Boring is making holes or hollows through hard materials, such as rock, that are in the way.

legs called stabilizers steady the crane

▽ The mobile crane has a long arm called a boom. It is worked by a driver in the cab. The load is lifted on wires which go around pulley wheels.

pulley wheel

load

△ Before construction begins, the foundations must be made. Deep holes are bored into the ground. They are filled with steel beams and concrete.

△ A steel frame is built up from the foundations, piece by piece. The steel beams are lifted up by tall cranes.

pulley

the boom can be made longer or shorter

load

cab

H376 DNK

MACHINES • On the Construction Site

Roads, bridges, and tunnels

Huge machines are used to build roads, bridges, and tunnels. Different machines are needed for different jobs. There are bulldozers, scrapers, graders, rollers, and many more. They clear the earth, carry away waste, and lay asphalt. Special tunneling machines can cut away the rock.

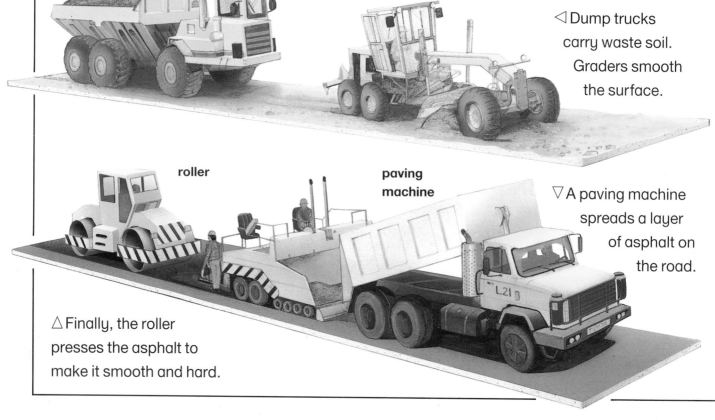

▽ Bulldozers clear away piles of rocks and earth.

bulldozer

scraper

◁ Machines called scrapers level the ground to make it flat.

dump truck

grader

◁ Dump trucks carry waste soil. Graders smooth the surface.

roller

paving machine

▽ A paving machine spreads a layer of asphalt on the road.

△ Finally, the roller presses the asphalt to make it smooth and hard.

Find the answers

What does a bulldozer do?

Which machine levels the ground?

◁ Bridges and tunnels shorten our trips. They let us go over or under rivers or other roads. Some go right through mountainsides.

▷ To build a tunnel through hard rock, machines bore holes and put explosives in them. The explosives blast huge holes in the rock so that the tunnel can be built.

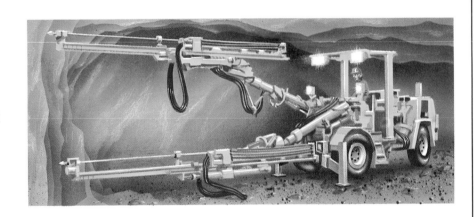

conveyor belt removes rubble

◁ If the rock is soft, explosives are not needed. This tunnel boring machine can cut through softer rock.

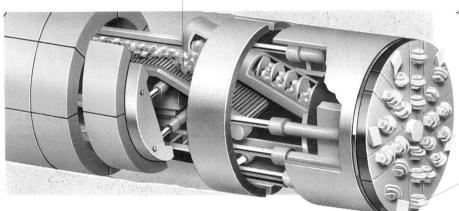

cutting face

363

Ocean liners

Ocean liners are large ships that carry many passengers across the sea. The captain and crew control the liner from a room called the bridge. Huge engines drive the propellers, which push the liner through the water. Most ocean liners are powered by enormous diesel engines.

△ The captain and crew make sure the ship is going the right way. This is called navigation.

pilot boat

△ Taking a liner in and out of port can be difficult. A pilot boat guides the liner through the deeper channels of water.

▽ Some parts of a ship have special names. The front of a ship is called the bow and the back is the stern. The kitchen is called the galley and the bedrooms are called cabins.

Word box
Navigation is the way ships find their way safely to where they are going. **Propellers** push ships through the water. The engines make their blades spin very fast.

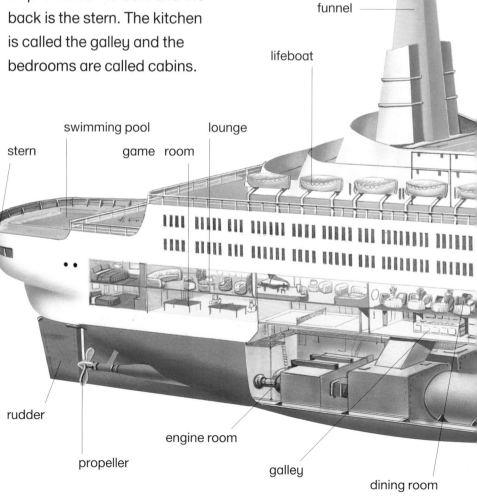

funnel

lifeboat

swimming pool

lounge

stern

game room

rudder

engine room

propeller

galley

dining room

△ The engine room is in the bottom part of the hull. Here, the engineers make sure the engines are running smoothly.

Make a soap boat

Cut a boat shape from a styrofoam tile. Cut a V-shape in the back of the boat. Fill a clean bowl with warm water. Put your boat on the surface of the water. Squeeze a drop of dishwashing liquid into the V-shape of the boat and watch it move forward.

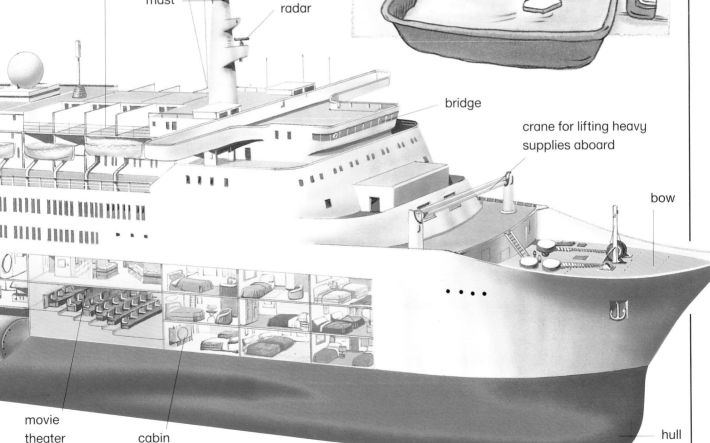

tennis court

mast

radar

bridge

crane for lifting heavy supplies aboard

bow

movie theater

cabin

hull

365

Other watercraft

There are many different kinds of watercraft. Supertankers carry oil. Ferries and hovercraft carry people and cars. Fishing trawlers catch fish. Ships go to sea, but paddle steamers and canal boats travel on rivers and canals.

Most watercraft have engines, but some are powered by the wind.

▽ Canal boats are long and thin so they can move along narrow canals easily. Some people live on board all the time. Other people hire them for short trips or vacations.

▽ Paddle steamers travel up and down rivers. They are driven by a wheel at the back.

▷ Fishing trawlers have a winding engine at the back to haul in their heavy nets.

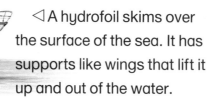

▽ This racing yacht can go very fast. The big sail at the front is called a spinnaker.

◁ A hydrofoil skims over the surface of the sea. It has supports like wings that lift it up and out of the water.

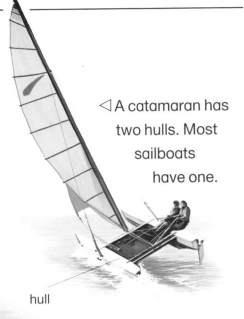

◁ A catamaran has two hulls. Most sailboats have one.

hull

Treasure Island
(A story by Robert Louis Stevenson)

Young Jim Hawkins and his friends have a map showing a treasure island. Long John Silver and his pirate crew try to get to the treasure first, but after many exciting adventures on land and sea, it is Jim and his friends who succeed.

▷ The junk is a Chinese sailing ship. It has from two to five masts. The sails are made from cotton or matting.

mast

◁ Hovercraft float on a cushion of air. Fans blow air downward and lift the hovercraft off the water.

▽ Supertankers carry oil in huge tanks. They are the biggest ships in the world.

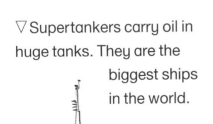

Jumbo jets

Planes are complicated machines. Jumbo jets are the largest planes to carry passengers. They are used to fly long distances all over the world.

Pilots are the people who fly the planes. They have computers to help them. At airports, air traffic controllers use radar to help them keep track of jumbo jets and all other planes.

△ Computers help the pilot. They can show how high and fast the plane is flying.

▽ When a plane lands, baggage is taken from the plane and delivered to passengers waiting inside the airport building.

▷ The main part of the jumbo jet is called the fuselage. Attached to this are strong wings and a big tailfin. Its four jet engines push it through the air at more than 600 miles an hour.

Word box
Jet engines push a blast of hot air out the back of a plane, which pushes it forward.
Radar is used to tell exactly where things are.

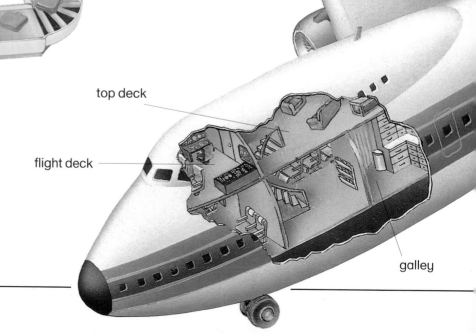

top deck

flight deck

galley

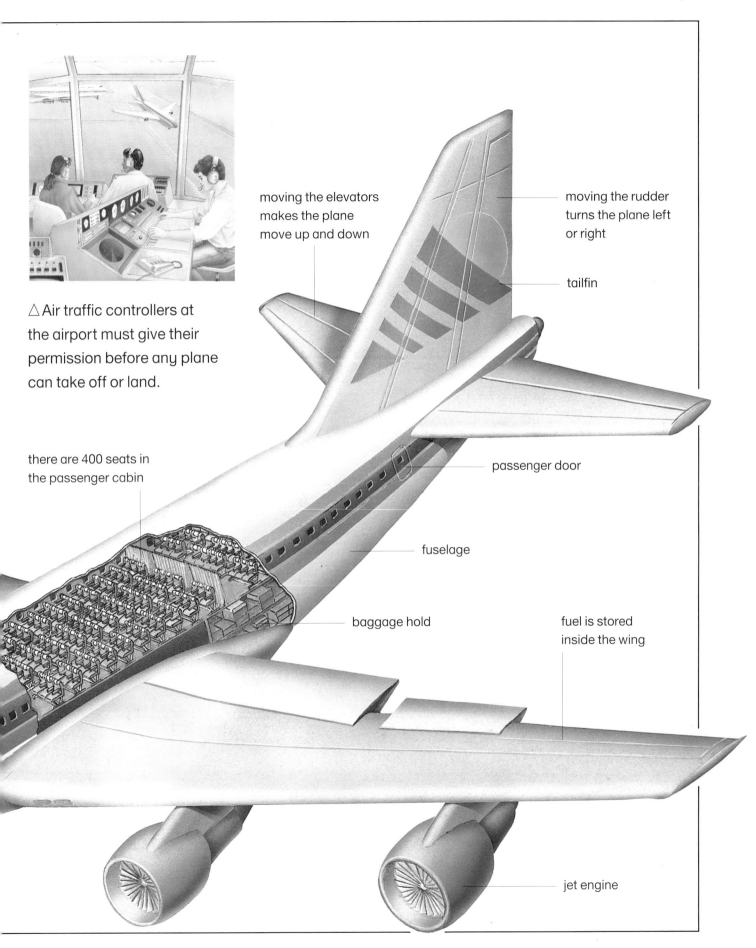

△ Air traffic controllers at the airport must give their permission before any plane can take off or land.

moving the elevators makes the plane move up and down

moving the rudder turns the plane left or right

tailfin

there are 400 seats in the passenger cabin

passenger door

fuselage

baggage hold

fuel is stored inside the wing

jet engine

Other aircraft

Any flying machine is an aircraft. Some aircraft are so big, they are used to carry parts of other aircraft. Some are so small, they can carry only one person. Most have wings, but helicopters have rotor blades. Unlike most other aircraft, helicopters can hover and fly backward.

△ A glider does not have an engine. It glides along on currents of air.

△ The Super Guppy looks like a flying whale. This enormous plane was built to carry parts of other aircraft.

△ This plane scoops up water to put out fires.

△ An ultralight is a tiny one-person plane.

▽ A helicopter uses spinning rotor blades to fly up, down, sideways, or to hover in mid-air. The pilot controls it with a joystick, a lever, and foot pedals.

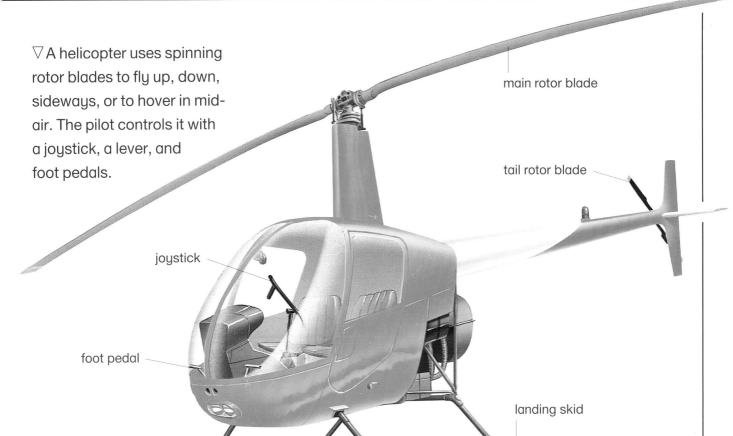

main rotor blade

tail rotor blade

joystick

foot pedal

landing skid

▽ Concorde is the world's only supersonic passenger aircraft. Supersonic means faster than the speed of sound.

▽ This small jet carries people on short business trips.

Make a gyrocopter

Take a piece of paper, 6 inches long and 1½ inches wide. Cut one slit, 3 inches long, down through the middle. Fold the two wings down, as shown below. Attach a paperclip pointing straight up at the bottom. Drop your gyrocopter from a height. It should spin to the ground.

Machines for emergencies

In emergencies, there are machines that help us save lives and buildings. Police use cars and motorcycles to reach emergencies quickly. Fire engines carry fire fighters and equipment to put out fires. Ambulances carry medical help and injured people to the hospital. Lifeboats and special helicopters are built for use in rescues at sea.

Find the answers

Which machines are used during sea rescues?

How do fire fighters reach fires in tall buildings?

▽ In an emergency on land, police, fire engines, and ambulances are called. An elevating platform truck lifts fire fighters to the fire.

load

effort

lever

pivot

lever

pivot

lever

▷Helicopters are often used for sea rescues. The pilot steadies the helicopter while a rescuer is lowered on a winch to the person in the water. Then they are winched to safety.

winch

load

△ In some parts of the world, lifeboats are used for sea rescues. They have specially trained crews, who can work in very rough seas.

Word box
Crews work together in a team. They often save lives in emergencies.
Winches lift things up with a rope or chain attached to a winding wheel.

Spacecraft

Spacecraft are machines that are launched into space by rockets. Some spacecraft circle the Earth, while others have visited distant planets.

The space shuttle is a spacecraft that carries astronauts into space. It can also launch satellites or carry a spacelab in its payload bay.

robot arm

flight deck

spacelab

small thruster rockets move the shuttle while it is in space

living area

tunnel to spacelab

Word box
Rockets burn fuel to push themselves up into space at great speed.
Payloads are the things rockets carry, such as laboratories or satellites.

Thunderbirds
This Thunderbird 3 *rocket model was designed by Derek Meddings. In the Thunderbirds stories, a rescue team used* Thunderbird 3 *to rescue people who were in trouble in space.*

space shuttle

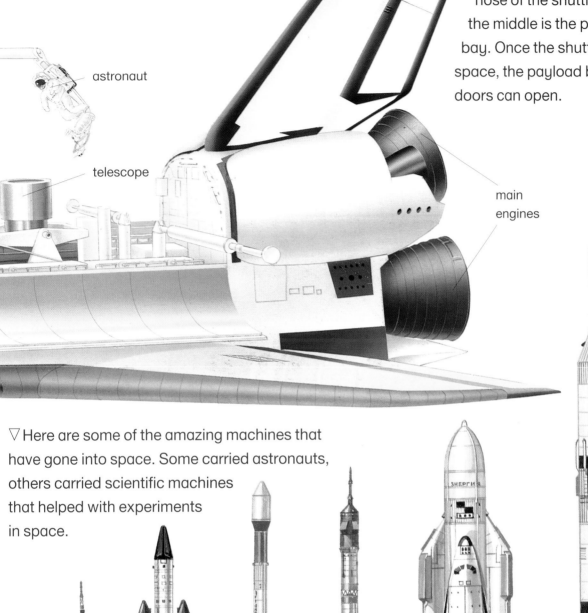

astronaut

telescope

◁ The living area and flight deck are in the nose of the shuttle. In the middle is the payload bay. Once the shuttle is in space, the payload bay doors can open.

main engines

▽ Here are some of the amazing machines that have gone into space. Some carried astronauts, others carried scientific machines that helped with experiments in space.

V2 *Atlas* *Titan 3* *Ariane* *Vostok* *Energiya* *Saturn V*

375

Bread

Most bread is made from wheat. It is gathered by a machine called a combine harvester. At the flour mill, a grinding machine turns the wheat into flour. This is made into bread by all sorts of machines at a bakery.

loaf

grain

flour

△ Farmers grow wheat in huge fields. When it is ripe, combine harvesters cut and gather the wheat seeds. This is called grain.

△ Bread begins as grain, which is ground into flour.

△ At the bakery, flour, yeast, salt, and water are poured into a mixing machine.

△ Next, a machine called a divider cuts the dough into lumps called loaves.

△ The loaves are put on trays and baked in a very hot oven until they are done.

△ The baked loaves are lifted off the trays and moved along on a conveyor belt.

△ Some loaves are sold whole, but most are cut in slicing machines. This machine wraps bread in plastic to keep it fresh.

Make party sandwiches
Cut crusts off sliced bread and spread with fillings. Roll slices, wrap in plastic film, and refrigerate. After two hours, slice the rolls. Striped sandwiches can be made with alternate layers of white and brown bread.

Little Red Hen
(An English folk tale)

When Little Red Hen found some grain, she asked the other animals to help her plant it. But they were lazy and said, "No." She asked for help at harvest time and they lazily said, "No." She asked for help milling the grain, and making and baking the bread. The lazy animals said, "No." But when the bread was ready to eat, all the animals wanted to help. This time, Little Red Hen said, "No."

△ Bread can be made in different ways. This bread from India, called roti, is baked in a clay oven.

Word box
Factories are places where things are made.
Conveyor belts are flat moving pathways that carry things in factories.

377

Peanuts

Peanuts are grown on farms. There are special machines to plant them and pull them out of the ground when they are ripe. Then the peanuts are taken to factories where other machines sort, clean, and roast them for eating.

Make peanut clusters

Ask an adult to melt a bar of chocolate in a bowl, over steaming water. Add 6 ounces of unsalted peanuts. Stir. Pour into cake cups. Leave to set. Do not make or eat these if you are allergic to peanuts.

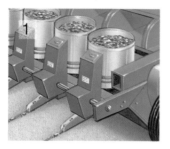

▷A combine pulls peanuts off plants, tips them into a trailer, and takes them to the factory.

△ Machines are used to plant peanut seeds.

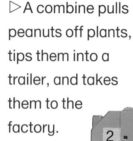

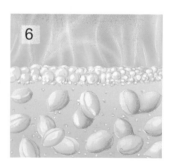

△At the factory, the peanuts are shelled.

△Electronic sorting machines check them.

△Metal rollers shake off the peanut skins.

△The peanuts are roasted in hot oil.

▷Bagging machines weigh and wrap them. Then they are ready to sell in the stores.

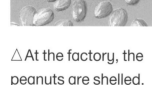

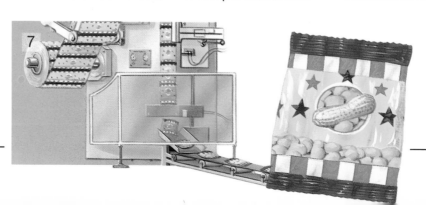

Milk

Cows produce milk to feed their calves. Farmers sell some of this milk for people to drink. The cows are milked by machine in a special milking parlor. The milk flows to a cold tank to keep fresh. Then a tanker takes the milk to the dairy, where it is put into containers.

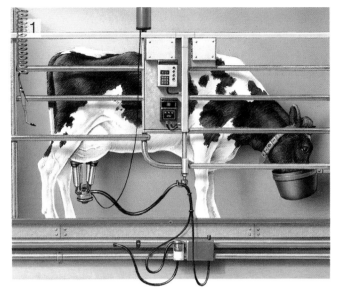

△ The milking machine is attached to the cow. It takes about ten minutes to milk each cow.

△ A milk tanker collects milk each day. The tanker is spotlessly clean inside.

△ The tanker takes the milk to the dairy.

△ The milk is tested to make sure it is fresh.

△ It is heated in tanks to kill any germs.

△ Filling machines put the milk in containers.

Find the answers

Where are cows milked?

Why is the milk tested?

Wood, pencils, and paper

Wood comes from trees in the forest. Lumberjacks chop down the trees. Trucks take the wood to a sawmill, where it is cut up into planks.

Wood is used to make many things, including pencils and paper. Pencil leads are made from clay and graphite. These materials are mined out of the ground. Paper is made at a paper mill.

△ In the forest, a lumberjack uses a chain saw to cut down a tree. A young tree will be planted to replace it.

△ At the sawmill, the bark is cut away from the tree trunk. Then it is sawn into planks.

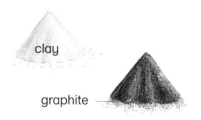

clay

graphite

△ Clay is a type of earth. Graphite is a soft, black rock, mined from under the ground.

▽ At the pencil factory, graphite and clay paste is baked to make leads.

1

▽ Leads are glued between two pieces of wood, or slats. These will be cut up.

2

3

△ When cut up, the separate pencils are put onto a huge frame. As the frame turns, the pencils are dipped in paint. This coats the wood and helps to strengthen them.

△ At the paper mill, machines cut the wood into small pieces called wood chips.

△ The pulp is cleaned and rinsed with water. Then it is spread on a moving wire screen. Most of the water drips away, leaving a thick, soggy layer of pulp.

△ The wood chips are mixed and cooked into a pasty pulp.

Find the answers

What is graphite?

What does a lumberjack use to cut down trees?

What are wood chips?

△ Heavy rollers press the pulp into a thin sheet and squeeze out more water. Hot rollers dry the paper. Finally, the paper is wound onto an enormous roll called a reel.

Clothes

Most of the clothes that we buy in stores are made in factories. Clothes are made from different types of material, such as cotton and silk. Cotton comes from a plant and silk comes from silkworms. It takes a lot of different machines to turn them into different types of clothing.

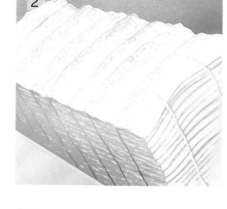

△ The cotton is cleaned and pressed into bales.

◁ Cotton harvesters collect the cotton from the fields.

△ Spinning machines twist the cotton into long threads.

△ To make material for blue jeans, the thread is dyed blue.

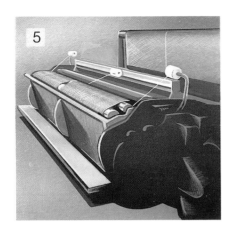

△ Looms weave the thread into denim cloth.

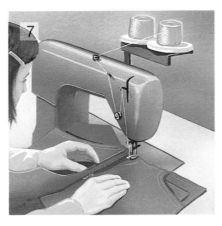

△ Then machinists sew the pieces together to make jeans.

Rumpelstiltskin
(A story by the Brothers Grimm)

A little man helped a girl spin straw into gold, but in return she promised him her first child. The girl married the King and had a baby. The little man said the baby was his, unless she guessed his name. At the last minute, she found out he was called Rumpelstiltskin.

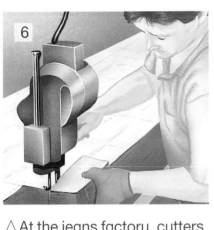

△ At the jeans factory, cutters cut the denim to shape.

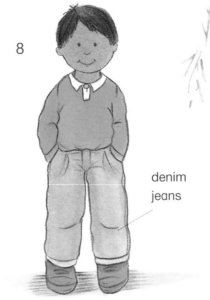

denim jeans

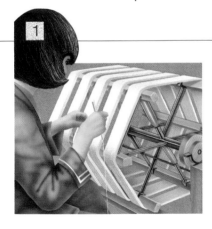

△ Silk from silkworms' cocoons is wound into thread on reeling frames.

▽ The thread is dyed and woven into cloth on a loom.

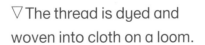

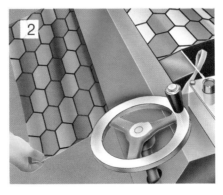

silk pajamas

Sneakers

All sorts of shoes are made by machines in shoe factories. Shoes may look simple, but making them can be a complicated process. There are many different pieces in just one pair of sneakers, so it takes several machines to make them.

The Elves and the Shoemaker
(A story by the Brothers Grimm)

Before machines made shoes, they were sewn by hand. An old shoemaker cut pieces of leather every night, ready to sew the next day. Each morning he found the shoes made. He hid and found out that elves had been making up the shoes for him.

△A cutting machine cuts out all the pieces.

△A machinist sews the pieces together.

△Eyelets are punched for the laces.

△Another machinist attaches the insole.

△The shoe is dipped in hot liquid plastic.

△As the plastic cools it makes a hard sole.

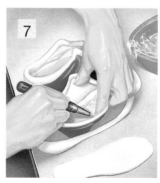

△Finally, a lining is glued in place.

sneakers

Glass

Most of the glass we use is made by machines at a glassworks. Glass is made up of a mixture of a type of sand called silica, limestone, soda ash, and cullet, or scrap glass. These are melted in a furnace. Liquid glass is molded before it cools and hardens.

Find the answers

Where is most glass made?

What are the four main ingredients of glass?

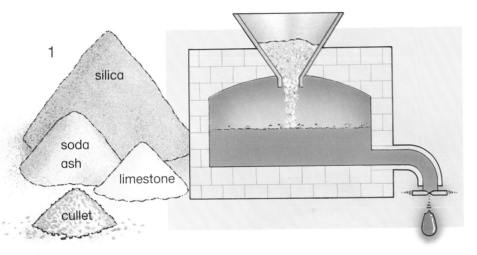

△ These are the main ingredients of glass.

△ They are mixed together and melted down in a furnace.

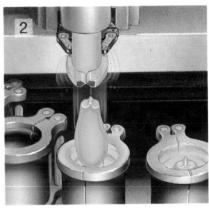

△ For a jar, a blob of liquid glass is dropped into a mold.

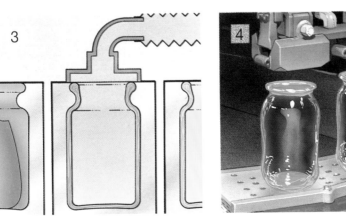

△ Air blows the glass blob into the shape of the mold.

△ The jar is put into an oven, which strengthens it.

△ Now the jar is strong enough to use.

385

Recycling cans

Recycling means making new things out of used materials.

Steel is one material that can be recycled easily. Steel is made from iron. Iron is mined from under the ground. Recycling steel means that less iron needs to be mined.

Recycled steel can be used to make new drinks cans in a soft drinks factory.

△ A big magnet picks out steel from garbage.

△ The cans are crushed into big bales.

△ The bales are melted in a furnace.

△ Rolling mills flatten the steel as it cools.

△ A press pushes out circles from the steel.

△ The steel is shaped into a can.

△ Printing rollers add color to the can.

△ Another machine shapes the can lid.

◁ Finally a machine squirts soft drink into the cans. The machine can fill 8,000 cans each minute. A machine called a seamer puts the lids on.

Coins

Money is made in a place called the mint. Coins are made from mixtures of metals, called alloys. These alloys are melted together in a furnace, then pressed into thin sheets by rollers. Designs are stamped on the coins to tell us how much each coin is worth.

Scrooge
(From a story by Charles Dickens)

Scrooge had lots of money. He often counted his money, but never spent it. He loved money more than people. Then, three ghosts showed him how miserable he was. He stopped being stingy and used his money to help others.

△ The mint buys bars of different metals.

△ The bars are melted together in a furnace.

△ The hot, soft metal is rolled into sheets.

△ Disks called blanks are punched out.

△ A coining press stamps each blank.

△ This puts a pattern on each coin.

Find the answers

Which machine stamps patterns on the blanks?

What do we call a mixture of metals?

Where are coins made?

In the home

Our homes contain a lot of machines. They make our lives easier and more comfortable. Machines in the home help us keep warm, work, and play. We use washing machines and vacuum cleaners to take the hard work out of cleaning. We watch television to learn and to relax. We communicate, or talk, on the telephone. We even use machines to open cans of food.

△ Before washing machines were invented, people set aside a whole day each week to wash their clothes by hand.

◁ Drying your hair with a hairdryer takes much less time than waiting for it to dry by itself.

Word box
Digital displays show information in the form of numbers on a screen.
Communication is when people pass facts, information, and ideas to each other. We may communicate using many different machines.

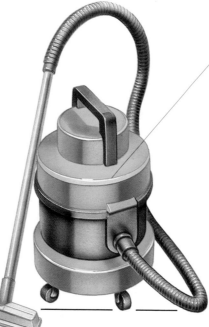

◁ Before vacuum cleaners were invented, floors had to be swept with a broom or scrubbed with a brush.

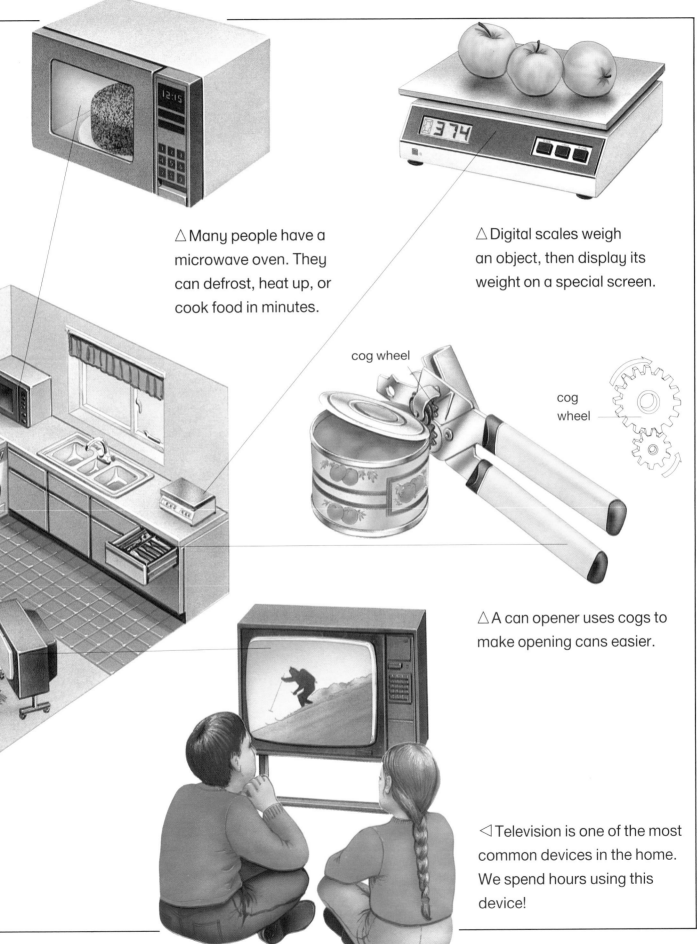

△ Many people have a microwave oven. They can defrost, heat up, or cook food in minutes.

△ Digital scales weigh an object, then display its weight on a special screen.

cog wheel

cog wheel

△ A can opener uses cogs to make opening cans easier.

◁ Television is one of the most common devices in the home. We spend hours using this device!

389

Communication

Communication is exchanging ideas and feelings. We communicate with each other by using sound or pictures, or sound and pictures together.

We often use machines to communicate. Many machines found in an office are used to communicate. These include telephones, fax machines, computers, and dictaphones.

▽ Radios pick up sound waves sent from a radio station and turn them into sounds we know, such as words and music.

◁ A fax machine can copy writing or pictures, and send them to another fax machine hundreds of miles away.

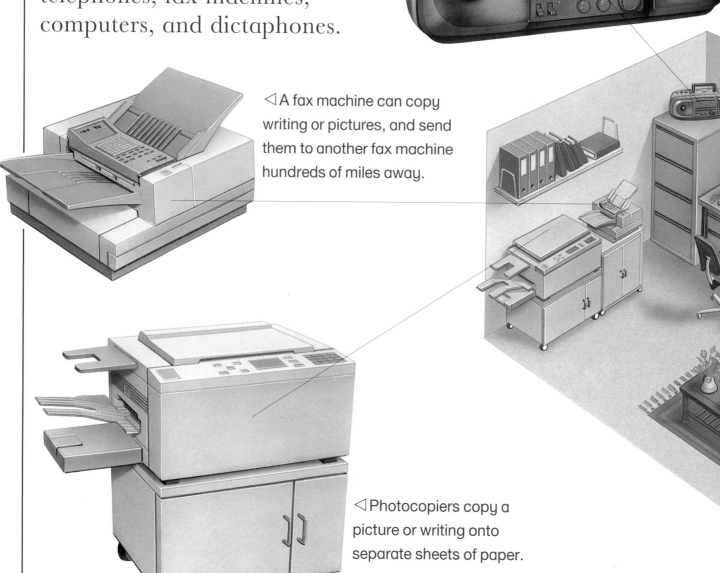

◁ Photocopiers copy a picture or writing onto separate sheets of paper.

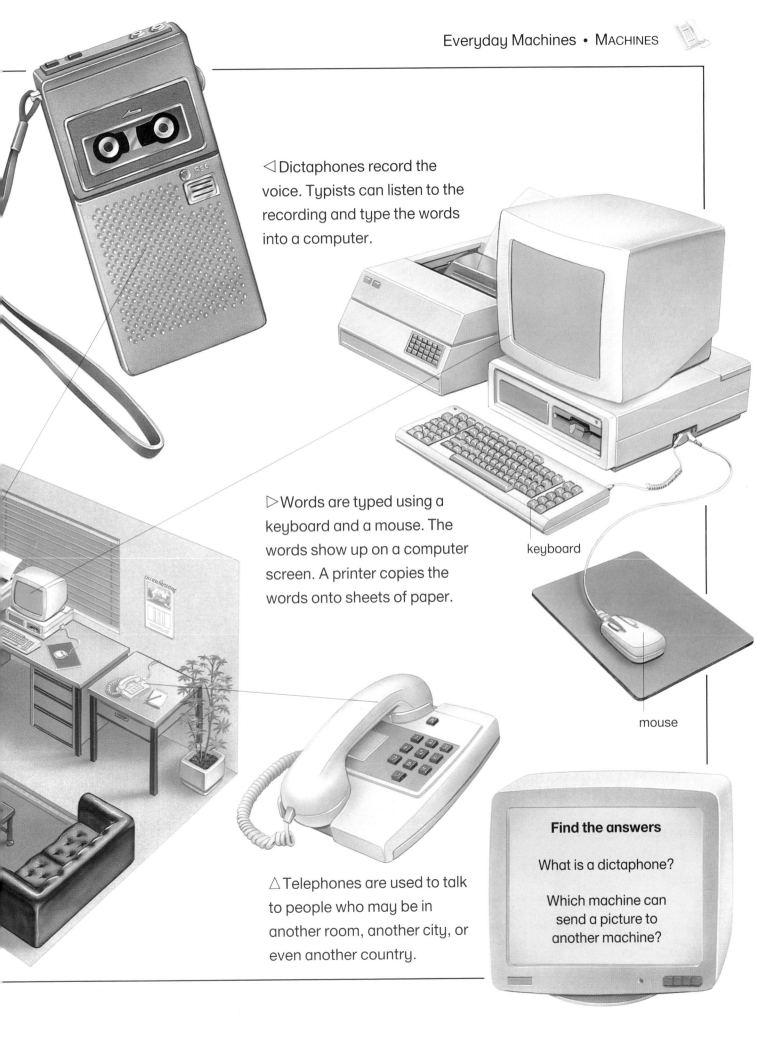

◁ Dictaphones record the voice. Typists can listen to the recording and type the words into a computer.

▷ Words are typed using a keyboard and a mouse. The words show up on a computer screen. A printer copies the words onto sheets of paper.

keyboard

mouse

△ Telephones are used to talk to people who may be in another room, another city, or even another country.

Find the answers

What is a dictaphone?

Which machine can send a picture to another machine?

In the hospital

Many machines are used in hospitals. They can help us get better when we are sick. They can also find out what is wrong with us, so that doctors know how to look after us.

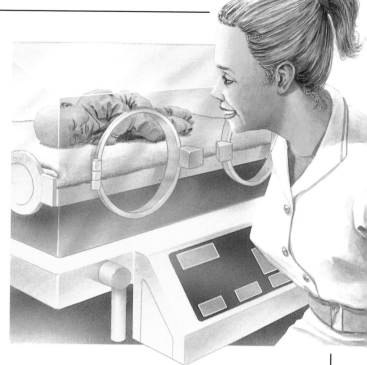

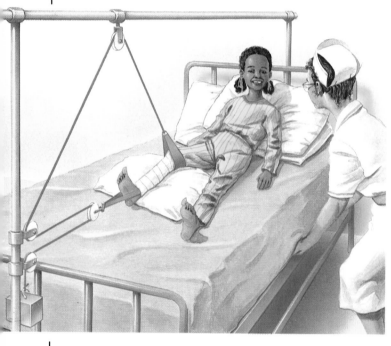

△ Some babies that are born too early are not ready to live in the outside world. They are put in an incubator to keep them warm and protect them from germs.

◁ Sometimes a broken leg has to be mended in a special way. It is kept in the right position by traction until it is strong enough to use.

▷ Some machines monitor, or watch and record, what is happening to the heart. Information from electronic pads shows up as a picture on a screen.

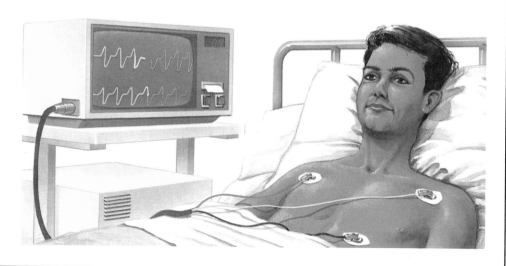

392

Science

What is science?

Science is about finding out. It helps us make sense of our world. Science begins with observation. This means looking at things very carefully. Scientists work in different ways and study many subjects, such as biology, astronomy, medicine, geology, and chemistry. Much has been discovered through science, but there is a lot left to find out about our world.

△ Scientists often use special tools, such as microscopes, to help them observe.

The senses

Observation means using not just our eyes, but all our senses to find out things.

touching a tree to see if it is smooth or rough

smelling an egg to see if it is bad

tasting a lemon to find out if it is sweet or sour

looking in a book to find answers to questions

△ We can all be scientists. These children are studying the wildlife in a pond.

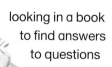

listening for high and low sounds

▷This scientist is a marine biologist. She is studying sea life.

△Astronomers use telescopes to study the stars. They find out about the universe.

▽ Doctors study medicine. They do experiments, or tests, to find out if new drugs can fight diseases.

▷Geologists study rocks to see what the Earth is made of. Rocks can tell us a lot about the history of the Earth.

▷Chemists use special symbols, or signs, to study chemistry. Doctors and other scientists use these symbols, too.

Word box
Observation is how we find out about the world around us. We need to use our senses to do this. **Experiments** are the tests scientists carry out to see if their ideas are correct.

How to be a scientist

Scientists see things happening and start to ask questions. Sometimes they guess at possible answers. Then they carry out experiments, or tests, to see if they were right. When scientists carry out experiments, they measure and record what is happening. They might do the same test several times. The results are often worked out with the help of computers.

△ We all ask questions. This boy is asking how heavy planes manage to stay up in the sky.

◁ His sister is trying to find out about planes by looking up the information in a book.

graph

▷ Computers may be used by scientists to record and make sense of information. This scientist is using a computer to make a graph with the results of his experiment.

△An exciting way of finding out answers is to test things for yourself. The question on the clipboard is to be tested.

△Equal amounts of dry soil are put into two trays. The same number of seeds are sown in each tray. The trays are placed side by side.

Can you stop an apple from turning brown?

You can be a scientist too! Try this experiment. Ask an adult to cut an apple into four pieces. Put each piece on a plate. Place one piece in the refrigerator. Wrap the second piece in foil, and sprinkle lemon juice on the third. Leave the fourth alone. Do they all turn brown?

△Every day the right-hand tray is watered. The left-hand tray is not watered at all.

△The watered tray has seedlings growing. The other tray has none. The test has shown that seeds will not grow without water.

Time

Time is very important to scientists. They often need to measure exactly how long it takes something to happen.

Over thousands of years, people have invented different clocks. Candles, shadows, and sand have been used to measure the passing of hours and minutes. Today, scientists can measure in seconds and even tiny parts of a second, so their results can be extremely accurate.

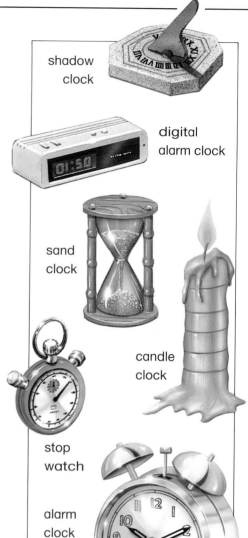

shadow clock

digital alarm clock

sand clock

candle clock

stop watch

alarm clock

◁ These children are using a watch to time the number of drips in a minute.

▷ This boy has found out that the girl's skipping is slowing down as she gets tired.

Clocks

These are all different kinds of clocks. Which ones have you used?

Make a water clock

Ask an adult to make a hole in the bottom of a plastic tub. Tape on a string handle. Pin to an old table. Put another tub below. Pour water into top tub. After each minute, mark water level on bottom tub. Empty and refill to use as a minute clock.

Temperature

Thermometers are used to measure temperature, or how hot something is.

Scientists have to think about temperature when they are carrying out experiments. If two things are being compared, it is important that they are kept at the same temperature.

When scientists work in very hot or very cold places, they need to wear and use materials that are not damaged by these temperatures.

△ Different thermometers measure temperatures in different places. A wall thermometer measures the temperature of air in a room.

▽ Scientists in cold places, such as Antarctica, work in below-freezing temperatures. They have to wear special clothes to keep them warm.

△ Scientists who work near hot volcanoes must wear heat-resistant suits. This scientist is using a special thermometer that can measure high temperatures.

Materials and structures

The things around us are made from different materials, such as wood, plastic, and metal. Different materials do different jobs. A sponge soaks up water. A metal saucepan is strong and can stand up to heat.

The way something is put together is called its structure.

△ These objects are made from many materials. Some are strong, some are soft, and others stand up to heat.

△ This lighthouse is made from materials that can stand up to stormy weather.

△ The glass in a greenhouse lets the sun's rays pass through and traps heat, so the plants stay warm.

Word box
Materials are used to make things. Materials are carefully chosen to suit the jobs they have to do.
Structure is the way materials are put together to make things strong.

△ This bridge has stood for years. The stone it is made from is a strong material.

△ Skyscrapers are made from strong, hard materials that will last a long time.

Build a roof

Arrange two cereal boxes alongside each other. These are your walls. Open a hardback book in the middle and try to balance it on the walls to make a roof. You will find that the weight of the roof pushes the two walls apart. Now lay two rulers across the cereal boxes, as shown. Does the book balance now?

△ The shape of a structure is important. Cylinders look like tubes. They are very strong. A tree's cylinder-shaped trunk supports its heavy branches.

◁ Triangles are strong because no one side can bend away from the other two. The Eiffel Tower is made of many triangles.

▽ Spiders spin strong webs. Can you see the triangles in this web?

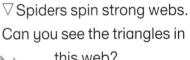

△ Stone columns on buildings are cylinder-shaped. They are able to hold up a lot of weight, such as roofs.

Solids, liquids, and gases

All materials are either solids, liquids, or gases. Solids keep their shape and can be hard or soft. Liquids take the shape of their container. If we pour a liquid, it will run. Gases will not even stay in their container. If they escape, they spread out all over the room.

△ Can you pick out the solids, gases, and liquids in this picture?

Icarus
(A Greek myth)

Icarus and his father were imprisoned on the island of Crete. They escaped by making wings of feathers held together with wax. Icarus's father warned him not to fly too near the Sun. But Icarus ignored him. The Sun melted the wax, and Icarus fell.

△ Some materials can turn from solid to liquid to gas. This water is liquid.

△ If we freeze water, it becomes a solid called ice. Ice melts back into water.

△ If we heat water enough, it becomes a gas called steam. This change is called boiling.

△ If we let steam cool, it turns back into a liquid. This change is called condensation.

▷Many materials change when they are heated or cooled. Lava comes out of a volcano as a liquid. As lava cools, it turns into solid rock.

lava

△As wax gets hot, it melts and becomes runny. When it cools it becomes solid. Wax can change again and again.

◁Some things change when they are heated, but cannot change back. A fried egg cannot go back to being raw.

▽Milk left for a long time turns lumpy and smelly. You cannot undo this change.

Make an ice pop freezer
Put about 20 ice cubes in a bowl. Push a liquid ice pop into bowl and cover with ice. Sprinkle a tablespoon of salt over ice so ice melts. A mixture of salt and ice is colder than ice on its own. After 15 minutes the ice pop will be solid.

▽A cake cannot go back to being the runny mixture it was before it was baked.

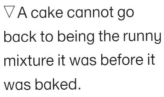

Mixing and dissolving

We often mix things together when we are cooking, but not everything mixes in the same way. Some things seem to disappear in water or other liquids. They have dissolved. Others soak up some of the liquid and get lumpy. Some do not mix at all, but float on top of liquids. Oil does not dissolve in water; it floats on the water's surface.

△ In cold water, salt dissolves quickly, sugar takes a longer time, and flour gets lumpy.

How The Donkey Got Away
(A story by Jean de La Fontaine)

Two donkeys were being driven home from market. One carried heavy bags of salt, the other light sponges. The donkey carrying salt was forced to cross a stream. The salt dissolved in the water and the donkey escaped. The second donkey jumped in the stream, thinking he could escape too. But the sponges soaked up water and he had to be rescued from sinking.

△ Hot water helps things dissolve more easily, such as sugar in hot coffee.

△ Cleaning gets rid of dirt by dispersing it. Mud from muddy boots disperses in water. This means that tiny bits of mud are in the water that is carried away down the drain.

▽ We wash dirty plates in a mixture of water and detergent, or dishwashing liquid. The detergent loosens the bits of food on the plates so they disperse in water more easily.

▷ Large tankers carry tons of oil. Sometimes there is an accident and oil leaks. Here you can see an oil slick floating on top of the sea.

Evaporation

When something dissolves, it does not disappear. In the sun, the water in salty water evaporates, leaving the salt behind.

◁ Oil slicks affect all of our wildlife. This bird has been rescued and is being bathed in detergent to disperse the oil covering its feathers.

405

Energy

Energy is all around us. We cannot see it, but we can see, hear, and feel its effects. When we watch the television, listen to the radio, or feel a room warm up, energy is being used.

Energy does not disappear, it changes from one kind to another. Gasoline has energy stored in it. When it is used in a car, gasoline burns and gives out heat energy. As it makes the car go, the heat energy is turned into movement energy.

Make a pinwheel

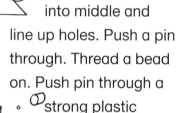

Cut slits in a square of cardboard, 10 inches by 10 inches. Make holes in the middle and corners, as shown. Fold corners into middle and line up holes. Push a pin through. Thread a bead on. Push pin through a strong plastic straw, a bead, and a piece of cork. Blow pinwheel to spin it.

△ A sailboat uses wind energy. This wind energy is caught in the boat's sails and pushes the boat forward.

◁ People and animals turn energy from the food they eat into movement energy.

△ Hairdryers work by turning electrical energy into heat and movement energy.

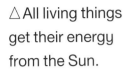

△ All living things get their energy from the Sun.

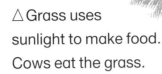

△ Grass uses sunlight to make food. Cows eat the grass.

◁ Cows use energy from the grass to make milk.

◁ This energy helps us to lead an active life.

◁ We drink the milk, which contains energy.

▽ Plants use the Sun's energy to grow.

▷ Cars use the gasoline to make them go.

◁ Today we drill for oil and turn it into other fuels, such as gasoline.

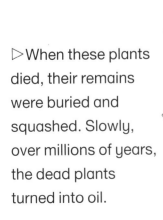

▷ When these plants died, their remains were buried and squashed. Slowly, over millions of years, the dead plants turned into oil.

Word box
Energy is the ability to do work. Everything needs energy to move, work, breathe, or grow.
Fuel is stored energy. It is burned to release heat energy to power machines.

Heat energy

Holding a mug of hot chocolate warms up your hands. When you hold a snowball, it makes your hands very cold. This is because hot things pass their heat to their surroundings and lose some heat themselves. Heat always moves from a warmer place to a colder one. Heat energy moves through radiation, conduction, or convection.

△ Conduction heats food in a pan. The heat from the stove moves to the pan, and from the pan it moves to the food.

▽ The Sun gives off rays of heat, which warm up Earth. This is called radiation.

△ Heat from hot drinks warms up your hands by conduction.

▷ Animals, such as reptiles, use radiation. The sun's rays warm their bodies up. After basking in the sun, this lizard will be warm enough to move around and search for food.

△ Heat from your hands is lost through conduction when you hold a snowball.

408

▽This room is being heated by convection. Air near the radiator becomes warm. This warm air rises and is replaced by cooler air, which in turn is heated itself.

Conduction experiment
Some materials conduct heat better than others. To test this, put a wooden spoon, a plastic spoon, and a metal spoon into some warm water. Leave for two minutes. Feel the handles. The one that is the warmest conducts heat the best.

▷Convection is important in heating homes. The warmest place is usually at the top because warm air rises.

▷The middle of the house is warm, but not as warm as upstairs. The bottom of the house is coolest because cold air sinks. In old houses, the basement was often used as a store for keeping things cool.

Bigger and smaller

Most materials get bigger, or expand, when they get hotter. When materials get colder they usually get smaller, or contract. Solids, liquids, and gases all expand and contract. It is important to know how materials will behave when we build different structures. The size of pipes, wires, and buildings must allow for expansion and contraction.

△ Electric power cables contract in the winter, so they are almost straight.

△ In the summer heat, electric power cables expand and hang lower and looser.

△ Water is unusual. It expands as it freezes. This is why pipes can burst in winter.

△ Expanding ice in a water pipe cracks it. When the ice melts, water spurts out.

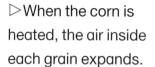

◁ Popcorn is made by expansion. Inside each grain of corn is a small amount of air.

▷ When the corn is heated, the air inside each grain expands.

◁ The air inside expands so much that the grain pops open. Popped grains of corn are bigger because the air has puffed them up.

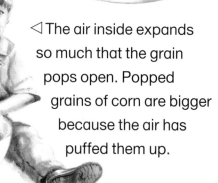

Expand water
Fill a plastic tub to the brim with water. Put the lid on. Ask an adult to put the tub in the freezer. As it freezes, the ice will expand and push the lid off the tub.

Saving energy

Most of the energy we use comes from fuels such as coal, gas, or oil. But the Earth's supply of fuel will run out one day. Also, when we burn fuel to release its energy, we pollute, or poison, the air around us. So we must save energy when we can.

▽ Gasoline for cars is made from oil. If we walked more, instead of driving, we could save oil.

▽ We can save energy so that fuels last longer and pollute less. We can switch off lights when they are not needed.

▽ Heating water takes up energy. A shower uses less hot water than a bath, so saves energy.

▽ Homes can be insulated to keep heat in. Gaps in between walls stop heat from being conducted through the bricks. The gaps are often filled with insulating materials. Double-glazed windows and attic insulation also stop warmth escaping.

▽ We can stop wasting heat by making sure that windows are closed when the heating is on.

double-glazed window

attic insulation

space in between walls

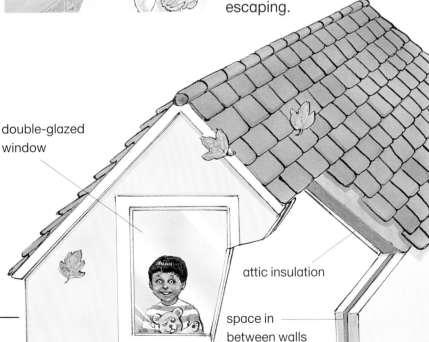

Electricity

There are two types of electricity. They are static electricity and current electricity. Current electricity can flow along wires. This means that it can travel from a battery or a power station to where it is needed. Current electricity is very important in our everyday world. Think of all the things that stop working if there is a power failure!

△ If you comb your hair quickly, it will become charged with static electricity.

Never play with, or go near, current electricity. It could kill you.

▷ These machines work by using current electricity. Without them, our lives would be very different, and much more difficult.

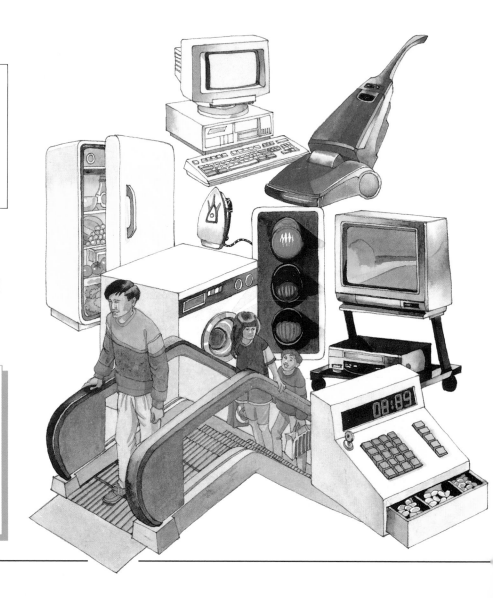

Word box
Power stations burn fuel to make current electricity for use at home and work.
Batteries make current electricity from chemicals stored inside them.

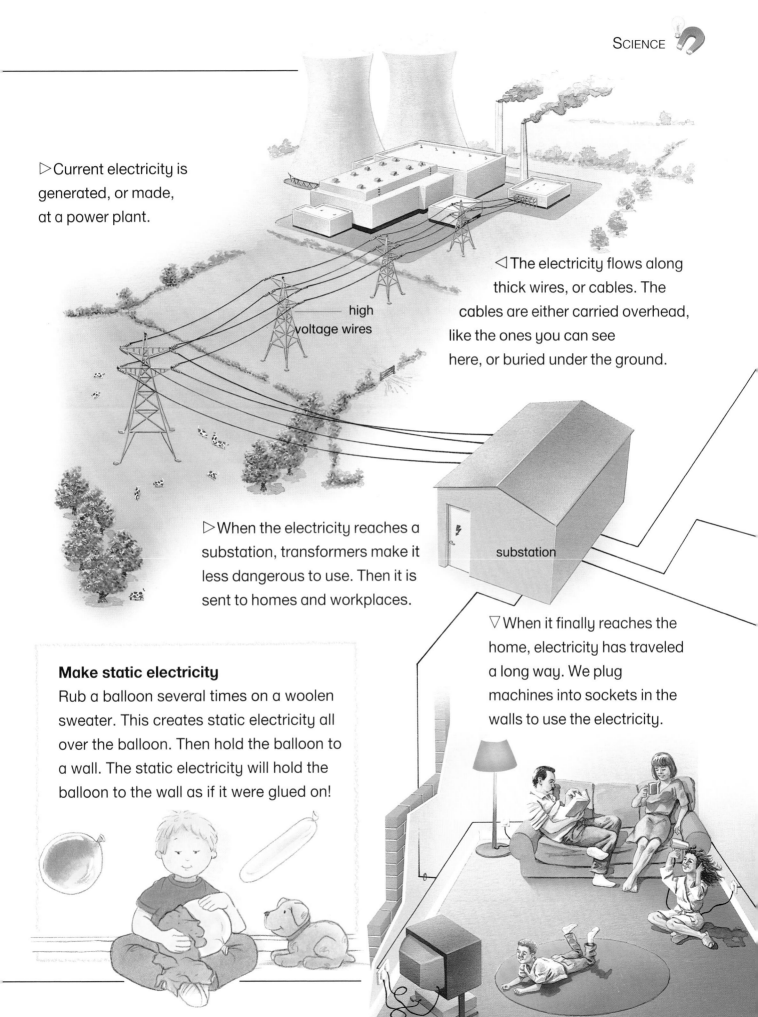

▷ Current electricity is generated, or made, at a power plant.

◁ The electricity flows along thick wires, or cables. The cables are either carried overhead, like the ones you can see here, or buried under the ground.

high voltage wires

▷ When the electricity reaches a substation, transformers make it less dangerous to use. Then it is sent to homes and workplaces.

substation

▽ When it finally reaches the home, electricity has traveled a long way. We plug machines into sockets in the walls to use the electricity.

Make static electricity
Rub a balloon several times on a woolen sweater. This creates static electricity all over the balloon. Then hold the balloon to a wall. The static electricity will hold the balloon to the wall as if it were glued on!

Batteries and circuits

Batteries make and store small amounts of electricity that can be carried anywhere. Chemicals inside a battery make the electricity. Some batteries can be recharged so they last longer. Others are finished once the chemicals have been used up.

Batteries are used in circuits. A circuit is a pathway that allows electricity to flow. As long as a circuit is complete, electricity will keep flowing.

△ Batteries are sold in many shapes and sizes. All these batteries use chemicals to make electricity. Once the chemicals are used up, the batteries stop working and should be thrown away.

▽ A car battery can be recharged. The battery stores electricity to start the car, and then is recharged when the engine is running.

Never take a battery apart. The chemicals inside are dangerous.

△ Batteries are used to power many things. Watches and calculators have tiny batteries. A much larger one is needed to run an electric wheelchair.

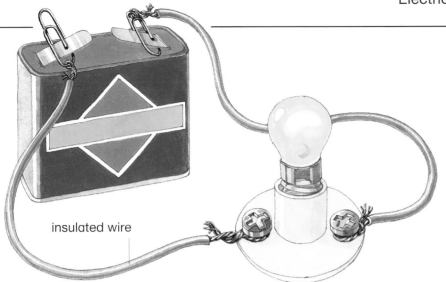

insulated wire

◁ This is a complete circuit. Electricity flows along a wire from one terminal, or end, of the battery. It passes through a light bulb and lights it up. Then it travels along the other wire, back to the other terminal of the battery.

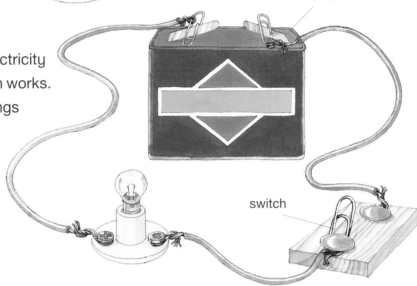

terminal

switch

▷ If there is a gap in a circuit, electricity cannot flow. This is how a switch works. It connects the circuit to turn things on and breaks the circuit to turn things off. Here, the switch is a paperclip. When both ends are no longer connected, it breaks the circuit and the light bulb goes out.

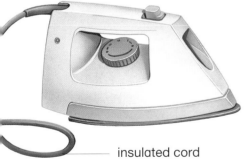

insulated cord

△ Electricity cannot flow through some materials. These are called insulators and make using electricity safer. The wires carrying electricity to this iron are covered by insulating material.

Make a simple circuit
Ask an adult to help with this activity. Screw a small bulb into a bulb holder. Strip ½ inch of insulating plastic from each end of two pieces of insulated wire. Attach to the bulb holder, as shown in pictures above. Attach a paperclip to the other ends. Clip them onto each terminal to light up the bulb.

415

Magnets

A magnet attracts, or pulls, some materials toward it. This is called magnetism and the materials are magnetic. Not everything is magnetic, so there are some things that you cannot pick up with a magnet.

Every magnet has a north pole and a south pole. These poles are at the ends of a magnet. The north pole of one magnet attracts the south pole of another magnet. Two north poles or two south poles repel, or push apart.

△ If you put the north pole of one magnet near the south pole of another, they are attracted and pull together.

▽ These materials are magnetic. When you put a magnet near them, they are attracted to it.

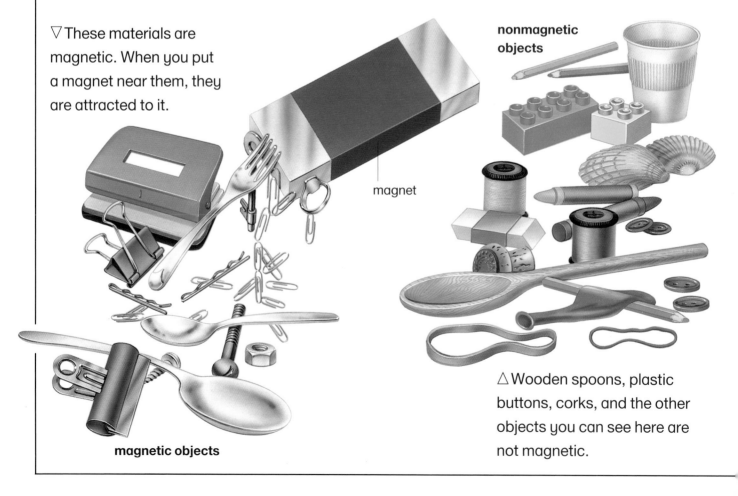

magnet

nonmagnetic objects

magnetic objects

△ Wooden spoons, plastic buttons, corks, and the other objects you can see here are not magnetic.

▷Compasses are used to help people find their way. The needle in a compass is a magnet. As the Earth is magnetic, the north-seeking pole of the compass turns to the North Pole of the Earth.

△ The Earth itself is magnetic.

▷Magnets come in all sorts of shapes and sizes. This enormous magnet works in a scrapyard. The magnet picks up and moves huge pieces of scrap metal. It would be difficult to pick up this car without it!

Make a magnetic theater

Cut slits in four short cardboard tubes. Splay out ends and glue to the bottom corners of a thin cardboard box. Decorate to look like a theater. Add old material for curtains. Draw characters on cardboard. Cut out, leaving a tab, as shown. Fold back tabs and tape on paperclips. Tape strong magnets to sticks. To move the characters, move one magnet under each character.

417

Backward and forward

Things move when something pushes or pulls them. These pushes and pulls are called forces. A force can make something start to move, speed up, slow down, change direction, or stop moving. Every force has another force that pushes in the opposite direction.

△ All these children are using forces to make things move.

◁ Three children cannot make the seesaw work. This is because the force pushing down on one end is bigger than the force pushing down on the other end. So, one child is getting off.

Word box
Forces can make things move. Pushes and pulls are forces.
Pendulum is any weight that hangs from a fixed point and swings freely.

△ Two children make the seesaw work. The forces pushing on each end are the same.

418

Can you find?

1 push	4 pull
2 pull	5 push
3 push	6 pull

Make a pendulum

Tie string around a spool of thread. Thumbtack the loose end of string to a block of wood. Fix block to the edge of a table with modeling clay. Push your pendulum so it swings.

Use a stopwatch to see how many swings it makes in 30 seconds. Try making the string longer and count the number of swings again. Are there more or less? The child in the picture can't make her pendulum work because the block is not at the edge of the table.

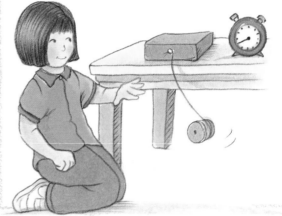

▷When the paddle is pulled back, the kayak is pushed forward.

419

Floating and sinking

An object floats on water because of balancing forces. As the weight of an object pulls it down, the water pushes it up. If an object is light for its size, the push of the water balances its weight and the object floats.

The shape of an object is also very important. It allows some heavy metal objects, such as ships, to float. This is because they push aside more water than they weigh themselves.

Find the answers

Do wooden spoons float?

What can we use to keep us afloat when swimming?

some objects float on top of the water's surface

some objects float almost completely under the water

some objects sink to the bottom

△ Some objects float on top of water, others sink to the bottom. Some float near the surface, just under the water.

Make a catamaran

A catamaran is a boat with two hulls. Ask an adult to cut a dishwashing liquid bottle in half for hulls. Use waterproof tape to attach thin strips of balsa wood across the hulls, to hold them together.

Float your catamaran in water. How many objects can you put into your catamaran before it sinks?

▽ Air-filled swimmies help you float. Air is lighter than water. Objects with lots of air trapped inside them float well.

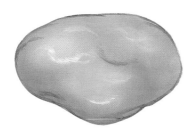

△ A lump of modeling clay sinks because it weighs more than the water pushing it up.

▽ The shape of a ship helps it float. This is because it has a lot of air inside it, so is light for its very large size. It pushes aside more water than it weighs itself.

△ If the clay is made into a boat, the water has a wider shape to push up. It floats because the clay is now lighter for its size.

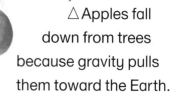

Gravity and weight

The Earth pulls everything toward its center, including us! This force is called gravity. It is the reason why things always fall down and not up. The Earth's gravity pulls on the Moon too, which keeps it circling around the Earth.

The weight of an object depends on gravity. We call the pull of the Earth's gravity on an object its weight.

△ Apples fall down from trees because gravity pulls them toward the Earth.

▷ You can throw a ball up into the air, but it will always fall back to the ground.

◁ When a scale measures your weight, it is measuring the pull of Earth's gravity on your body.

▷ In a spaceship far from the Earth, there is so little gravity that things just float around. Astronauts have to tie themselves down, if they do not want to float around.

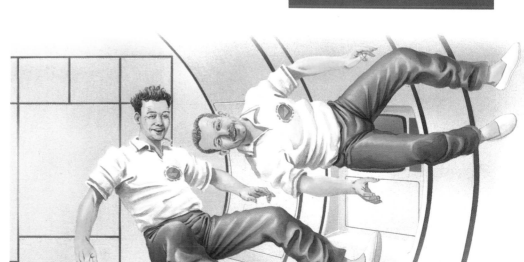

Pressure

When you press your fist into clay, you make a dent. But if you use your finger, you make a deep hole. This is because of the different amounts of pressure, or forces, pushing on each area of clay. The weight of your fist is spread over a larger area than your finger, so there is less pressure and a shallower print.

▽ Your shoes make deep footprints in the snow.

▷ Tires are full of air. The air's pressure keeps a truck moving along smoothly.

▽ Snowshoes make shallower footprints. Your weight is spread over a greater area, so there is less pressure.

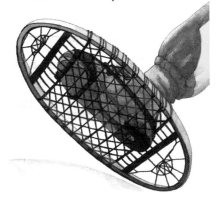

▽ You can see air pressure at work if you squeeze all the air out of a plastic tube.

△ If the lid is put on while the tube is still squeezed, the tube will stay squeezed.

▽ When the tube's lid is taken off again, air pressure forces air back into the tube.

423

Stick or slip

Have you ever slipped on a wet floor? If so, it was because there was so little friction. Friction is the force that stops two surfaces from sliding past each other easily. There is little friction between slippery surfaces, and more friction between rough surfaces. The more friction there is between two surfaces, the hotter they become.

△ It is easy to slip with wet feet. People use bath mats because they increase friction.

◁ Special grips increase friction. With more friction, tires and shoes are safer on slippery surfaces. Also, tennis rackets are less likely to slip out of a player's hand.

△ A smooth toboggan slides over slippery snow.

▷ We put oil in a car's engine to reduce the friction between its moving parts. This helps the parts move more easily and stops them getting too hot.

424

Have a friction race

Find objects that are made of different materials, but are about the same size. You could use an ice cube, a stone, a piece of sponge, and a block of wood.

Rest smooth cardboard against some books to make a slope. Hold the objects at the top of the slope. Let them go at the same time. The first to the bottom has less friction than the rest.

△ Squeaky doors need oil. The squeak is caused by friction in the metal hinges. Oil helps reduce friction and stop the squeak.

The Wizard of Oz
(A story by L. Frank Baum)

When Dorothy found the Tin Man, he was stuck. She had to ease the friction in his joints with oil before he could move.

△ You can feel the heat that friction makes when you rub your hands. Soapy hands have much less friction, so they do not warm up as much.

425

Moving through air

Moving through air slows things down. We call this air resistance. To make things move more quickly we make them a special shape. Many of them have smooth, rounded edges, which let air flow under, over, and around them easily. These shapes are called streamlined.

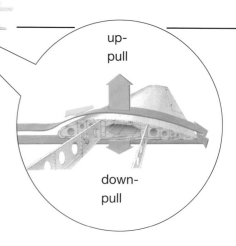

up-pull

down-pull

△ The streamlined wings of a plane help keep it in the air. The up-pull of the air flowing over the wing balances the down-pull of its weight.

◁ Planes have a streamlined shape. This helps them fly easily through the air.

◁ This cyclist's helmet, clothes, and bike have streamlined shapes that help her move more quickly.

△ The flying lemur does not actually fly. It has streamlined flaps of skin and a tail that help it glide through the air.

Machines for moving

Simple machines can make moving things easier. Machines such as rollers and wheels help reduce friction.

Levers are simple machines that help us lift heavy weights. A lever is a bar that swings on a fixed point, like a seesaw. Pushing one end of the lever down lifts a weight at the other end.

△ Stonehenge, England, was built 4,000 years ago. Its huge stones were probably pulled on rollers made of tree trunks.

▷These clowns are using a lever. A clown jumping on one end provides the force to push the other clown up into the air.

△A wheelbarrow is a simple machine that uses a lever and a wheel to move things. Have you ever used a wheelbarrow to make moving things easier?

427

Light and color

Sunlight is a kind of energy that comes from the Sun. It travels through space as light waves. Sunlight seems to be colorless or white. But really it is made up of several colors mixed together.

▽ You can see the colors of sunlight in a rainbow. Light passing through raindrops is split up into red, orange, yellow, green, blue, indigo, and violet.

▽ Things are different colors. This is because they soak up some of the colors from light and let the others bounce off them.

△ Transparent materials, such as glass, let nearly all light through.

△ Translucent materials, such as plastic, let some light through.

△ Opaque materials, such as wrapping paper, do not let any light through.

◁ A tomato soaks up all colors except red, which bounces back off it into our eyes. So we see a red tomato.

Make a rainbow

You can split up light into different colors. On a sunny day, fill a tub with water and put it by a window. Rest a flat mirror against one side of the tub. Angle the mirror to catch the sunlight until a rainbow appears on the ceiling. You can use modeling clay to hold the mirror in place once you have made the rainbow.

△ Sunlight travels through space very quickly. Nothing travels faster than light.

△ At night there is only starlight and moonlight. Long ago, people used fire for light.

△ Later, people used wax candles and oil lamps. Now we mainly use electricity.

Rain's son, the Rainbow
(An Australian folk tale)

Rainbow was Rain's son. He only came out to stop his father from falling from the sky. People had to chase Rainbow away to allow Rain to fall, otherwise there would be a drought.

Word box
Transparent materials let most light pass through.
Translucent materials only let some light through.
Opaque materials do not let any light through.

429

Shadows

Light waves travel in straight lines. They cannot bend around things. If something gets in the way of a light wave, it blocks the light and casts a shadow. The Earth spins as it goes around the Sun. This makes outdoor shadows point in different directions and change length at different times of the day.

Find the answers

When is your shadow longest?

When is the Sun high in the sky?

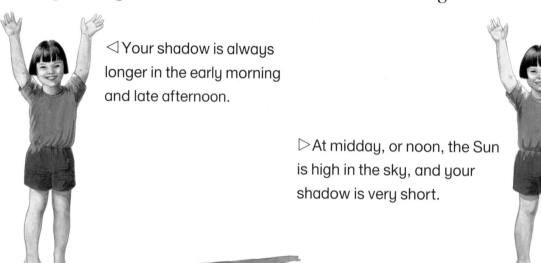

◁ Your shadow is always longer in the early morning and late afternoon.

▷ At midday, or noon, the Sun is high in the sky, and your shadow is very short.

dog   rabbit

giraffe   bird

Make shadow shapes
In a darkened room, ask a friend to shine a flashlight onto a wall beside you. Make sure your hands are in between the light rays and the wall. By holding your hands as shown here, you can cast different animal-shaped shadows.

430

Reflections

When light hits any smooth, shiny surface, it bounces back, making a reflection. When you look into a mirror, light bounces off your body, then off the mirror back at you, so you can see your reflection.

The light from the Sun bounces off the Moon, giving us moonlight.

▷ Lots of shiny surfaces reflect light. This boy can see his reflection in an empty saucepan. Can you see yourself in any objects at home?

△ Mirrors are made of a sheet of glass in front of a thin piece of shiny metal.

△ Moonlight is sunlight reflected from the Moon. It can be reflected again in the shiny surface of water.

The Rain Puddle
(A story by Adelaide Holl)

The barnyard animals see their own reflections in a rain puddle and think there are other animals drowning in it. When the Sun comes out and dries up the puddle, they foolishly think the reflected animals have been saved.

Refraction and lenses

If you put a straw in a glass of water, it seems to bend. This is called refraction. Refraction is caused by light traveling at different speeds. Light moves faster through air than it does through water. When it changes speed it can change direction too.

Lenses use refraction. They are specially shaped to bend light and make things seem smaller and farther away, or bigger and closer.

△ Refraction can make things look bigger. A goldfish in a round, glass bowl seems to grow as it swims toward you.

▽ The lens in a telescope can help you to see distant stars.

zoom lens

△ You can photograph things that are far away and make them look nearer with the zoom lens of a camera.

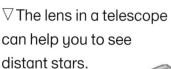

△ The lenses in a pair of binoculars help you to see things that are far away.

△ If you put a straw in a glass, it seems to change shape and size because of refraction.

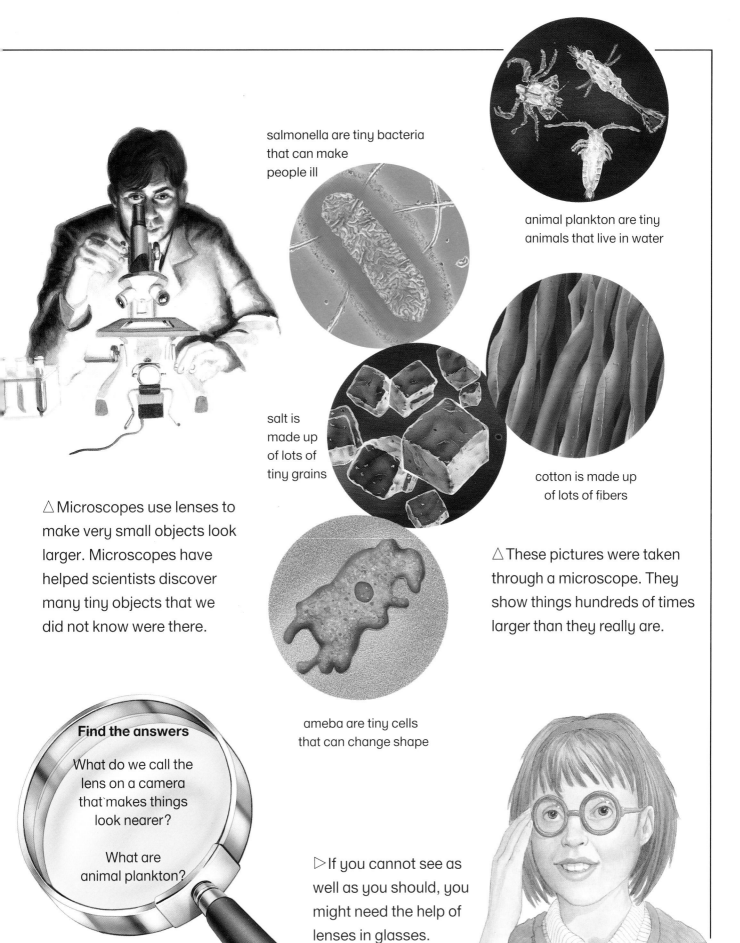

salmonella are tiny bacteria that can make people ill

animal plankton are tiny animals that live in water

salt is made up of lots of tiny grains

cotton is made up of lots of fibers

△ Microscopes use lenses to make very small objects look larger. Microscopes have helped scientists discover many tiny objects that we did not know were there.

△ These pictures were taken through a microscope. They show things hundreds of times larger than they really are.

ameba are tiny cells that can change shape

Find the answers

What do we call the lens on a camera that makes things look nearer?

What are animal plankton?

▷ If you cannot see as well as you should, you might need the help of lenses in glasses.

Sound

Every noise you hear is made by something vibrating, or moving backward and forward very quickly.

Sound travels in waves. Sound waves need to have something to move through. They can travel through solids, liquids, or gases.

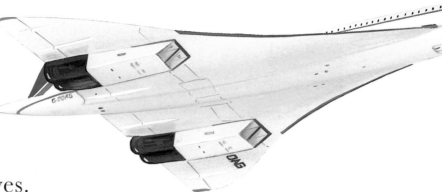

△ Sound travels through the air at about 760 miles an hour. Concorde is supersonic: it can travel faster than sound.

▽ When someone speaks to you, vibrations pass through their mouth into the air, making the air vibrate. The vibrations travel to your ear in sound waves and you hear them as sound.

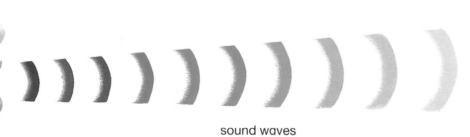

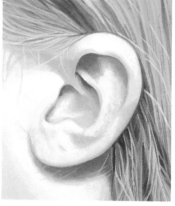

sound waves

Seeing sounds

You cannot see sound waves, but you can see their effects. Make a drum by stretching foil tightly over a bowl. Attach with a rubber band. Put some grains of uncooked rice on the drum. Then bang on the lid of a tin. The sound waves will make the rice bounce.

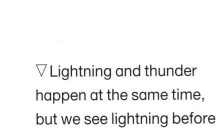

▽ Lightning and thunder happen at the same time, but we see lightning before we hear thunder. This is because sound travels more slowly than light.

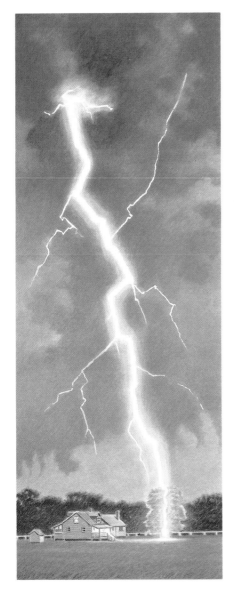

△ Sound travels faster and farther through water than air. Whales sing to each other. They can hear each other's songs from up to 60 miles away.

△ You can hear sound that has traveled through a solid by putting your ear to a table and asking a friend to bang a saucepan at the other end.

Word box
Vibrations are fast, regular, backward and forward movements in solids, liquids, and gases.
Sound waves are produced by vibrations. They carry sounds at different speeds through solids, liquids, and gases.

435

High and low

Some sounds are higher than others. The more vibrations there are in a second, the higher the sound. So there are fewer vibrations in low sounds than high sounds.

Humans hear sounds between 20 and 20,000 vibrations a second, but some animals can hear higher sounds.

△ This man is playing a double bass, which makes a low sound. The boy is making a high sound with his tin whistle.

▽ The numbers below tell you how many vibrations each of these animals can hear in a second.

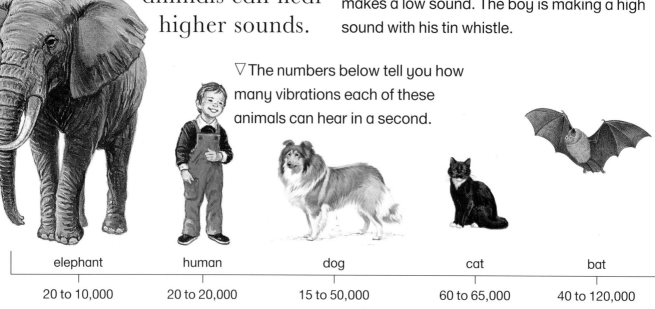

elephant	human	dog	cat	bat
20 to 10,000	20 to 20,000	15 to 50,000	60 to 65,000	40 to 120,000

▷ Female opera singers usually have higher voices than male opera singers. The higher the voice, the higher the number of vibrations in a second.

How loud?

The loudness of a sound depends on the size of the sound waves. Big sound waves are louder than smaller ones.

Loudness is measured in decibels. A sound that can only just be heard measures one decibel. We whisper at about 20 decibels. Blue whales can sing at 188 decibels, which is louder than any other animal.

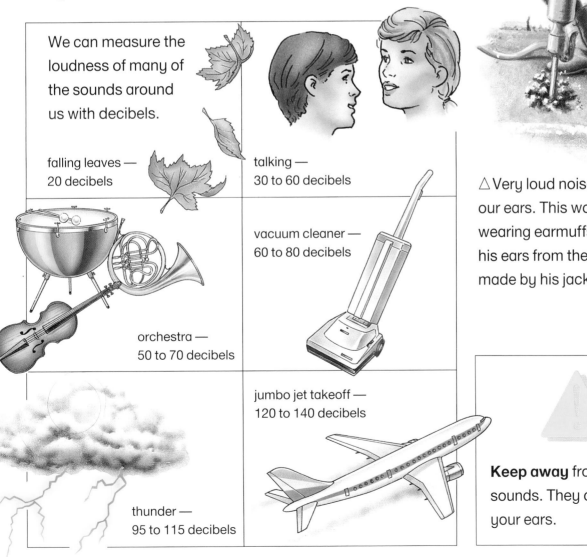

We can measure the loudness of many of the sounds around us with decibels.

falling leaves — 20 decibels

talking — 30 to 60 decibels

vacuum cleaner — 60 to 80 decibels

orchestra — 50 to 70 decibels

jumbo jet takeoff — 120 to 140 decibels

thunder — 95 to 115 decibels

△ Very loud noises can harm our ears. This worker is wearing earmuffs to protect his ears from the loud sound made by his jackhammer.

Keep away from very loud sounds. They can damage your ears.

Echoes

An echo is the sound you hear when sound waves reflect back from a wall or another hard object.

It takes the sound waves a certain amount of time to hit the walls and bounce back again. By measuring this time, we can find out how far away something is. This is how submarines find things on the seabed.

sound waves

△ The sound waves made by this girl's voice have bounced off the mountain wall, so she can hear her echo.

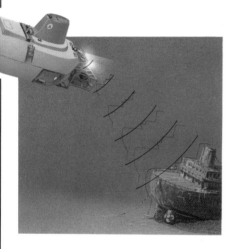

△ This minisub sends out sound waves, measures the echoes' time, and records where the shipwreck is below.

Echo's fate
(A Roman myth)

Echo was one of the great goddess Juno's maids. She got into trouble for talking too much and almost lost her voice. Later, she fell in love with Narcissus but he did not return her love. Broken-hearted, she changed into a stone and was only able to repeat words that others said first, just like an echo.

◁ If you shout into an empty bucket, your voice bounces off the sides, loudly.

▷ Swiftlets call out and use echoes to find their way in dark caves.

Making music

One of the most wonderful things about sound is music. Different people think of different things as music. Some people hear music in a babbling brook or the wind rustling through leaves. Others prefer music made by musical instruments. It is easy to make simple instruments and form a band.

△ This boy has made a shaker by putting dried peas into two plastic pots. It rattles when he shakes it up and down.

◁ Stretching thick rubber bands over a can and plucking them makes low sounds. Thinner rubber bands make higher sounds.

▽ Blowing down different lengths of drinking straws, stuck onto cardboard, makes the sound of Pan pipes.

△ A scraper can easily be made from an empty, ridged plastic bottle and a pencil.

▽ A piece of thin paper wrapped around a comb sounds like a harmonica when it is blown hard.

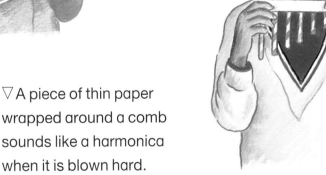
▷ These children are playing a tune using their homemade musical instruments.

439

Everyday science

Your bike is full of science! It uses many of the scientific ideas already explained. Look at the bike below and the science that each different part uses.

△ The frame is made of strong metal. Its shape is made of triangles, which make the structure strong.

▷ The cyclist uses her energy to push the pedals, which move the bike forward.

the helmet is streamlined so air does not hold the cyclist back

the bell rings to make a warning sound

◁ The bicycle light is powered by a battery.

the light helps the cyclist to see and be seen in the dark

▷ Air is pumped into the tires to keep up the pressure.

▽ Oil is used to reduce friction, so the bike's parts run smoothly.

tire

brake pad

△ The brakes use friction to slow down the wheels.

People and Places

Where do people live?

The world we live in is made up of many different environments, or surroundings. These include deserts, grasslands, woodlands, rain forests, and mountains. Some of these areas are shown on the map. People can live in almost every area.

Since early times, people have built homes with natural materials that grew or were found close by. Today, many homes are built with materials made in factories.

▽ Inuit people in North America once used igloos as homes. Igloos were built of blocks of snow.

Key to map

hot desert		evergreen forest	
grassland		deciduous wood	
cold desert		rain forest	
		mountains	

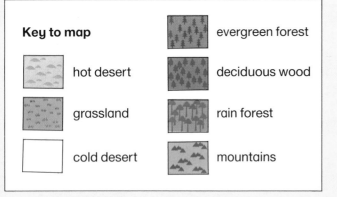

△ People live in reed houses on Lake Titicaca in South America. They are built on a floor of flattened reeds.

Word box
Environments are our surroundings. They affect the way we live.
Manufactured materials are made in a factory.

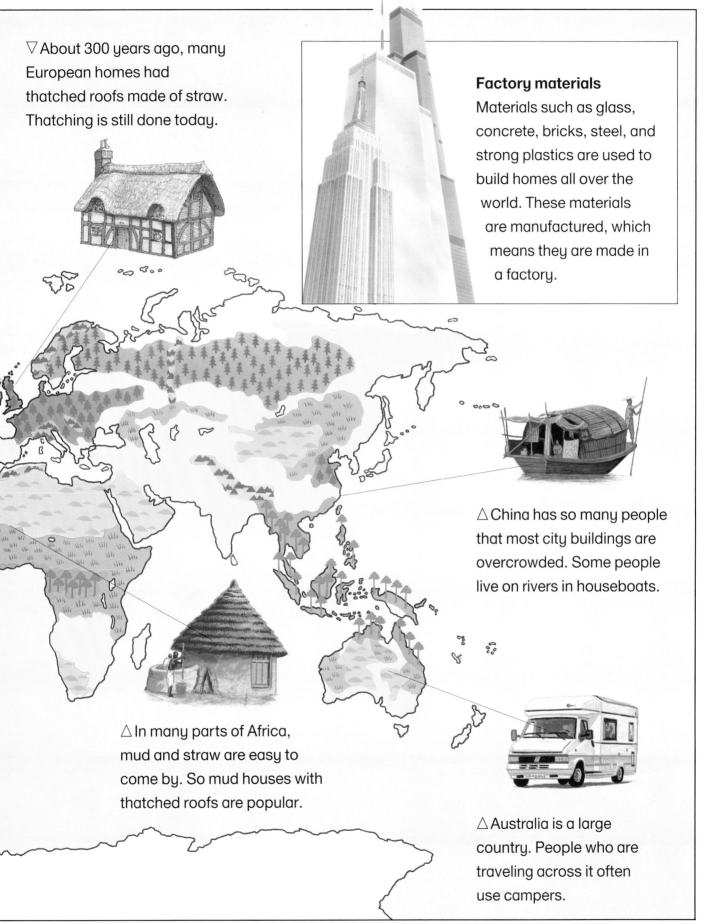

▽ About 300 years ago, many European homes had thatched roofs made of straw. Thatching is still done today.

Factory materials
Materials such as glass, concrete, bricks, steel, and strong plastics are used to build homes all over the world. These materials are manufactured, which means they are made in a factory.

△ China has so many people that most city buildings are overcrowded. Some people live on rivers in houseboats.

△ In many parts of Africa, mud and straw are easy to come by. So mud houses with thatched roofs are popular.

△ Australia is a large country. People who are traveling across it often use campers.

Languages

Language is made up of spoken and written words. Without words it would be difficult for us to tell others what we mean. We would have to act out what we were trying to say, which would take a long time. It is hard to understand people from other countries, because they use different words to say the same thing.

Whispering game
One player whispers to a neighbor. They repeat what was said to the person next to them, and so on. The last person says it out loud. Usually, the words have changed.

▷ Throughout the world, hands are used in different ways as a greeting, and as a sign of welcome and respect.

▽ The children below are all saying good morning. The different languages are written above them. How many do you know?

你好嗎

আস্সালামু

günaydın

안녕

Buenos días

おはよう

שָׁלוֹם בֹּקֶר טוֹב

здрáвствуй

GOOD MORNING

السلام عَلَيْكُم

jamm nga fёnaan

नमस्कार

καλημέρα

မင်္ဂလာနံနက်ခင်း။

BONJOUR!

Religious beliefs

Many things have happened in the world that we do not understand. Religious beliefs are one way of helping to explain them. Most religions have a god or gods and laws to tell people how to behave. Some people's special religious buildings are shown here.

△ There are many gods in the Hindu religion. One god, Shiva, is carved on the walls of this Hindu temple.

△ Buddhists follow the sayings of the Buddha. They worship in a temple.

△ In Jerusalem, the Western Wall is visited by Jews, who believe in one god only.

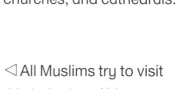

△ Christians worship one god and Jesus Christ in chapels, churches, and cathedrals.

◁ All Muslims try to visit this holy city of Mecca. The Muslim name for god is Allah.

△ Shinto symbols are important to Japanese people, who worship gods of nature.

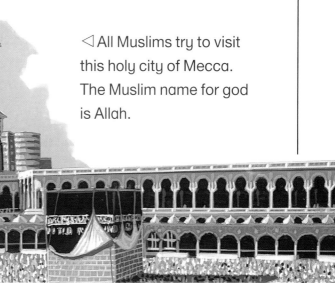

Food from far and wide

All kinds of delicious foods are grown throughout the world. Different types of weather, called climate, help to decide how people live and what sort of food they grow.

Once, certain foods were eaten only by the people who grew them. Today, food can be transported to markets all over the world.

Make a fruit salad
Buy some brightly colored fruits and wash them. Ask an adult to cut them into cubes and slices. Place in a bowl and mix together. Add a little fresh fruit juice.

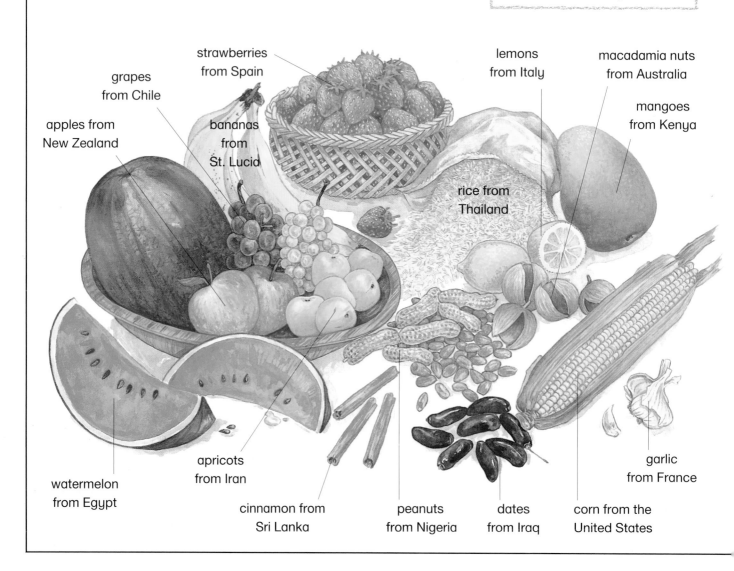

strawberries from Spain

grapes from Chile

lemons from Italy

macadamia nuts from Australia

apples from New Zealand

bananas from St. Lucia

mangoes from Kenya

rice from Thailand

watermelon from Egypt

apricots from Iran

cinnamon from Sri Lanka

peanuts from Nigeria

dates from Iraq

corn from the United States

garlic from France

446

Sports and games

People all over the world play sports and games all through the year. Some are played alone, while others are played with a partner or in teams. Soccer and basketball are sports that are played between teams from many countries, to decide which country's team is the winner. Which sports and games do you enjoy playing?

△ Ice hockey is a fast and tough game.

△ Volleyball is played on beaches worldwide.

▽ Every four years, sportsmen and women from different countries meet to compete against each other at the Olympic Games. The winners are given medals.

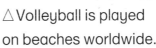

△ In Katanga, Zaire, children play a game like marbles, using fruits.

▷ Children and adults all over the world enjoy kicking a ball and playing soccer.

Traditions

A tradition is something that is done in the same way, year after year. It may be a celebration, a storytelling, or a way of making something. Different places and groups of people have their own traditional festivals, stories, and crafts.

In the following pages, we will be looking at five large areas of the world: the Americas, Europe, Africa, Asia, Australasia, and the Pacific Islands. Each is made up of many countries that all have their own traditions.

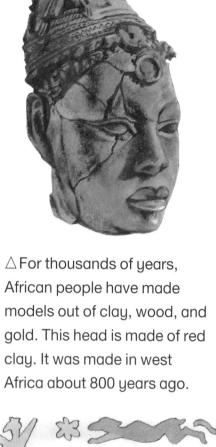

△ For thousands of years, African people have made models out of clay, wood, and gold. This head is made of red clay. It was made in west Africa about 800 years ago.

◁ Every year, people in Belgium, in Europe, dress as giants for a parade around the town streets. Each costume has a peephole, so the person inside can see where they are going. Can you see the people's faces in this picture?

Snowmaiden
(A Russian folk tale)

Once upon a time, a couple who longed to have a child carved a young girl out of snow. When she magically came alive they were delighted and called her Snowmaiden.

▷These traditional rod puppets are from Java, in Asia. They are made of wood and used to tell stories. A puppeteer works them by moving the long sticks attached to their bodies.

△ The Aborigine people in Australia tell their children wonderful stories as they paint Dreamtime pictures. The children learn to paint the pictures and remember the stories so they can tell them to their own children one day. This way, the stories will never be forgotten.

▷For hundreds of years, people have ridden horses to round up cattle. Today, cowgirls and cowboys show off their riding skills to crowds of people at shows called rodeos. They are popular in both the United States and Canada.

The Americas

For hundreds of years, the Americas have drawn people from all over the world. Amazing landscapes and different climates still attract millions of visitors each year. Some decide to stay after their vacation. All of these peoples add to the richness and colorful style of American life.

△ The area called the Americas is shown in red.

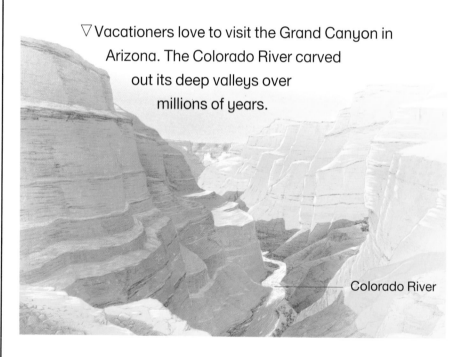

▽ Vacationers love to visit the Grand Canyon in Arizona. The Colorado River carved out its deep valleys over millions of years.

Colorado River

△ Many people go to see the famous Statue of Liberty, in New York City.

▷ Fruit and vegetables are sold in this busy market, high in the Andes Mountains.

△ The Horseshoe Falls in Canada are part of the group of waterfalls called Niagara Falls. Some of the falls are in Canada, the rest are in the United States.

▽ Sugarloaf Mountain rises above the bay in Rio de Janeiro, Brazil. The city is a lively place to live, surrounded by magnificent views.

△ Alaska is the northernmost state of the United States. Much of the land is frozen with massive rivers of ice, called glaciers.

Word box
Glaciers are huge rivers of ice that move very slowly down valleys. They follow the easiest way to the sea.
Canyons are deep, steep-sided valleys. They are usually in dry areas where the sides do not get worn away by the beating rain.

The frozen north

The Inuit people came from Asia to Canada thousands of years ago. The early Inuits used dogsleds to get around and made homes from snow or animal skins. There was no soil for growing food, so they hunted caribou and seals for food and clothing. Today, some Inuits hunt, but most work in offices and factories.

How Ishdaka found Summer
(An Inuit folk tale)

There was once a time when a giant called Winter ruled Ishdaka's northern land, keeping it frozen all year round. Ishdaka traveled south to ask Summer for her help. She agreed, and together they tricked Winter and were able to melt all the ice and snow. Thereafter, the giant only ruled for part of the year, so that Summer had a chance to visit and bring warmth to Ishdaka's people.

△ Rubbing noses is an Inuit sign of affection, like a kiss.

◁ This Inuit fisherman is spearing fish through an ice hole.

▷Today, most Inuits live in wooden houses and drive snowmobiles and cars. Planes bring supplies and medicines.

snowmobile

Native Americans

Native Americans were the first people to live in North America. They spoke many languages and hunted, fished, and farmed. When Europeans arrived, Native Americans were forced to live in areas known as reservations.

△ The Pueblo people are Native Americans. Some still perform traditional dances to make the rains come and bring them a good harvest.

▷ The medicine man used magic to help heal sick people. He drew magic signs in the sand and chanted.

▽ White settlers from Europe first arrived more than 350 years ago. At first, they were friends with the Native Americans, but later fought many wars against them.

Find the answers

Who were the first people to live in North America?

What did the medicine man use to help heal people?

Forestry

British Columbia in Canada is one of the world's largest timber producers. Timber is wood from trees. It is needed to make building materials, furniture, and paper.

These Pacific forests are looked after carefully, so that new tree seedlings are always growing to replace the trees that are cut down.

△ Trees are cut down by forest workers called lumberjacks. They use power saws.

△ Huge trucks take the trees away to sawmills. Then the bark is removed from the trees and they are sawed into planks.

◁ Trunks of sugar maples are drilled to collect a watery sap. When this is boiled it turns into the sweet, sticky liquid known as maple syrup.

▷ Maple syrup is delicious on waffles and pancakes.

Find the answers

What is made from timber?

Where is British Columbia?

Cattle ranches

There are many large cattle ranches in the western United States and Canada. There, cattle graze on the open range. Many are also fed on special food to make them grow bigger. Lassos are used to round up the cattle.

◁ The South American cowboy is called a gaucho. He wears a broad hat, baggy pants, a decorated belt, and spurs on his boots.

spurs

Make a gaucho hat

Cut a circle of cardboard with a hole the size of your head. Cut a strip 2 inches wide, for a headband. Cut edges of band, as shown. Tape ends to fit your head. Fold bottom edges and glue over hole. Cut a circle the size of your headband and glue on top.

▽ Cattle in North America have been rounded up on horseback since the early days of the Wild West.

lasso

◁ On some large ranches, trucks and helicopters are used to find lost cattle.

West Indies

The West Indies is made up of thousands of islands in the Caribbean Sea. Cuba is the largest of these islands.

Bananas, coconuts, coffee, cotton, tobacco, and sugarcane grow well in the warm weather on these islands.

It is sunny all year round, so people can work and relax outside.

▽ Puerto Rico is an island in the West Indies. Puerto Rican fishermen go out to sea in small boats. They often have to repair nets that have torn on rocks below the sea.

Make Caribbean bananas

Peel some bananas. Ask an adult to cut them into two. For each, mix two tablespoons of orange juice with a teaspoon of lemon juice and two teaspoons of brown sugar. Pour on top. Sprinkle a tablespoon of coconut over each. Ask an adult to broil them for five minutes.

Find the answers

Which is the largest island in the West Indies?

What grows well in the West Indies?

Amazon Indians

Amazon Indians live in the South American rain forests. They look after the forest because it gives them all the food, medicine, and building materials they need.

Other people are not looking after the land. They are cutting down many of the trees to sell as timber or to make space for new farms.

How the birds got their colors
(A South American folk tale)

Once all birds were white, until a wicked rainbow snake was killed. The cormorant who had killed the snake was supposed to have its skin as a prize, but he was told it was only his if he could carry it. All the birds helped, and were given the piece of skin they had carried. Their feathers changed to similar colors, and are the same today.

▽ Many Amazon Indians sleep in hammocks and cook food outside.

△ These men are fishing with a bow and arrow. They must have sharp eyes and move quickly to catch fish this way.

◁ The forest people live in clearings. They get all their food from the forest and rivers. Hunters often go away for many days at a time.

Mexico

More people live in Mexico City, Mexico's busy capital, than in any other city in the world. Other Mexican towns are quieter, especially during the hottest part of the day, when most people rest.

Many visitors travel to Mexico to see the amazing temples that were built by the Aztecs.

△ The Aztecs lived in Mexico hundreds of years ago. They built great cities, which probably looked like this. The ruins of these temples are visited by people today.

▽ It is noon, the hottest part of the day, in this small Mexican town. Some people have gone inside to rest, away from the sun. Others go about their daily business.

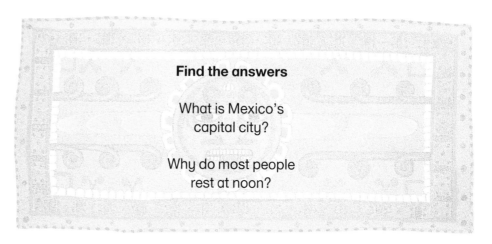

Find the answers

What is Mexico's capital city?

Why do most people rest at noon?

Traditions

Carnival, Thanksgiving, and the Canadian Winter Festival are just a few of the many traditions that take place in the Americas today. They are happy times, when people celebrate with their friends, family, and neighbors.

△ Each year, a giant ice palace is built for the Winter Festival in Quebec, Canada.

△ Carnival is a famous and colorful street festival. It takes place in Rio de Janeiro, Brazil, every year. People parade and dance in bright costumes.

▷ The first Thanksgiving was a feast to give thanks for a good harvest. Native Americans who had helped the settlers were also invited.

Europe

Europe is made up of many countries. The northernmost areas in the Arctic are cold and snowy all year round. In the south, by the Mediterranean Sea, it can be very hot and dry.

People from northern Europe, such as Scandinavia, are often fair-skinned with light hair. People from southern Europe, such as Italy, are usually darker.

△ Europe's many countries make up the red shape shown on this map.

◁ People from all over the world visit the Mediterranean countries to lie in the sun on sandy beaches and swim in the warm, blue sea.

▽ Iceland has many geysers. They blast jets of hot water into the air.

△ Some Sami, or Lapp people, keep reindeer. They take them farther south in the spring. On the way, they live in tents called lavos.

▷St. Basil's Cathedral in Moscow, Russia, is famous for its many brightly colored, onion-shaped domes. Russia is such a large country that it stretches across both Europe and Asia. Moscow is in Europe.

▽ Prague, the capital of the Czech Republic, is full of many old and beautiful buildings. It is called the city of 100 spires because it has so many churches.

▷The Netherlands has thousands of fields filled with brightly colored tulips that are sold abroad.

△ Edinburgh Castle in Scotland stands high above the city on a volcanic rock.

Word box
Geysers are hot springs that throw up jets of hot water. In volcanic areas, hot water underground turns to steam and pushes out into the air.
Mediterranean areas include all the lands surrounding the Mediterranean Sea.

461

Farming

Some European farmers keep animals, others grow crops, and many do both.

Machines can be used to plant and harvest crops on flatter land. Farming hilly ground is more difficult. These areas are often used to graze sheep and goats.

Make a sheep picture
Draw a sheep using this shape as a guide. Color in its face and legs. Glue cotton balls onto its back. Glue used matchsticks to make a sheep pen, as shown.

▽ A lot of wheat is grown in Europe. Tractors and combine harvesters gather in the crop toward the end of summer.

△ On a small farm, everyone helps look after the animals. The chickens are given grain to eat and their eggs are collected each day.

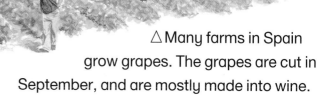

△ Many farms in Spain grow grapes. The grapes are cut in September, and are mostly made into wine.

462

Fishing

The fishing industry in Europe is huge. Thousands of tons of fish are sent to the fish markets every day.

Shellfish, such as lobsters and crabs, are trapped in baskets. Other fish are caught by floating nets.

Find the answers

What are large fishing boats called?

How are shellfish caught?

▽ Fishing is often a family business. These two Greek brothers fish every day. Sometimes they let vacationers rent their boat.

△ These fishermen are from Brittany, in France. They go out to sea for several days in large boats. They sell the fish they catch in a fish market in their home port.

▷ Large fishing boats are called trawlers. The fishermen on this Russian trawler will freeze the fish on board to keep it fresh until they return.

Mountains

Europe has many beautiful mountains. In Norway, inlets of sea, called fjords, cut into mountainous coastlines. The world-famous Alps stretch through many countries. Thousands of people climb and ski on them every year.

Dogs to the rescue!
The St. Bernard dog is named after the St. Bernard monastery in the Swiss Alps. Many years ago, the monks in this monastery reared and trained these dogs to rescue people trapped on the mountains in blizzards.

▷The countries of Scandinavia have warm summers. People on vacation sometimes swim in low mountain lakes. They also take special baths, called saunas, inside wooden cabins.

◁These people have come to a ski resort for a vacation. Those who are used to skiing will climb the mountain in a chair lift and ski down. Beginners will ski on gentle slopes, or practice on flatter areas in the resort's village. Others prefer to sled or toboggan.

Traditions

As Europe is made up of so many countries, there are hundreds of different festivals and celebrations.

Certain festivals, such as New Year, are celebrated by groups of people everywhere. Some traditions belong to one area or country only.

△ In Switzerland, there is an opening parade every fall for the onion festival.

△ Russian dancing is famous throughout the world. The dancers have to be very fit and strong. They kick their legs out while squatting, leap high in the air, and touch their toes.

△ In Italy, more than 300 years ago, a puppet called Pulcinella became so well loved, the show spread to France. From there it went to England, where Pulcinella became Mr. Punch.

465

Africa

Africa is an area of many landscapes and climates. It includes tropical rain forests and the world's largest and hottest desert, the Sahara.

Three-fourths of all Africans live in the countryside, earning their living by farming. More and more people are moving to the cities to work in shops, offices, and factories.

△Africa is shown in red. It is made up of many countries.

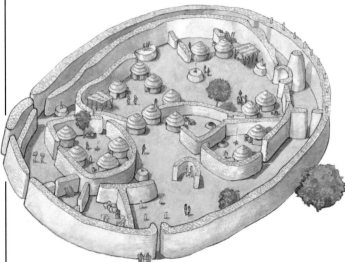

◁About 900 years ago, the Shona people built the city of Great Zimbabwe in southern Africa. Its ruins are still there today.

Word box
Safaris are journeys into the wild to see and photograph wild animals in their natural surroundings.
Pyramids were built in Egypt thousands of years ago as places to bury important people when they died.

▷In Morocco, north Africa, the old part of some towns have walls around them. Souks, or town markets, are within these walls.

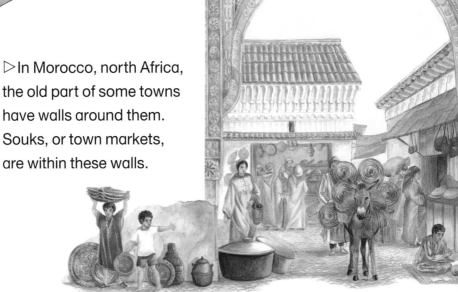

466

◁ In ancient Egypt, pharaohs, or kings, were buried in pyramid tombs with their treasure.

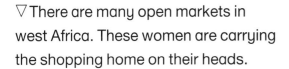

▽ There are many open markets in west Africa. These women are carrying the shopping home on their heads.

△ Some African towns are on rivers, so boats can be used to carry people and goods.

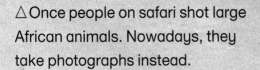

△ Once people on safari shot large African animals. Nowadays, they take photographs instead.

Village and nomadic life

In the towns, many people live in modern houses built from manufactured materials. In the villages, houses are often made of sun-dried mud with roofs of straw or leaves.

Tuareg and Masai people do not live in towns or villages. They live a nomadic life, which means they travel from place to place.

△ This Tuareg man is lowering a bucket on a rope to scoop water from a well below the desert sand.

▽ The Tuareg people wander the Sahara Desert with their camels and goats. Their homes are tents carried on the camels' backs.

△ Camels are used to carry goods across the desert. They can travel for days without a drink.

Snake magic
(A folk tale from east Africa)

A poor, hungry woman and her son helped a snake. They were rewarded with a magic ring and a casket that always gave them a home, riches, and delicious food.

△ In many African villages, women prepare meals together outside their homes. They pound millet or cassava into flour.

△ Bridges made from branches and vines cross some rivers. They look wobbly, but local people use them easily.

▷ The greatest day in a young Masai warrior's life is when he becomes a junior elder. Young women dress up in colorful beaded collars for the warrior's procession.

◁ Masai women build a holy house, called an osinkira, for the young warrior's ceremony. An altar inside it is made from three wooden stakes cut from sacred trees. The house is always burned afterward.

Farming

In some parts of Africa modern machinery is used to farm the land, but most farmers use simple tools. In eastern and southern grassland areas, peanuts, corn, and millet are grown. In warm, wet areas, bananas, rice, and yams grow well. Coffee, cocoa beans, coconuts, and cotton are grown mainly to sell abroad.

△ Ostriches are very strong and can be ridden like horses. They can give a nasty kick if they are in a bad mood!

△ Ostriches are kept in South Africa for their eggs, feathers, and meat. The females have special shelters where they lay their eggs.

▽ In Zaire, central Africa, the farmers grow tea bushes on hillsides. The leaves are picked by hand. They are dried before being packed.

▽ Coffee plants produce fruits called berries. Each berry has two beans. Some of these are roasted and ground to make coffee powder.

Find the answers

Why are ostriches kept in South Africa?

In which part of Africa are peanuts grown?

▽ Some farmers are lucky enough to have land near Africa's longest river, the river Nile. Waterwheel pumps, worked by animals, keep the Nile's water flowing along ditches to water crops.

Make an ostrich
Draw an ostrich on stiff paper, using this shape as a guide. Color it in. Glue on a bead for its eye.

Cut out feather shapes from black and white paper. Cut edges as shown. Glue the feathers onto your ostrich's body.

Life on the water

Some people in Africa live in villages by the sea and rivers. There are few streets, but people move around easily in small boats.

The houses are built on high stilts, so that when the river rises during the rainy season, the houses are kept dry. Children here are more used to water than dry land!

Make a stilt house
Cut and fold the ends of four tubes, as shown. Tape to the bottom of a cardboard box. Fold a piece of cardboard in half. Tape over box to make roof. Paint doors and windows. Glue straws onto the roof.

▷ This is a fishing village in Benin, west Africa. Local people can buy vegetables and fruit from boats that visit their homes.

The pumpkin boat
(A folk tale from Madagascar)

One day a pumpkin fell into the river. A group of small animals thought it would make a wonderful boat to sail down river. But Rat became hungry and secretly began to nibble the bottom. When water flooded in, the boat tipped over and all the animals had to swim for the shore. They were all very angry with Rat!

Traditions

Many of the African countries are famous for their traditional crafts. Beautiful masks and colorful fabrics have been made in the same way for thousands of years.

There are also exciting festivals and celebrations all over Africa.

△ This colorful cloth is from Ghana in west Africa. It is woven from dyed cotton. Traditional clothes in Africa often have bright colors and bold patterns.

◁ African people have made masks out of materials such as clay, wood, bronze, and gold for thousands of years. This mask was made in central Africa. It was used for special ceremonies.

◁ Every year, men from Argungu in Nigeria hold a fishing festival. They fish for giant perches, using dried gourds, or calabashes, as floats.

473

Asia

Asia covers a vast area. Its lands vary from freezing Siberia in the north to warm, tropical India and Thailand in the southeast.

More than half of the people in the world live in Asia. Many of them live in busy cities. Very few people live in the dry desert and rocky mountain areas.

△ Asia's enormous land area is shown in red.

▷ Many people living in the Middle East are Muslim. They worship in mosques, like this one in Dubai. It looks spectacular when it is lit up at night.

▽ These Hindus are bathing in the holy waters of the river Ganges in Varanasi, northern India.

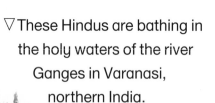

△ Over half of Thailand is covered in teak forest. Teak is a very important timber tree. Elephants move the teak logs to the river, where they are floated down to the sawmills in the capital city, Bangkok.

◁ There are many bazaars, or markets, in Afghanistan. People from the hills and mountains come to sell their goods.

△ China's city streets are busy. Bicycles are often the quickest way to travel around.

△ The Himalayas are the highest mountain range in the world. Many people try to climb them every year.

◁ The Great Wall of China was built over 1,000 years ago to protect China. It is the longest wall in the world.

Word box
Teak timber comes from forests in Southeast Asia. It polishes well, so is used to make furniture.
Bazaars are eastern markets where goods are sold or traded.

Different ways of life

Most Asian people live and work in villages, towns, or cities, but some people choose to lead a different way of life. This may be because they have special beliefs, such as the Buddhist monks. Other people, such as some Mongolian and Tibetan families travel around to work. A few of the unusual ways of life in Asia are shown on this page.

△ These people are from Mongolia. They wander the grassy plains with their animals. Their homes are felt tents called yurts.

◁ On the slopes of the Himalayan mountains, Buddhist monks live in monasteries. They have chosen to live apart from other people so they can pray and study in peace.

▷In Israel there are farms called kibbutzim. Everyone works together to grow food for the people of the kibbutz and to sell at markets. Here, workers are picking oranges.

◁This is a whole village under one roof. The Iban people of Sarawak, Malaysia, often live in a longhouse like this. Inside, as many as 70 families have separate rooms, off a long corridor.

◁In Chang Tang, Tibet, some families live in tents made of yak skin. They sell salt to China. These bags have been filled from a salt pan and are ready for the long trek back to camp.

477

Industry

People who manufacture, or make, similar products are said to work in the same industry. There are a huge number of industries in Asia. Some Asian industries make very complicated electrical goods. Others are simple industries, such as farming rice, cotton, and tea.

△ Rice grows best in flooded fields, so all of the work has to be done by hand or with the help of animals.

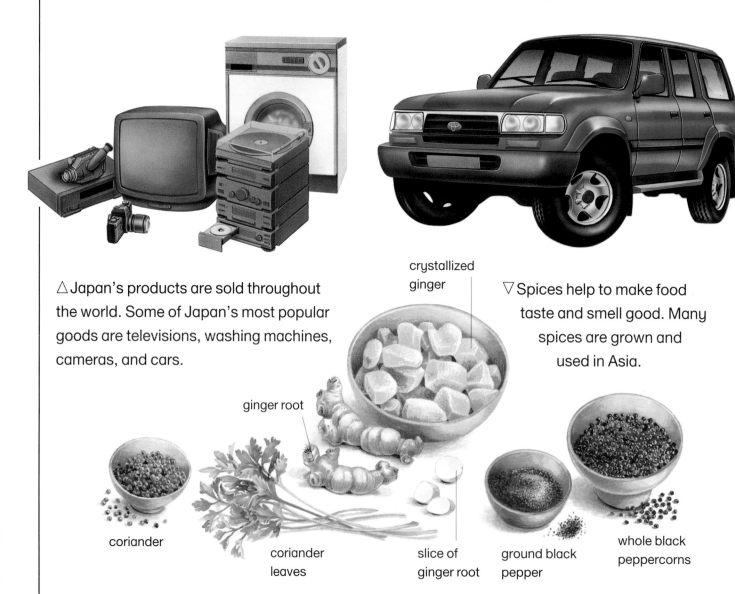

△ Japan's products are sold throughout the world. Some of Japan's most popular goods are televisions, washing machines, cameras, and cars.

crystallized ginger

▽ Spices help to make food taste and smell good. Many spices are grown and used in Asia.

ginger root

coriander

coriander leaves

slice of ginger root

ground black pepper

whole black peppercorns

△ Oil is one of Asia's biggest industries.
Over half the world's oil is found in Asia, with
a quarter of it drilled in Saudi Arabia alone.

▷ The movie industry is very
busy in India. Several hundred
films are made each year.

Weave a rug
Fold a piece of thin cardboard in half. Cut slits as
shown. Open out. Tape
strips of colored paper
to one edge. Weave strips
in and out until you reach the
end. Tape in place. Weave strips
until you have a colorful rug.

▽ Woven Persian rugs
are famous around
the world.

Traditions

There are many celebrations and traditions to be found throughout the different countries in Asia. All are fun to watch or take part in. You can see people dressing up in costumes, an exciting fireworks display, and a colorful painting on these pages. Perhaps you have been lucky enough to see some of them before.

▽ During the Chinese New Year, some adults dress in a dragon costume and dance through the streets collecting gifts for those in need.

△ Islamic art is based on the Muslim religion. Many beautiful patterns and designs are created.

▽ On the island of Bali, in Indonesia, the women and children offer gifts of flowers and fruit to the gods, to help protect their villages.

▷ In Thailand, villagers hold a festival called Bun Bang Fai, to make sure the rains come. They light enormous rockets.

Make a Bun Bang Fai picture

Draw a firework picture with wax crayons. Use your brightest colors and draw plenty of rockets. Place it on an old newspaper and cover your picture with black paint. Watch what happens to your fireworks.

◁ The Kabuki theater, in Japan, began over 300 years ago. All the parts were played by men. Many Kabuki plays are still performed in Japan today.

△ The Japanese tea ceremony teaches that even everyday actions should be thought about deeply.

Australasia and the Pacific Islands

Australasia's largest countries are Australia, Papua New Guinea, and New Zealand. In the Pacific Ocean there are thousands of islands that we call the Pacific Islands. Some are too tiny to see on a map. Over this enormous area, there are hot deserts, cold mountains, and warm tropical seas.

△ Australasia and the Pacific Islands cover the enormous red area shown above.

▷ The Sydney Opera House, Australia, is a very famous landmark. It was built to look like sailboats in the harbor. The bridge behind it links north and south Sydney, the largest city in Australia.

∇ Wellington is the capital of New Zealand. The city is famous for its steep hills and its very strong winds.

Word box
National Parks are large, protected areas where wildlife can live in safety.
Reefs are ridges of coral that build up below the surface of the sea.
Aborigines are people who lived in Australia long before Europeans arrived.

◁ Fjordland is a National Park along the southwest coast of New Zealand. It is a protected area, so people are not allowed to build on it. It is known for its beautiful mountains and scenery.

▷ The Great Barrier Reef, off the Australian coast, is the largest coral reef in the world. Thousands of tourists visit the colorful coral reef each year.

▽ Uluru, or Ayers Rock, is sacred to the Australian Aborigines. Its caves are covered with ancient paintings.

▷ These giant stone statues are on Easter Island in Polynesia. No one knows who carved them. Traditional stories tell of the statues walking to their resting place, helped by a magical power.

Farming and industry

The farm and factory products from Australasia and the Pacific Islands are very popular in other countries. Japan is one of the main buyers of goods from Australia, New Zealand, and Papua New Guinea.

New Zealand has more sheep than people. The sheep are sold worldwide.

△ Sheep shearers in New Zealand often travel from farm to farm. Some can shear a sheep in under a minute!

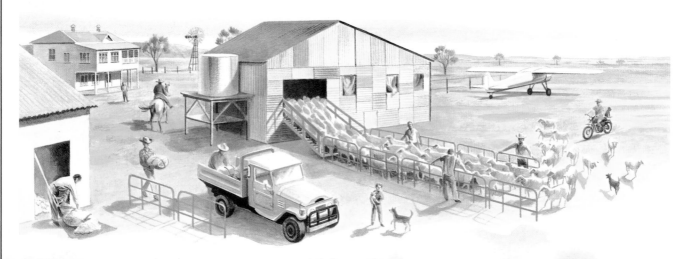

△ Australian sheep farms are so large that farmers use planes and trucks to get around them. At shearing time, sheep are driven into sheds to have their wool cut off.

◁ Sugar is the island of Fiji's most important crop. Many people earn their living by working on sugar plantations.

▷One of the world's largest copper mines is on the island of Bougainville, Papua New Guinea. Apart from the pure copper sold, small amounts of gold also come from this mine.

Find the answers

What is an opal?

What is Fiji's most important crop?

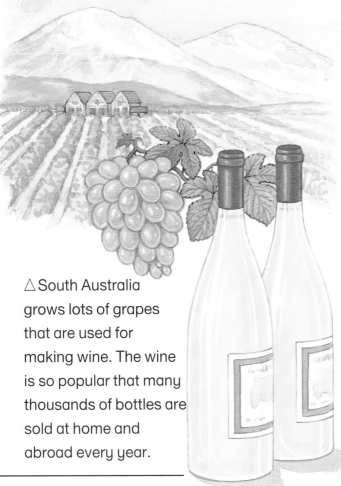

△South Australia grows lots of grapes that are used for making wine. The wine is so popular that many thousands of bottles are sold at home and abroad every year.

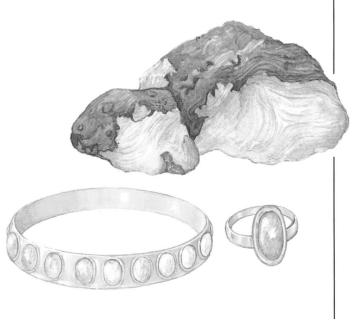

△Almost all the world's opals come from Australia. Opals are milky-colored gemstones with threads of other colors in them. They are used in jewelry, such as rings and bracelets.

485

Australian traditions

The first people settled in Australia about 40,000 years ago. These people were called Aborigines. Although many Aboriginal people now live in cities, there are a number who live in the outback, or areas of wilderness. These people have followed their own traditions for thousands of years.

Many Australians came from Europe and Asia and still follow the traditions of their original countries.

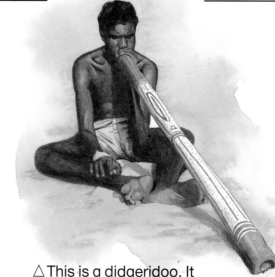

△ This is a didgeridoo. It is a musical instrument that makes a long, droning sound, like a loud bee. Didgeridoos play the background sound to many Aborigine songs.

Make a rock painting
Stuff a large, strong paper bag with newspaper and seal top edges with tape. Brush glue over the front. Cover with sand. Leave to dry. Draw simple stick figures and animals with wax crayons on sandy side.

△ Paintings and carvings created thousands of years ago can be seen on rocks and in caves today. Many of them tell old Aborigine stories.

▷Aborigines have used boomerangs for hunting and sport for thousands of years. If thrown properly, they come right back to the thrower.

◁This camel race is part of a big sports day. Watching and taking part in sports competitions is an important part of Australian life.

▷Surfing is a favorite sport in Australia.

Island traditions

Early Polynesians were adventurous sailors. They braved the unknown seas in small, light boats, searching for new lands. Finally, they settled on many of the Pacific Islands.

Traditions were handed down from family to family and are still part of everyday life today.

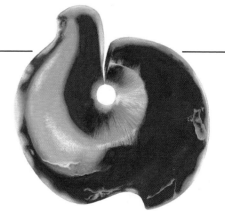

△ Amulets, or lucky pendants, have been worn by Maori people for hundreds of years. This one is worn, or placed in the water while fishing, to help the owner catch many fish.

◁ In Papua New Guinea, men hold meetings and ceremonies in spirit houses called Haus Tambarans. These have life-size wooden figures, or spirits, that watch over the village.

▷ Hawaiian dancing is called hula. Hula dancers have special costumes and often wear garlands around their necks. Stories are chanted while the dancing takes place.

Index

This index will help you to find out where you can read about a subject. It is in alphabetical order. Each section is under a large letter of the alphabet. A main entry and its page numbers are printed in **dark**, or **bold**, letters. This is where you will find the most information. Below a main entry, there may be a second list. This shows other places in the book where you can find further information on your subject.

The publishers would like to thank the following artists for their contribution to this book:

Hemesh Alles (Maggie Mundy Agency Ltd.); Jonathan Adams; Marion Appleton; Mike Atkinson (Garden Studio Illustrators Agents); Craig Austin; Graham Austin; Janet Baker; Julian Baker; Bob Bampton; Julie Banyard; John Barber; Shirley Barker (Artist Partners Ltd.); Denise Bazin; Tim Beer (Maggie Mundy Agency Ltd.); Pierre Bon; Maggie Brand; Derek Brazell; Brihton Illustration Agency; Peter Bull Art Studios; John Butler; Vanessa Card; Diana Catchpole (Linda Rogers Associates); Jonathan Cate; David Cook (Linden Artists); Bob Corley (Artist Partners Ltd.); Joanne Cowne; Jim Channell; Caroline Jayne Church; Peter Dennis (Linda Rogers Associates); Kay Dixey; Maggie Downer; Richard Draper; Bernard Duhem; Jean-Philippe Duponq; David Eddington (Maggie Mundy Agency Ltd.); Luc Favreau; Diane Fawcett; Catherine Fichaux; Michael Fisher; Roy Flooks; Chris Forsey; Rosamund Fowler (Artist Partners Ltd.); Andrew French; Tony Gibbons; Mick Gillah; Peter Goodfellow; Matthew Gore; Ray Grinaway; Terry Hadler; Rebecca Hardy; Nick Hawken; Tim Hayward; Ron Haywood; Pierre Hezard; Kay Hodges; Stephen Holmes; Mark Iley; Ian Jackson; John James; Rhian Nest James (Maggie Mundy Agency Ltd.); Ron Jobson; Kevin Jones Associates; David Kearney; Pete Kelly; Roger Kent (Garden Studio Illustrators Agents); Tony Kenyon; Kevin Kimber (B.L. Kearley Ltd.); Deborah Kindred; Stuart Lafford (Linden Artists); Marc Lagarde; Terence Lambert; Stephen Lings (Linden Artists); Bernard Long (Temple Rogers Artists Agents); John Lupton (Linden Artists); Gilbert Macé; Kevin Maddison; Alan Male (Linden Artists); Shirley Mallinson; Maltings Partnership; Josephine Martin (Garden Studio Illustrators Agents); Barry Mitchell; Robert Morton; Patrick Mulrey; David McAllister; Dee McClean (Linden Artists); Polly Noakes (Linda Rogers Associates); Steve Noon (Garden Studio Illustrators Agents); Oxford Illustrators; Darren Pattenden (Garden Studio Illustrators Agents); Jean-Marc Pau; Bruce Pearson; Jane Pickering (Linden Artists); Stephen Player; Sebastian Quigley (Linden Artists); Bernard Robinson; Eric Robson; Michael Roffe; Michelle Ross (Linden Artists); Eric Rowe (Linden Artists); Susan Rowe (Garden Studio Illustrators Agents); Martin Salisbury; Danièle Schulthess; Stephen Seymour; Brian Smith; Guy Smith (Mainline Design); Lesley Smith (John Martin and Artists); Étienne Souppart; John Spires; Clive Spong (Linden Artists); Valérie Stetton; Roger Stewart (Kevin Jones Associates); Tess Stone; Swanston Graphics; Eva Styner; Treve Tamblin (John Martin and Artists); Jean Torton; Shirley Tourret (B.L. Kearley Ltd.); Simon Tegg; Guy Troughton; Michèle Trumel; Visage Design; Vincent Wakely; Ross Watton (Garden Studio Illustrators Agents); Phil Weare (Linden Artists); Graham White; Joanna Williams; Ann Winterbotham; David Wright

The publishers wish to thank the following for supplying photographs for this book:

Page 47 Hergé/Casterman; 60 Frederick Warne & Co., 1902, 1987; 122 Mary Evans Picture Library; 145 National Maritime Museum, Greenwich; 162 Mansell Collection; 169 BATMAN is a trademark of DC Comics © 1991. All Rights Reserved. Reprinted by permission of DC Comics; 206 Mary Evans Picture Library; 222 Victoria & Albert Museum, London/Bridgeman Art Library; 226 Private Collection/Bridgeman Art Library; 233 1973 by E.H. Shepard and Methuen Children's Books Ltd.; 250 Ronald Grant Archive; 252 Ronald Grant Archive; 299 Mansell Collection; 302 Ronald Grant Archive/DC Comics; 306 Mary Evans Picture Library; 311 Ronald Grant Archive; 341 Mary Evans Picture Library; 374 "Thunderbirds" I.T.C. Entertainment Group Ltd.; 425 Ronald Grant Archive

Thanks also to photographer David Rudkin and models Felicity Lea and Kane Tunmore of Scallywags; and to the World Conservation Monitoring Centre for their kind help